HUMAN RIGHTS FOR CHILDREN AND YOUTH: SOCIOCULTURAL DIFFERENTIATION, RESISTANCE AND UNITY

SOCIOLOGICAL STUDIES OF CHILDREN AND YOUTH

Series Editor: David A. Kinney (from 1999)

Series Editors: David A. Kinney and
Katherine Brown Rosier (2004–2010)

Series Editors: David A. Kinney and
Loretta E. Bass (from 2011)

Series Editor: Loretta E. Bass (from 2012)

Recent Volumes:

Volume 14: 2011 – David A. Kinney & Loretta E. Bass, Series Editors; Loretta E. Bass & David A. Kinney, Guest Editors

Volume 15: 2012 – Loretta E. Bass, Series Editor; Susan Danby & Maryanne Theobald, Guest Editors

Volume 16: 2013 – Loretta E. Bass, Series Editor; Sandi Kawecka Nenga & Jessica K. Taft, Guest Editors

Volume 17: 2014 – Loretta E. Bass, Series Editor; Paul Close, Guest Editor

Volume 18: 2014 – Loretta E. Bass, Series Editor; M. Nicole Warehime, Guest Editor

Volume 19: 2015 – Loretta E. Bass, Series Editor; Sampson Lee Blair, Patricia Neff Claster and Samuel M. Claster, Guest Editors

Volume 20: 2016 – Loretta E. Bass, Series Editor; Yasemin Besen-Cassino, Guest Editor

Volume 21: 2016 – Loretta E. Bass, Series Editor; Maryanne Theobald, Guest Editor

Volume 22: 2016 – Loretta E. Bass, Series Editor; Ingrid E. Castro, Melissa Swauger & Brent Harger, Guest Editors

Volume 23: 2017 – Loretta E. Bass, Series Editor; Patricia Neff Claster & Sampson Lee Blair, Guest Editors

SOCIOLOGICAL STUDIES OF CHILDREN AND YOUTH
VOLUME 24

HUMAN RIGHTS FOR CHILDREN AND YOUTH: SOCIOCULTURAL DIFFERENTIATION, RESISTANCE AND UNITY

EDITED BY

MAGALI REIS
Pontifical Catholic University of Minas Gerais, Brazil

MARCELO S. ISIDÓRIO
Pontifical Catholic University of Minas Gerais, Brazil

SERIES EDITOR

LORETTA E. BASS
The University of Oklahoma, USA

emerald PUBLISHING

United Kingdom – North America – Japan
India – Malaysia – China

Emerald Publishing Limited
Howard House, Wagon Lane, Bingley BD16 1WA, UK

First edition 2019

British Library Cataloguing in Publication Data
A catalogue record for this book is available from the British Library

ISBN: 978-1-78973-048-7 (Print)
ISBN: 978-1-78973-047-0 (Online)
ISBN: 978-1-78973-049-4 (EPub)

ISSN: 1537-4661 (Series)

Printed and bound by CPI Group (UK) Ltd, Croydon, CR0 4YY

ISOQAR REGISTERED

ISOQAR certified Management System, awarded to Emerald for adherence to Environmental standard ISO 14001:2004.

Certificate Number 1985
ISO 14001

INVESTOR IN PEOPLE

CONTENTS

ABOUT THE CONTRIBUTORS

Anete Abramowicz, PhD, Senior Professor at University of São Paulo – USP/ Brazil. He is a graduate at Ciências Sociais from Universidade de São Paulo (1979), PhD at Education from Universidade Estadual de Campinas (1996), Senior Professor at University of São Paulo – USP. (from 2018 up to now), Senior Professor at Center of Education and Humanities at São Carlos Federal University – UFSCar (from 2012 up to 2018). He got a scholarship for productivity National Council for Scientific and Technological Development, level 1C (since 2010). His published works are books: 26; articles in indexed journals: 36; book chapters: 59; guided dissertations: 18, guided thesis: 18.

Imola Antal, PhD, is a Psychologist, an Associate Professor in the Social Work Program in Babes-Bolyai University, Romania. Her teaching focuses on child protection, trauma, family therapy and mental health issues. Her main research interest is in child abuse and neglect, child protection systems, and gender-based violence. She successfully contributed to publications in the area of trauma therapy.

Raneesh Chakalakkal is a PhD Scholar, Department of Social Work, Central University of Kerala, India. In the last two years, the scholar has been working on the subject of "reintegration of institutionalized children." Along with researcher is also interested in the field of rights of children in public care. He presented several articles in national and international seminars on Child Rights-related topics.

Valdete Côco is a Professor at the Federal University of Espírito Santo; Coordinator of GT07: Education of children from 0 to 6 years old, from the National Association of Postgraduate and Research in Education (2016/2019) and coordinator of the Research Group "Education and Training of Educators." Tutor of the Education Tutorial Program Connections of Knowledge: Education Project.

Ágnes Dávid-Kacsó, PhD, is a Psychologist, a Therapist and has a Doctoral degree in Sociology. Currently, she works as a lecturer at the Department of Social Work in Babes-Bolyai University, Romania, and teaches topics related to vulnerable young persons in residential or foster care or marginalized children, with minority background.

Marle Aparecida Fidéles de Oliveira Vieira is a Doctoral Student in Education at the Graduate Program in Education, Federal University of Espírito Santo; member of the Research and Training Group of Educators; teacher of the Municipal Education in Vitória city, Espírito Santo.

Ingrid Engdahl is an Associate Professor in Child and Youth Sciences, Stockholm University, Sweden. Vice President for OMEP in Europe, Organisation Mondiale pour l'Éducation Préscolaire. Prof Engdahl's is a preschool teacher and psychologist, with a PhD in Child and Youth Sciences. Her main research interests are the holistic development of early childhood education, focusing on toddlers and play, the perspective of the child, education for sustainability and the rights of the child.

Rocío Fatyass, PhD student in Social Sciences-CONICET (National Council for Scientific and Technical Research), has a degree in Sociology from the National University of Villa María (UNVM), Argentina and a scholar of the National Council of Scientific and Technical Research (CONICET). His line of research refers to the experiences of childhoods in contexts of poverty.

Aldrie Henry-Lee, PhD, is a Professor of Social Policy, University of the West Indies, Mona Campus, Kingston, Jamaica.

Yhanore Johnson-Coke, MSc, is a Research Assistant in Sir Arthur Lewis Institute of Social and Economic Studies (SALISES).

Éva László, PhD, Psychologist, is a Lecturer in the Social Work Programme at Babes-Bolyai University, Romania. She has been working on several projects, including child abuse and neglect, child protection, violence against women, trafficking, domestic violence, and online risks for children. She has a vast experience in prevention, intervention, lobbying and advocacy for women's and children's rights.

Letícia Mendonça Lopes Ribeiro is a Teacher at the Federal University of Acre (Universidade Federal do Acre), in the city of Rio Branco, State of Acre, Brazil. She currently teaches and researches topics related to teacher training and teaching work, in basic and higher education. Her most important publications are related to the professional practice of teachers. She has worked in child education classes for six years, in public schools in the metropolitan area of Belo Horizonte, Minas Gerais, Brazil.

Mariela Losso is a Professor Adjunct, Department of Education Policy, Faculty of Educational Sciences National University of Comahue, Argentina. She is a Doctoral Student about to finish her doctoral thesis, with the preliminary title "Configurations of the Civil Society and State Relationship to the demand for Early Childhood Education and Care" in contexts of social inequality in the province of Río Negro.

Charlotte McPherson is an ESRC-funded Doctoral Researcher at the University of Stirling in Scotland. Her doctoral qualitative research explores the lives and perspectives of working-class young people in urban and rural communities in Scotland through the lens of social justice. More broadly, her research interests lie in youth, place, social justice, social class, intergenerational relations and the future.

Dr Mohan A. K., is an Associate Professor and Head, Department of Social Work, Central University of Kerala, Kasaragod and the affiliated Institute is Department of Social Work, Central University of Kerala.

Noel Rosana Rafer, PhD, is currently a Professor at the Sociology Department, College of Social Sciences and Philosophy, Bicol University, Daraga Campus, Daraga, Albay, Philippines, and a member of the International Sociological Association. This is his first publication on children and youth, but he has also published or presented articles locally and internationally on armed conflict, extra-judicial killings, higher education, and religion in the Philippines.

Tatiane Cosentino Rodrigues, PhD is an Assistant Professor in the Department of Pedagogical Theories and Practices at the Federal University of São Carlos (UFSCar), São Paulo, Brazil. Coordinates the UFSCar Center for Afro-Brazilian Studies. She is the leader and coordinator of the Research Group Ethnic-Racial Relations and Education at the National Council for Scientific and Technological Development of Brazil (CNPq). Has experience in coordinating different research projects on Ethnic-Racial Relationships, Didactics, Teacher Education and Higher Education.

Maria Roth, PhD, is a Professor in the Social Work Program in Babes-Bolyai University, Romania, and the director of the European Master in Children's Rights. Before entering the academic field, she has worked with children in schools, hospitals, and orphanages. Along with her academic career, she did research and published in the area of child well-being and adverse childhood experiences in Romania.

Gabriela Guarnieri de C. Tebet, is a PhD Professor at Department of Social Sciences in Education and of Post-Graduation Program on Education of Faculty of Education, State University of Campinas – UNICAMP/Brazil. While she was teacher in early childhood education and care, working directly with babies and young children, in 2007 she won the prize "Educar para a igualdade racial" (To educate for racial equality) promoted by CEERT. In her docotoral studies Tebet studies Childhood Sociology and Babies. Her recent researches interests focus on babies, differences, early childhood education polices and practices and cartographies of babies. Since 2018 she coordinates a research project named "Babies, individuation, subjectivation and singularization process experienced by them in different spaces" founded by FAPESP.

INTRODUCTION

HUMAN RIGHTS FOR CHILDREN AND YOUTH: SOCIOCULTURAL DIFFERENTIATION, RESISTANCE AND UNITY

Magali Reis and Marcelo S. Isidório

We present to the academic community the dossier *Human Rights for Children and Youth: Sociocultural Differentiation, Resistance and Unity*, specially organized for volume 24 of the magazine Sociological Studies of Children and Youth – SSCY.

The set of chapters presented under the theme of childhood and youth, brought together researchers from three continents – India, Philippines, Sweden, Romania, Scotland, Brazil, Argentina, Jamaica – and configures an important mapping on the condition of childhood and youth in different sociocultural realities.

We structured the dossier from two problematizing keys, being the first fixed in the fundamental rights of children and young people, in which the limits and possibilities of guaranteeing and effecting rights are presented, as well as the ways in which the new generations have resisted the waves of exclusion and marginalization; the second problematizing key is based on the idea of sociocultural differentiation and unity, presented through studies that reflect the similarities and differences in the living conditions of children and young people in different contexts.

The scientific discussions that articulate the two parts of this volume reveal aspects related to the analysis of children and young people's rights, the performance of public policies and the materialization of the norms in certain contexts and their precariousness in different incidence *foci* of the analyzed societies.

Human Rights for Children and Youth: Sociocultural Differentiation, Resistance and Unity
Sociological Studies of Children and Youth, Volume 24, 1–8

ISSN: 1537-4661/doi:10.1108/S1537-466120190000024001

We highlight the social struggles, by improving the living conditions of the new generations, taking into account the elementary role of social role, which is placed both as an inalienable right and a challenge, from the perspective of participation in the spaces of decision towards the self-policy of children and young people, in different parts of the world.

The political-theoretical position of working with the analytical categories childhood and youth was intended to highlight the field of questioning to contemporary production about them, which sedimented the historical construction of identities and their rights.

In this way, we seek to challenge the inequalities that permeate the political-juridical instruments and the social conditions of life of children and young people, especially of the poorest strata of different societies, directing our criticism of the causes and factors that impede the real realization of rights and the realization of public policies that overcome social inequalities.

We also seek to question the social reproduction, the normative of political vision centred much more on the productive adult than in the newer ones considered 'unproductive' from the economic point of view, as well as other social oppressions, which were not exhausted or were overcome with the change of legal paradigms.

At the heart of the proposition of this thematic dossier, we put to the reader the challenge of dialoguing in theoretical, academic and normative fields, which do not always arise from the perspective of analyzing the similarities and differences of their objects of study.

In other words, the fields of inquiry about children and young people are structured as two sides of the same question, that is, they are based on the generational problem, however, with independent theoretical, methodological and practical referents, and what unites them are, in particular, the theoretical reflections on certain common themes such as the absence or lack of scope of policies aimed at those generational segments, child-juvenile work, violence against young people, exploitation, exclusion, and even the social role of young people, or even their absence.

The authors discuss relevant and current aspects of one or both fields of knowledge production, but seek to do this from a perspective of enrichment of social, geopolitical, sociological and pedagogical analysis in order to broaden the focus of appropriation and interdisciplinary discussion and problematize the conditions of production and application of children and young people rights in the Asian, European and Ibero-American sphere.

Let us know the chapters that compose the dossier Human Rights for Children and Youth: Sociocultural Differentiation, Resistance and Unity. In the first part entitled 'Children, Youth, Human Rights and Resistance' are presented four studies that are articulated by the question of children and young people rights, the limits and possibilities for effecting their guarantee, with special focus on young children.

By opening the work, we place the chapter by Ingrid Engdahl and Mariela Losso, entitled 'The Human Rights of Children and Young People from the Beginning: Early Childhood Care and Education for All', a comparative study between Sweden and Argentina. The authors present a descriptive analysis on care and education in early childhood as a significant basis for guaranteeing the fundamental rights of children from birth.

According to the authors, this is 'the first stage and the most solid basis considering the relevance of the development processes from birth to the age of six'. For both the initial education from the tender age must be compromised with the reality of the community where it is inserted, which, according to them, would facilitate the formation of the new generations as citizens, that is, subjects of full rights. They affirm that 'education and care in early childhood are indispensable'.

The intentionality of the researchers showed in this study was to produce a descriptive synthesis of the current state of Early Childhood Care and Education (ECCE) in the regulations in force in various regions and countries, especially in Latin America – Argentina – and in Europe –Sweden. To this end, the authors analyze topics that are interacting in the totality of the ECCE proposal, but organized according to the comprehensive priority of each reality. They present the theoretical contribution on childhood and the new perspectives that discuss conventional conceptions of children and childhoods. In this analytical line, the educational process is recognized as fundamental and is described as Early Education (EE), presenting a synthesis of the ECCE from its normative conformation which stems from the declarations of Jomtien (1990). The concept of Educare is presented as a holistic approach to educating and caring in early childhood. The objective is to highlight the differences in the scope of childhood inequalities, describing 'fragmented territories' in terms of guaranteeing rights. At the end, the authors emphasize the importance of early childhood education, recovering current studies on Educare, that project the guarantee of rights from birth.

Although the right to education and care is a universal guarantee, we emphasize that not all children enjoy this right in the same way, under the same conditions and with the same quality. In contrast, the study showed that in some realities the principle of Educare is still distant from the daily lives of children especially the poorest.

The second chapter entitled 'The Convention on the Rights of the Children (CRC), the Global Developmental Agenda and Children in Small Island Developing States (SIDs)' is authored by the Jamaicans Aldrie Henry-Lee and Yhanore Johnson-Coke, and analyzes the 30 full years in this year 2019, the adoption of the Convention on the Rights of the Child (CRC), in the United Nations. For the authors, the significance of this temporal milestone lies in the fact that we are a decade to meet the specific goals of UN2030, in which it was established that no country or child would cease to be supported by their rights. Therefore, we are at a significant historical moment to assess the situation of children in the small island developing states, in particular as Small Island Developing States (SIDs), as they show.

With primary and secondary data, the authors evaluate the status of children after 30 years of CRC in four SIDs in the Caribbean; Barbados, Jamaica, Haiti and Saint Lucia. The focus of the study is on the basic living conditions of children with emphasis on poverty, education, health and issues related to climate change. Data analysis revealed that SIDS vulnerabilities preclude adherence to fundamental rights by large proportions of children at risk of suffering from public policies.

Climate change increases their vulnerabilities and disparities persist in accessing basic social services. The situation of children is exacerbated by the lack of substantive data to inform the political process; in addition to inadequate programmatic coordination; lack of financial support; limited liability and little political will. Children's cultural perceptions and inadequate recognition of their importance for any Development Agenda also prevent children's progress in SIDs. For the authors, urgent action is still needed in order to fulfill all the commitments we have taken with the new generations since 1989 with the adoption of the CRC.

The relevance of this study lies in the problem of the reach of rights that is achieved unevenly by the new generations, putting the issue of poverty and inequality as still persistent and difficult issues to overcome in many sociocultural realities.

The third chapter comes from Brazil and consists of a bibliographic research developed by Anete Abramowicz, Gabriela Guarnieri de C. Tebet, Tatiane Cosentino Rodrigues, entitled 'Brazilian Childhood Studies and Relations to Children's Rights', and discusses scientific advances with regard to childhood as an analytical category, restricted to the so-called childhood studies, in various regions of Brazil 'from the understanding that childhood is a social discursive construct', as well as the Human rights, and both concepts interconnect when the subject in focus is the rights of children.

According to the authors, the evidence of the research reveals advances in the affirmation of the concept of childhood, and that those have supported specific policies of protection for subjects of little age, focusing on issues such as the marginalization of children in society, the persistence of inequalities affecting them, which are central themes developed in studies on childhood in Brazil. The authors make a mapping of the advances of those studies and their relationship with the rights of the child and conclude that neither childhood nor children's rights are a reality for all Brazilian children, especially when considering other markers who have challenged their rights as race, ethnicity, social class and gender.

In the fourth chapter developed by Marle Aparecida Fidéles de Oliveira Vieira and Valdete Côco, entitled 'Early Children's Education: Institutionality and the Right to Education', the authors discuss the right to education of small children in Brazil, with particular emphasis on the institution of early childhood education, highlighting the legal frameworks and educational indicators of a federative unit in the country. The field researched was a settlement of the Landless Rural Workers' Movement (Movimento dos Trabalhadores Rurais sem Terra- MST), from which are highlighted the processes of inequalities that elicit childhood in the rural environment. The evidences of the study presented in this chapter reaffirm the need to combat and overcome the logic of precariousness affecting the education system in the field, as well as guiding the specificities of the education of small children and the transition thought and dialogued for elementary school. The authors reaffirm the need to create early childhood education institutions centred on the fundamental rights of children, guaranteeing all the right to education in different contexts where it can occur and particularly in the settlements.

In this first part of the dossier the studies showed the low effectiveness of public policies especially in the Ibero-American context, to guarantee the primary right to education of the youngest, triggering a series of gaps in the guarantee of rights that extend to other social life spheres of the new generations. The studies reaffirm the need to resist the waves of exclusion and to combat social and educational inequalities that condemn millions of children to a life of deprivation and reproduction of situations of extreme poverty. What mobilizes us in this sense is the idea that human rights can be placed at the service of a progressive and emancipatory policy capable of creating the objective conditions so that the dignity of the human person can be respected in their primordial needs (Santos, 2013).[1]

What we envied in the studies presented is that the effectiveness of actions based on the rights of children and young people is an essential issue that is the guarantee of the right to education, or as analyzed by Cury (2014)[2]:

> [...] the right to school education, which, more than a contemporary requirement linked to productive processes and professional insertion, responds to values of social and political citizenship. (p. 1057)

We recognize that we are still facing the 'dilemma with which human rights are faced today in their relationship with democracy and development policies that constitute the dominant agenda of the contemporary world' (Santos, 2013).

What moves, to some extent, the militant action of the rights and the processes of resistance is the idea of recognizing that sociocultural differentiation cannot produce the gap between the rights and its realization for much of mankind, which leads us to fight for unit, object of analysis of the next section of this dossier.

In this second part of this dossier, 'Children, Youth, Sociocultural Differentiation and Unity', we find the dialogue with the studies of the Romanian Maria Roth, Imola Antal, Ágnes Dávid-Kacsó, Éva László, entitled 'Forms, Impact and Consequences of Violence against Children in Romanian Child Protection Settings'. The authors analyze that after three decades of universal recognition of the rights of the child, dating from 1989, as the foundation of child protection, it would be justifiable and necessary that child protection systems around the world had undergone a thorough analysis of their previous failures and from that point they would have rebuilt their institutions based on principles of human rights.

However, their studies show that data from Global Violence Reports carried out between 2006 and 2015 reflect that children placed in care institutions, including residential care, family welfare, prison establishments and environments for children with disabilities remain at high risk for violence against them. Although there has apparently been progress in different parts of the world due to the global commitment of government agencies and civil society to the Convention on the Rights of the Child (CRC), the analysis often pointed to the multiple victimization faced by the tutored children, by the institutions that should take care of them.

In 2006, the report of the UN Secretariat-General on violence, drew the attention of the public that child protection authorities and justice systems around the world are responsible for supervising and controlling the lives of millions of children under their care and risk of violence by employees and colleagues, and also to develop effective reporting mechanisms. In the last two decades, researchers have often found that residential facilities are poorly funded, endangering the lives and development of many children. Children in large institutions and people with disabilities are especially at risk because they may not have met their basic needs.

The relevance of this study is to show that the contemporary systems of custody and care of children and young people in vulnerable situations have significant flaws being incapable in many cases to ensure that millions of children and young people sheltered in families or different forms of residential or even institutional care, spend their childhood in a stimulating environment, for the full realization of their potential.

In the sequence, we present the study of Rocío Fatyass, from Argentina, whose title is 'Contributions and Limits of the "Childhood Studies" for the Research of the Children's Agency in Latin America', which analyzes theoretical elements of the sociology of childhood in the Anglo-Saxon field, to discuss their contributions, scopes and limits on the child agency in children living in poor and urban contexts in Latin America. According to the author, his objective was to contribute to the debates in the field of childhood from a sociological perspective that accentuating the capacity of action and resistance of children even in the framework of structural constraints, without taking an approach decontextualized and ideal about the agency. The concept of 'agency' translates into a series of meanings, for example, the ability of children and young people to make decisions about issues affecting their lives, expressing their ideas, or even the possibility of having some degree of control over the direction of their own lives, and evidently play a relevant role in the changes that occur in society, it is therefore the intrinsic capacity of the new generations to act independently of the social structures, institutions that impose on the newest, or even the system of values that regulate their actions.

The seventh chapter that makes up this dossier is Brazilian: 'Child's Play in and out of School: Bodies Control of Slum Children'; it was written by Letícia Mendonça Lopes Ribeiro, and analyzes the most common pranks of children, approximately seven years of age, during the recreation period and when they are not in the school, located in a small favela (slum) in the metropolitan region of Belo Horizonte in Minas Gerais, Brazil. According to the author, her analyses considered the issues that involve the recognition of the essentiality of childhood in the context of the reality and affectivity of children at the site called Favela, as well as in aspects that show the control of their bodies, through the child's play performed at school.

The research procedures were based on participant observation, whose purpose was to record the important experiences and reflections of the research participants, to know their actions and to observe them in their behaviours and attitudes in routine situations. For the author, the research evidences indicated that children's play, both in school and outside it, is different between boys and girls. In the open areas of the favela, boys explore more spaces than girls, who prefer to play children in the domestic sphere. At school, educators tend to censor some behaviours and attitudes of children, suggesting the search for obedient postures and disciplined bodies.

The fundamental aspect of this study was to understand that the school in different situations acts in a censor way, leading to the restraint of children's actions constituting, sometimes, in another social space of domestication of the bodies since childhood.

In another context, the Scottish researcher Charlotte McPherson, argues that young people in Scotland, as well as in other parts of the world, are known to have results, social status and political representation inferior to those of adults. In her chapter 'Economically, Culturally and Politically Disadvantaged: Perspectives on, and Experiences of, Social Justice Amongst Working-class Youth in Mainland Scotland's Smallest Council Area through the Lens of Nancy Fraser', the author analyzes that those disadvantages between adults and young people have come to be broadly normalized in the contemporary context, and can be further aggravated by other factors, however, are particularly amplified by coming from a lower social class context.

An additional challenge for young people is associated with the place, with young people living in more remote and less urban areas at greater risk of being socially excluded to face complex and multiple barriers to employment and education than their peers living in better structured urban centres. Based on interviews and focus groups on a qualitative project with 16 young people and five practitioners and using the tripartite theory of social justice by Nancy Fraser, the chapter highlights the various and interconnected disadvantages experienced by working-class youth who become adults in Clackmannanshire, Scotland's smallest council area.

The author concludes that the young people surveyed felt, in a certain way, invisible, stigmatized and marginalized and for this reason, they were more hurt and irritated by feeling guilty at their own disadvantage. The participants were also living highly precarious lives, in which they had insufficient security, resources or opportunities to achieve distributive justice. Some were largely unemployed for several years, at the age of twenty-two, and most had erratic employment histories, characterized by agitation and instability. In this sense, the participants felt largely without voice and without representation or visibility, both as individuals and as a legitimate social group.

Closing the dossier, we present the study of the Indians Raneesh C. and Mohan A.K., named 'Reluctance to Register under the JJ Act among Child Care Institutions in Malappuram district of Kerala'. In this chapter, the authors analyze the Juvenile Justice Act dated from 2015, which provides for the care and protection of young Indians and obliges the registration of Child Care

Institutions (CCIs). However, according to the study, non-governmental organizations and private agencies are reluctant to proceed with such registration. Through an exploratory approach, the authors sought to understand the reasons why institutions intended for the care and protection of children and young people act in a manner contrary to the record itself and in disagreement with the law. They take as an example the district of Malappuram, that among 112 institutions 40 did not register or had their records denied. The authors conclude that there are several misconceptions against the juvenile law of justice between the CCIs, because they consider that their organizational freedom would be limited in the registry. Another observation is that most children's homes are administered by religious organizations, and for this reason they feel that the record may affect their religious values. About 60% of the CCIs are concerned about the financial burdens and 85% of them have difficulty in implementing the new rules and regulations related to the JJ law of 2015 in the respective institutions.

A study of this nature is important for us to understand what can in fact occur within institutions protection, care, and education of children and young people and the need for oversight by the public authorities of the practices and structure in which it takes place within those, given that education, protection and care are fundamental rights of the youngest.

As we gather those ten studies in a dossier, we conclude that the condition of childhood and youth is still quite controversial and is far from being benefited by their rights, even though in contexts of more developed countries and with public policies known to be more efficient, the disadvantages and inequalities are more intensely affecting children and poorer young people.

Thus, we hope that the studies presented in this dossier can stimulate critical reflection and political, social and academic actions engaged in transforming the current living conditions of the new generations in particular of children and young people from the most marginalized society, and that the materialization of their rights and public policies aimed at them, are in fact guaranteed by stimulating, also, the consolidation of the academic debate and the democratization of production and communication of knowledge on such matters, especially with the direct stakeholders who are children and young people.

NOTES

1. Santos (2013).
2. Cury (2014).

REFERENCES

Cury, C. R. J. (2014). A Qualidade da Educação como Direito. *Educação & Sociedade*, Campinas, *35*(129), 1053–1066, out.- dez.

Santos, B. S. (2013). *Se Deus fosse um ativista dos direitos humanos*. São Paulo: Cortez Editora.

PART I
CHILDREN, YOUTH, HUMAN RIGHTS AND RESISTENCE

THE HUMAN RIGHTS OF CHILDREN AND YOUNG PEOPLE FROM THE BEGINNING: EARLY CHILDHOOD CARE AND EDUCATION FOR ALL

Ingrid Engdahl and Mariela Losso

ABSTRACT

This article presents a description of Early Childhood Care and Education (ECCE) as a basis for guaranteeing fundamental human rights from birth. ECCE is the first stage and a solid base – considering the relevance of development processes from birth to six years. Active early education, committed to the reality of a community, facilitates the training of young citizens as rights' agents. In this sense, the education and care in early childhood is indispensable. This article communicates a descriptive synthesis of the current state of the ECCE in various regions and countries, especially in Latin America – Argentina – and in Europe – Sweden.

In the analysis, theoretical sustenance about childhood and new perspectives that discuss classical conceptions are presented. The educational process is fundamental and is described as Early Education (EE), presenting a synthesis of the ECCE from its normative conformation that arises from the statements of Jomtien (1990). The concept of Educare is presented, as a holistic approach to education and care within early childhood. This aspect is linked to highlight the inequality gaps for children, describing 'fragmented territories', in terms of guaranteeing rights. The final reflection summarizes the importance of

Human Rights for Children and Youth: Sociocultural Differentiation, Resistance and Unity
Sociological Studies of Children and Youth, Volume 24, 11–34

ISSN: 1537-4661/doi:10.1108/S1537-466120190000024002

Early Education, recovering the current studies on Educare, which project the guarantee of rights from birth.

Keywords: Early childhood education; human rights; equal access; Educare; Argentina; Sweden

INTRODUCTION

The article aims to analyze the relevance of Early Education (EE) as a basis for the guarantee of fundamental human rights from birth. The demands from the voice of the new generations are raised, emphasizing its potential for eloquence of children and young people as agents of rights. It is a fundamental part of education to promote the highest levels of autonomy, with the guidance of adult teachers. This guide is the temporary support that educates and cares for the youngest or the *new*[1] members of society.

Education is the possibility of interacting with others and deploying social action, expanding the ability to express and decide.

The demands from the voice of the new generations are raised, emphasizing its potential for eloquence of children and young people as agents of rights. We talk about 'eloquence'[2] (Cullen, 2009) as a practice that implies autonomy and decision-making power, according to the possibilities of the subject with agency in a community. Education is liberating (Freire, 1972), because in collective action there is reflective training and the teacher is the initial support that guides the praxis that will facilitate the awareness of the reality of that social group. In this process, each child strengthens her/his argumentative discursive capacity – education is based on communication and language and teaches it – and recognizes her/his agency and a growing responsibility and interest for sustainable development and to participate actively in the society.

Early Education is the first stage and the most solid base – considering the relevance of development processes from birth to six years – to guarantee Fundamental Human Rights from birth. Active early education that is committed to the reality of a community facilitates the training of young citizens as rights' agents.

It is also noted worldwide that Early Education quantitatively or qualitatively is an educational level that has not been strengthened enough; this will be one of the initial approaches of this article, relating the institutionalization of Early Education with international regulations that promote it. It is intended to produce and communicate a descriptive synthesis of the current state of the EE and ECCE in the regulations in force in various regions and countries.

The methodology is based on the qualitative treatment of the data. The methodology of the research is qualitative, focused on the analysis of legal discourses from a synchronic–critical diachronic perspective (Fairclough, Wodak & van Dijk, in Maxwell, 1996). Extensive ethnographic observations were made by Hammersley and Atkinson (2007) on the forms of institutionalization of educational practices in Early Childhood, and the collection of data with twenty semi-directed interviews with social agents linked to the processes of design and implementation of policies and advice on childhood rights. We proceeded to triangulate the data sources (Denzin & Lincoln, 1994), from which the analysis of the current state of the relationship between the functions and processes of institutionalization of the rights to early childhood education takes place.

Primary sources have been triangulated, for example, interviews with secondary sources – census data and documents, to produce a synthesis of ECCE in Latin America and Europe.

In the analysis, topics are displayed that are interacting in the totality of the proposal but are organized according to the comprehensive priority of each one and the relationship with the object of the work. In the first place, the theoretical sustenance about childhood and the new perspectives that discuss classical conceptions are presented. This is related to another point that is the capacity of discourse – action, the progressive autonomy and the relevance of the voice of the younger generations. The educational process is fundamental and is described from the Early Education, presenting a synthesis of the ECCE from a normative conformation that arises from the statements in the World Declaration on Education for All and the Framework for Action to Meet Basic Learning Needs, approved by the World Conference 1990 in Jomtien (UNESCO, 1990/1994)[3] and followed by presentations from Latin America, especially Argentina and Europe, especially Sweden. The concept of Educare is presented, as a holistic approach to educating and caring within early childhood: a fundamental process in an integral development from a rights' perspective. This aspect is linked to highlight the inequality gaps for children, describing 'fragmented territories'[4], in terms of guaranteeing rights, especially education and early care beyond the family nucleus.

The final reflection summarizes the importance of guaranteeing Early Education, recovering the current studies on Educare, which project the guarantee of rights from birth. This leads to strengthening the agency of children regarding their social rights and their ability to act for higher levels of social justice, especially in fragmented territories that are not considered in current projects, policies and institutions.

CHILDHOOD: THEORETICAL PERSPECTIVES

The research is carried out during the last years, and has been the subject of theories that begin to be considering the differences and naming 'the infancias'. De Mause (1982), Aries (1987), Gelis (1990), Lyotard (1991), Carli (1991, 2001, 2006), have allowed – from different perspectives – to construct more complex and inclusive conceptions, and girls begin to give space to diversity and contextualize the stories of the subjects in social, political, and economic processes that also determine the discourses that are written on them.

The peculiarity of children is that they have been enrolled in a diversity of discourses that characterize, analyze, and produce them; overflow pages and words about childhood but very few are children's voices. Even the adult voice prevails in the construction of these discourses and, in some way, maintains the power over the voiceless (infants).

As Carli (2006) states, in the last decades in Argentina numerous studies on 'childhood' have been developed; they come from different fields such as sociology, psychology, anthropology, history, etc. These studies have provided different perspectives to understand childhoods: the representations on the childhood in mass media, the childhood in situation of street, the children of the closed districts or countries, the policies and the rights for childhood, gender, ethnicity, class and child socialization, among others. The different childhoods begin to have a certain voice and existence and they come out of the shadows of the most closed representations to make their way as subjects with rights.

New theories constitute a significant step forward and brought about reliable grounds, displayed in innovative legal frameworks, for the re-consideration of children's rights. However, everyone knows that standard advances are not enough to produce radical changes in the ways of regarding childhoods and dealing with them.

Cullen (2009) contrasts the absence of voice of the infants with the interpellant eloquence of the facundia. Childhood is, from its reflection, a face that interpellates as exteriority, as an alterity that is not trapped by the relationship of language and culture. Before the withdrawal of the word, in front of the fragmentation of the subject and against the pretension of monopolization of the single thought postulates the taking of the word, the narrative construction of the identity and the intelligent resistance as challenges for the education. In the redefinition of childhood, she finds substantive keys to think about our time and responsibly assume the task of teaching: 'Ultimately, each child expects an unpublished adult. And in every adult a child lives, where the same, the passion to learn to live, is not the same' (Cullen, 2009).

Several investigations point out the relevance of early childhood, as the first time of life, with great importance for the subject and his community. Early childhood needs strong family ties, security and affection, togeether with care and education as a fundamental right that must be guaranteed by the states.

Early education is necessary to initiate social change and practices that guarantee the rights of young children. The role of adults is important in a context with adequate social, economic and political conditions for the change of view of childhoods. The new generations need those conditions to develop all their capacities, especially those to participate actively as citizens in public affairs. These new approaches to Early Education emphasize the principles of democracy and citizenship.

It is necessary to mention that adult voices still prevail in discouse constructions talking about children. There are plenty of pages and words describing childhoods, though few of them are actually children's voices or retrieve them authentically. In various social practices, the voice of adults still prevails. Some groups of children are less listened to, either because of their class, race or gender precedence (Losso, 2009a).

To build truly democratic and inclusive societies, it is essential to listen to the voices of all children. This implies promoting children to be active participants in community life. Here, early education – considered as a social and politic practice capable of becoming a privileged space for the construction of citizenship – plays an essential role. School practices – what happens in the educative space every day, the relations displayed – can foster and support this collective construction of citizenship. School is expected to be a democratic space, showing every citizen's engaged and transforming social behaviour already from childhood (Losso, 2009b).

Transforming action is precisely the basis on which an *emancipating civic education* – with the purpose of widening the scope of pupils' autonomy – rests. As Giroux (2000) says, educative contexts should encourage young people's imaginations, passions and intellects, for them to be able to challenge the structural conditioning factors which oppress them. 'This form of education is essentially political, and its goal is to achieve a true democratic society, a society able to answer for everyone's needs and not only for the needs of a few' (p. 202).

Democracy needs the support of an educative system that helps in the training of a critical awareness and the capacity of reflection. Democracy is and involves the childhood, too. In this sense, the conception of democracy guiding this task refers to it as 'a way of life', which implies active and public participation in common issues. Following Bárcena (1997), democracy promotes *freedom* (individual and collective self-determination), the *human development* (the capacity for practicing self-determination) and *moral equality* (the capacity to respect each other).

The EE approaches point to the necessary change in the representations and discourses that occur about young children. They encourage states to modify their regulations to expand access to care and education systems from an early age. While most states have ratified the UN Convention on the Rights of the Child (UN, 1989), not all have regulations that fully guarantee them.

The most recent universal step for EE was taken in 2015 by the General Assembly of the United Nations in the Sustainable Development Goals, more specifically by goal no 4 (UN, 2015). The goal is about education and states to ensure inclusive and equitable quality education and promote life-long learning opportunities for all. Goal 4.2 specifically addresses EE and says:

> 4.2 By 2030, ensure that all girls and boys have access to quality early childhood development, care and pre-primary education so that they are ready for primary education.

This is the first time that United Nations have decided on universal right to Early Education for all.

EARLY EDUCATION IN THE NATIONAL LAWS

Following the Convention on the Rights of the Child (CRC; UN, 1989), children have an unprecedented legal status, which includes the right to education, care, play, among other fundamental activities from birth, and the protection from discrimination and violence. Thus, we can consider these rights as fundamental in any study that addresses some legal exegesis linked to early childhood.

A total of 196 states have adhered to the CRC and the vast majority regulated the rights of children with national laws in line with the principles of the convention. In some cases, they have also been considered constitutionally – for example, Argentina, Norway and from January 1, 2020 also Sweden – and with correlation in certain aspects in educational laws in more countries. This article describes specifically the legislation of the province of Río Negro, Argentina, and the ways in which it promotes the rights from the initial level of the education system.

This province is the precursor of numerous pioneering regulations regarding education and children's rights since the recovery of the rule of law in Argentina (1983). Relevant examples are its current laws on children's rights and education and the first specific curricula for the Preschool (1988) and the curricular design for Maternal Cycle (1998). The initial level in the Argentine educational system is the first level of education. According to current legislation, it contemplates two cycles: Maternity (45 days of life to 3 years) and Preschool (3 to 5 years). The age division between the cycles is determined by the date of birth considering as the limit between one cycle and another on June 30 of each year. The school year in Argentina begins in the month of March and ends in December.

The importance of early childhood care and development emerges as a precept and foundation of the lines of action discussed at Jomtien World Conference (Myers, 2000). The universal agreement on ECCE emanates from the World Declaration on 'Education for All', which, in its article 5, holds that 'Learning begins at birth. This calls for early childhood care and initial education. These can be provided through arrangements involving families, communities, or institutional programs, as appropriate (UNESCO, 1994, p. 10).'

From the world conference, the *Framework for Action to Meet Basic Learning Needs* was drawn up, defining some objectives that should be included by the signatories, that is, governments, agencies, in the plans for the decade that began. The declaration provides a favourable conceptual framework for the definition of integral educational policies, inseparable from other social policies and economic policies (Coraggio, 1995, p. 63).

This declaration has been relevant worldwide. Countries in Europe and Latin America share the adherence to these regulations that have served as a framework for regional and state regulations. Organizations such as OAS, OEI, UNESCO, UNICEF, among others, have especially emphasized in the last four decades priority guidelines for early childhood care, and some advanced to integrate systematic education as part of their policies of action. Also, new credit support programs of the World Bank and the Inter-American Development Bank were implemented, especially for what they call developing countries, although their purposes can be interpreted with a more economic feature than rights. Analyzing these programs, they identify the priorities of projects that align with macro-economic programs, which aim to improve the quality of life of children with a projection to their productivity and insertion in the labour market of the capitalist model. Some calculations explicitly point out the benefits of an investment in early childhood, as Gabriela Fujimoto (2006) explains that children who participated in ECCE programs have been more successful in various aspects of their lives, such as better performance in schooling, at work and in social skills. The author states that, it has been shown that for every dollar invested in early childhood save more than 15 dollars in compensatory social programs.

In this article, EE is analyzed as a right of all children, in pursuit of their real and present well-being, a fundamental human and social right that will be consolidated throughout the child's life. During the last three decades, programs to establish or strengthen the EE have significantly increased, adhering to international regulations and proposing their own. In general, dependent care networks are organized by various state and private agencies.

EXAMPLES FROM LATIN AMERICA

Latin America presents a diversity of ECCE institutions and dependencies that make its study and identification very complex. There are child education programs that depend on the public and private sectors for the ages of four and five years with supervision of education areas in each country. For younger children, the proposals are diversified into institutions that depend less on the national and provincial states but to higher degree on the municipalities or local councils, generally linked to the sector of social welfare. More than 40% in most countries is run by private management with payment of tuition. EE initiatives were also broadened and strengthened by civil society organizations, most commonly in the territories with the low socio-economic status in each state.

The legal frameworks of most countries in the region – Latin America – are similar but the institutional mechanisms that are implemented vary. This diversity results from the crossing of different variables, among which the origins of educational institutions stand out – historically identified with the public sector or with the private sector. These programs for EE are managed through different state areas (Health, Labour, Social Welfare, Education and/or others), their actions are complemented with the support of community and/or private organizations (neighbourhood organizations, guilds, foundations, NGOs, etc.) (Table 1).

As already mentioned, Latin America has continuities in legislation, but strong differences in the institutionalization of early education. In this summary we can see the notable differences between countries that have developed education systems that include early childhood education and those that are in the process of doing so. The averages of the region also express the differences between the ages of three to five years with an attendance gap of more than 25% between the studied age extremes.

Case Argentina

An analysis of the laws and proposed curricula from 1980 to the present shows the correlation between EE principles and the political and economic processes prevailing in the regional and Argentinean context. With the return of democratic governments in the 1980s, debates on the contents of education and the

Table 1. School Attendance Rates for Three- to Five-years old in Selected[a] Countries in Latin America from 2001 to 2011.[b]

Countries	Age			
	3 years	4 years	5 years	3–5 years
Costa Rica	16%	38%	74%	42%
Argentina	40%	70%	92%	68%
Brasil	49%	73%	87%	70%
Uruguay	60%	83%	97%	80%
Total Region (16 countries)	34%	62%	82%	60%

Source: DiNIEE (2016).

[a]The criteria to choose these countries: Extreme percentages (highest and lowest) and the average percentages of the total table of 16 countries.

[b](2001–2011) it's the period between the last two population censuses. In general, in the countries of Latin America they are carried out every ten years, specifically in Argentina, the last census was carried out in 2010.The new censuses will start in 2020.

necessary reformulation of the curricula in line with democratic, deepened. The reforms focused on adjustments that responded to a general restructuring of the education system.

On Argentina, the National state recognized the Initial level as part of the educational system, legally established by law in 1993 (Law 24 195 Federal Law). The progress made with the 1993 law was the incorporation of the Preschool to the educational system as the first level: Initial Level and the compulsory nature of the five-year room. The following laws at the national and provincial levels proposed new goals, including the incorporation of the Maternal Cycle, the proposed curricula for this cycle in some provinces and the universalization of educational services for four-year-olds.

The 1993 law was extended in 2006 by the Law of National Education No. 26 206, Chapter II, Articles 18–25. In fact, the state – in joint actions with provinces and municipalities – guarantees access to the last section of the Initial Level, that is for the five-year-olds. EE for five-year-olds had the greatest expansion in the last decade.

The objectives of the 2006 legislation focus on expanding the coverage of the initial level and thus promote access to systematic learning. Goals are set to promote the development of principles of solidarity, trust, care, respect, creative ability and pleasure and play, vindicating the importance of the ludic perspective in early childhood. It strives to overcome the premises for primary school, determined in that expansion during the 1990s, thus reinforcing the principles of the objectives of EE (Table 2).

Although Law 26 206 states that 'Initial Education constitutes a pedagogical unit and includes children from forty-five (45) days to five (5) years of age inclusive', no legal mechanisms or institutions have been implemented that specify the guarantee of these rights for all children young children. These principles are reaffirmed and extended in 2014 with the enactment of Law No. 27045.

Table 2. Synthesis of Argentine Laws on Early Childhood and Education Since 1990.

Data	Law	Synthesis
1990	N° 23 849	Sanctioned: September 27, 1990 and enacted in fact: October 16, 1990 ARTICLE 1 – Approval of the CONVENTION ON THE RIGHTS OF THE CHILD, adopted by the General Assembly of the United Nations in New York (UNITED STATES OF AMERICA) on November 20, 1989, consisting of FIFTY-FOUR (54) articles, whose photocopy authenticated in Spanish language is part of this law.
1993	N° 24 195	Federal Education Law. Article 10: The structure of the educational system, which will be implemented in a gradual and progressive manner, will be integrated by (a) Initial Education, constituted by the kindergarten for children from three to five years of age, being mandatory last year. The provinces and the Municipality of the City of Buenos Aires will establish, when necessary, maternity garden services for children under three years of age and will provide support to the community institutions so that they can provide them and help the families that provide them require.
2006	N° 26 206	National Education Law. Article 19 The national State, the provinces and the Autonomous City of Buenos Aires have the obligation to universalize educational services for children of three (3) years of age, prioritizing the educational attention of the less favored sectors of the population.
2014	N° 27 045	ARTICLE 1 – Mandatory initial education for children of four (4) years in the national education system. [...] The Ministry of Education and the competent jurisdictional authorities will ensure compliance with the compulsory school through institutional, pedagogical and rights promotion alternatives, which comply with local and community requirements, urban and rural, through actions that allow achieve results of equivalent quality throughout the country and in all social situations. ARTICLE 3 [...] Initial education constitutes a pedagogical unit and includes children from forty-five (45) days up to and including five (5) years of age, with the last two (2) being mandatory years. ARTICLE 4 The National State, the provinces and the Autonomous City of Buenos Aires have the obligation to universalize the educational services for children of three (3) years of age, prioritizing the educational attention of the less favored sectors of the population.

Source: Ministry of Justice and Human Rights of Argentina, InfoLEG (2018).

Some progress can be perceived in the objectives set by the State for the population of three- and four-year-olds, an example is the explicitness of the intention to expand the coverage expressed in some legal instruments. The guidelines proposed in Law 26 075 of Educational Financing (enacted in 2005), aimed to increase access and investment in education in the period 2006–2010. This measure has as its main objective

> to guarantee equality of learning opportunities, support policies to improve the quality of education and strengthen scientific-technological research, reaffirming the strategic role of education, science and technology in the economic and socio-cultural development of the country. (Law 26 075, Article 1)

Within the framework of this objective, other priority goals are outlined, among them:

> "Include at the initial level one hundred percent (100%) of the population of FIVE (5) years of age and ensure the increasing incorporation of boys and girls of THREE (3) and FOUR (4) years, prioritizing the most disadvantaged social sectors. (Law 26 075, Article 2)

The law also gave directions about financing the EE expansion:

> The consolidated budget of the national Government, the provinces and the Autonomous City of Buenos Aires destined to education, science and technology will increase progressively until reaching, in the year 2010, a participation of SIX PERCENT (6%) in the Gross Domestic Product (GDP). (Law 26 075, Article 3)

In 2014 progress was made with proposals for educational services for three-year-olds.

In Argentina, the obligatory nature has become the bridge towards the quantitative expansion of the ECCE. In the 1990s, the mandatory five-year room was established as a way to initiate the extension of coverage. This obligation is intended for families, and the state accompanies, but unevenly depending on the territory. However, still in order to access the compulsory preschool section, the enrolment or reduction of enrolment of the three- and four-year sections or the multi-age rooms was used as regulators.

In 2016, the compulsory nature of the four-year section begins to be implemented. Again, some sections for three years and the maternal cycle regulates the expansion, and are reconverted or cease to exist to give place to enrolment of older children. Thus, the extension of legal rights of an age can violate the rights of other children. This shows the weakness of the national state and the provincials to genuinely guarantee the fulfillment of rights to EE, which fall on the possibilities of families and community.

These processes are being accommodated with the active participation of the educational communities – teachers, families, community, territorial organizations and municipalities – and after a few years the system is reorganized to increase enrolment quantitatively although the quality of the processes is not fully guaranteed. This condition highlights the difference in the realization of the right to EE, especially between children who live in different economic territories (Losso, 2016).

EXAMPLES FROM EUROPE

In Europe, all the states have ratified the CRC. Within EU, laws and reformulation about children's right, also in education and care, are stated in a foundational report by Delors (1996). EU writes early childhood education and care with the acronym ECCE, and we use ECCE when it is a direct quote emanating from EU. ECCE is defined in the following way:

> Provision for children from birth through to primary education that is subject to a national regulatory framework, i.e., it must comply with a set of rules, minimum standards and/or undergo accreditation procedures. It includes public, private and voluntary sectors. (Eurydice, 2016, p. 6)

The European Commission promotes that early childhood education is important to children's development, and that 'all young children to be able to access and benefit from high quality education and care'. In this perspective, the Commission shares reliable information 'on early childhood education and care (ECEC) systems in Europe, practice essential in order to understand what challenges are facing European countries, what we can learn from each other, and what new solutions might be developed to meet the needs of the youngest members of society' (Eurydice, 2016, p. 6).

In 2016, key principles were published as a result of a process for enhancing EE in the European Union. The selection drew on an analysis of research, which helped to identify the main elements of ECCE provision that contribute to providing children with the best possible start in life.

> The 'Proposal for key principles' [...] identified five main aspects of quality in early childhood education and care: access, workforce, curriculum, evaluation/monitoring and governance/funding. Seeing children as active participants in their own learning, the proposal highlights that parents are the most important partners and their participation is essential if high-quality ECEC is to be delivered. It also stresses that determining what constitutes high-quality ECEC should be a dynamic, continuous and democratic process. (Eurydice, 2016, p. 6)

Structural indicators for ECCE were described as; Guarantee of a place; Professionalization of staff (Requirement for tertiary education and Continuing professional development); Educational guidelines; Language support measures; and Support measures for parents (Eurydice, 2016, p. 6).

Most EE settings in Europe are provided and run by the municipalities. However, since the early 1990s, independent, grant-aided provision (organized by parent or staff co-operatives, foundations, limited companies, and other entities) has increased steadily (Eurydice, 2017). In Sweden, 60% of the children go to municipally run preschools (NAFE, 2018a).

Europe shows notable differences between countries, both in guaranteeing EE in legislation, but also in the organization of the services provided by each country. In some countries, such as Italy, notable progress in quality EE has been made, e.g. exemplified in Reggio Emilia, but there is no public access Italy is also one of the countries that does not guarantee places for young children aged zero to six years.

From a total of 33 European countries considered in Eurydice documents (2015–2017), approximately 30% legislate and guarantee some level of EE for children from three years. 37% suggest in their legislation EE from four years and a large part of this percentage guarantees EE for five-year-olds. 18% of the countries legislate and guarantee ECCE before three years and up to six years. The remaining 15% has no legislation or is in the process and does not guarantee any state education level for children under six years (Fig. 1).

A few European countries have had universal access to EE from three years for a century, e.g. France and England. Different research and documents on EE point out the numerous benefits of EE (see e.g. UNICEF, 2008), and several countries have reformulated their laws or are in the process of doing so to ensure greater access to early education. In 2014, only six European states (out of a

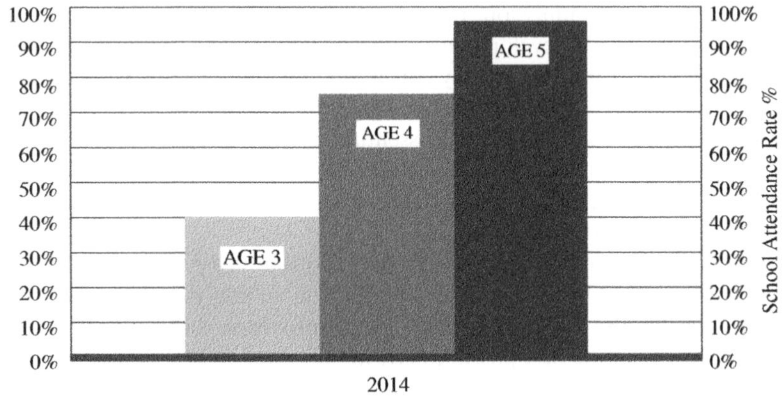

Fig. 1. School Attendance Rates According to Age. Study on 28 Urban Areas. *Source*: DiNIEE SICE, 2016, with data from the Permanent Household Survey-INDEC, 2006.

total of 28) did not guarantee early education coverage in their educational systems. EE is in focus for several political reforms, some of them are shown in Table 3 below.

In Europe, the organization of EE services in many countries also consider the age of the children. One example, the transition from the first cycle to the second is when children are around three years old. Some countries make the transition early (2½ years) or later (4 years) (Eurydice, 2015). As in Latin America, the European countries have several types of EE provisions and they are related to different areas (state, private, social, education programs or/and assistance areas).

Currently, in Europe, there are two approaches to providing universal access to EE. Some countries provide a legal entitlement to an ECCE place, while others make ECCE attendance compulsory. Access rights may also be attached to age:

> Legal entitlement to ECEC refers to a statutory duty on ECEC providers to secure publicly subsidised ECEC provision for all children living in a catchment area whose parents, regardless of their employment, socio-economic or family status, require a place for their child. It is important to note that a 'right to ECEC for every child' expressed in legislation in general terms, but without adequate funding and the necessary policies to ensure the delivery of sufficient places is not considered a legal entitlement. (Eurydice, 2016, p. 14)

This regulation promotes that every child has an enforceable right to benefit from ECCE provision. The public authorities guarantee a place for each child whose family request it (consider employment, socio-economic or family status) and the provision it is publicly subsidized and affordable.

As in Latin America, in most European countries there are significant differences in the age at which children qualify for a guaranteed ECCE place. Only seven of the 28 EU-countries (Denmark, Germany, Estonia, Latvia, Slovenia,

Table 3. Some National Political Initiatives to Expand EE within Europe.

Country	Reform
Czech Republic	From September 1, 2017, pre-primary education will be compulsory from age five, namely one year before primary education. At the same time, the legal entitlement will be extended to four-year-olds, and later on also to three-year-olds (from September 1, 2018) and two-year-olds (from September 1, 2020).
Estonia	A new legislation on ECCE is currently being prepared. The planned changes will give local governments the possibility to create new kindergarten or childcare places that meet the needs and preferences of families. EUR 47 million will be invested during the years 2014–2020 enabling to create approximately 3200 new ECCE places.
Finland	The right to ECCE was limited to 20 hours per week as from August 1, 2016. The full-time entitlement remains for children whose parents are working or studying. A child is also entitled to full-time ECCE if it is necessary due to his or her development, support needs or family circumstances, or if it is otherwise considered to be in the interest of the child.
Greece	Is planning legislation for lowering the starting age of compulsory ECCE years from five to four.
Hungary	From January 2017, every local government will have to provide care for children under three if there are 40 children under three living in the area, or the parents of at least five children express their wish for care. At present, this is a requirement for local governments where the population in the area is more than 10 000.
Ireland	From September 2016, children will be able to start in free preschool when they reach age three and to remain in free preschool until they transfer to primary school.
Italy	Is planning legislation to establish an integrated or unitary ECCE system catering for children from birth to six years of age. If the legislation is passed, a plan would be developed to guarantee more provision.
Lithuania	From 1 September 2016, pre-primary education will be compulsory (20 hours per week) for all children from one year before primary schooling.
Poland	From September 2016, compulsory ECCE starts at age five instead of six. From September 2017, the legal entitlement will be extended to three-year-olds.
Portugal	Will establish a legal entitlement for four-year-olds from 2016–2017 and for three-year-olds in the following years.

Source: European Commission/EACEA/Eurydice (2015).

Finland and Sweden) guarantee a legal right to a place in ECCE for each child soon after its birth, often immediately after the end of the parental leave period.

This, in general, does not coincide with the laws and treaties to which countries adhere so as to guarantee education for all. There is a gap between legal postulates and what countries can guarantee according to their policies and economic conditions. Also, some states have been able to adapt their systems to democratize access, significantly expanding the coverage and quality of early education processes.

> In Denmark, since 2001, the regulatory framework obliges municipalities to ensure ECEC provision for all children between the ages of six months and six years (when compulsory primary education begins). Municipalities are sanctioned financially if they fail to comply and therefore all municipalities now meet the requirements. Parents may have to meet up to of 25% of a centre's operating expenditure. (Eurydice, 2016, p. 8)

Case Sweden

Sweden was a slow starter, only offering EE to 10% of the children aged six months – six years in 1975 (Engdahl, 2011). Today, 84.5% of all children aged 1–5 years go to EE, most children starting during their second year of life. 89% of the two-year-olds and 95% or the five-year-olds participate today (NAFE, 2018a).

Today in Sweden, all children from the age of one are legally entitled to EE. The Education Act 2010 requires municipalities to provide preschool services for children from one year. When parents require a place for their child in ECCE, the municipality should offer one within four months. Parents may choose their EE-institution, run by the municipal or independently. In 2003, a flat fee system was introduced with a low monthly cost, lower than the monthly child allowance. 15 hours/week are free from three years (Table 4).

EE in Sweden is regulated by the Education Act of 2010 and establishes the first stage of education in Sweden. The task is to promote development and learning within a frame of secure care – Educare. A National Curriculum (Läroplan för förskolan Lpfö) was introduced in 1998 (NAFE, 2011) and has just been revised (NAFE, 2018b).

All preschools in Sweden are required to work according to this document. Philosophically, the early childhood curriculum is based on the notion of children as competent, active and engaged learners. The main approach is a play-based pedagogy, with a strong emphasis on children's participation at all levels. A holistic approach, which integrates education and care is foundational. The curriculum specifies the task and goals for EE in Swedish preschools, but the pedagogy, how to reach the goals, is locally decided in each preschool. The goals set down are goals to strive towards and to be aimed for and not goals to achieve. Consequently, they are formulated at a relatively abstract level, but preschool teachers are responsible for organizing the education in line with the curricular goals.

In a 2010 revised version of the curriculum, more specific objectives were included for children's development in language and mathematics, and in natural sciences and technology. The guidelines for staff responsibilities were

Table 4. Overview of EE-Institutions in Sweden.

Types	Characteristics
Preschool (förskola)	For children aged one to under six years
Preschool Class (förskoleklass)	One year of compulsory transition class for six- to seven-year-olds.
Open preschool (öppen förskola)	Community drop-in and advisory centres for parents and children.
Family day care (pedagogisk omsorg)	A home-based form of pedagogical care

Source: Engdahl (2011).

clarified, both at individual teacher level and at team level. New sections referred explicitly to documentation, evaluation and quality development, and also to the responsibilities of the head of the preschool.

The 2018 revision recognizes Sweden as a multi-cultural nation. It explicitly refers to the UN convention on the rights of the child and adds the task to contribute to sustainable development. Furthermore, the rights of the Swedish national minorities and of the Sami as indigenous people are added. A new section on the importance of play within EE clarifies that for children, play is the most important, and that teachers and all staff should recognize this in their attitudes and in the realization of the curriculum. Teaching is defined as a goal-directed intentional activity within the education. Education refers to the whole day, and any activity, as children's learning and development are continuous processes (Eidevald & Engdahl, 2018; Engdahl, 2011).

In Sweden, the number of preschool-aged children with a family language other than Swedish is large (around 25%, unevenly distributed) and growing. In some cities, for example, Malmö, half of the preschool children have another mother tongue that Swedish (NAFE, 2018a). With the curriculum aim of supporting active bilingualism and the children's bicultural identity, many municipalities have a policy of providing mother tongue support for these children. In the revision 2018, the task to support the development of the Swedish language as well as the mother tongue has been strengthened.

INEQUALITY AND 'FRAGMENTED TERRITORIES', EXAMPLE ARGENTINA[5]

The reality of Early Education shows notable differences in the different regions of the world, generally determined by the economic possibilities of each context. In the countries with the highest level of development, programs aimed at children set out more defined pedagogical objectives and have become a priority issue in the educational agendas.

To characterize the educational panorama in Argentina, and specifically the regional particularities, it is indispensable to consider the study carried out by Fernández, Lemos, and Wiñar (1997) *La Argentina Fragmentada. The case of Education.* The authors establish a correlation between the incorporation of children in EE and some socio-educational indicators, concluding that there is a close relationship between schooling of young children, the material conditions of life and the educational level of the parents. These conditions are contextualized in certain jurisdictions, generating a high degree of disparity regarding the possibility of attending EE in the different regions. The results of their investigation reveal the early mechanisms of exclusion of the public education system.

Social conditions have a strong impact on the ability of children to attend school or not. By analyzing the unequal distribution of wealth that is expressed territorially in Argentina, a correlation can be established between regions with higher poverty rates and those that have less assistance to educational institutions. To define the poverty parameters, the indicators of the permanent survey of households in Argentina are taken into account, specifically 'households with unsatisfied basic needs' (households with NBI)[6].

Official data indicate that in Argentina EE as in the Initial Level has a total enrolment of 1,485,899 students, 1,418,758 children are enrolled in the 'Ciclo Jardín de Infantes'[7] for three- to five-year-olds. Of these children, 702,158 attend the five-year room, 481,929 attend four-year-old rooms and 234,644 to the three-year section. It can be seen that children of three and four years have a much lower attendance, especially those of four years that do not reach 30% attendance in the whole country. According to the same source, 67,141 children enrolled in the 'Ciclo Jardín Maternal'[8] for children 45 days – 2 ½ years are registered throughout the country, which represents 4.5% of the total enrolment of the EE in Argentina. In Argentina it is necessary to guarantee access from 45 days of life of the baby, the maternity leave is very short.

To describe the inequalities in the territories in Argentina, data is taken from the Permanent Household Survey, which geographically covers the 28 main urban agglomerates of the country, surveying the 24 provincial capitals and other agglomerates that exceed one hundred thousand inhabitants. It highlights a significant heterogeneity in the specific attendance rates of three years of age (40%); four years (75%) and five years old (96%). It can be interpreted as a result of the historical evolution of the level that began by expanding from the top (five-year-olds) and then progressively to the first year in life (Fig. 2).

Since more than a decade, the five-year room of EE is mandatory in the country. According to official statistics, in Misiones there are 56,197 children between three and five years old waiting for the provincial government to guarantee their access to education. Many of these children who do not go to school live in rural areas and belong to poor families.

The analysis of the last censuses[9] shows that in the most economically depressed jurisdictions of Argentina, the development of the Initial Level is

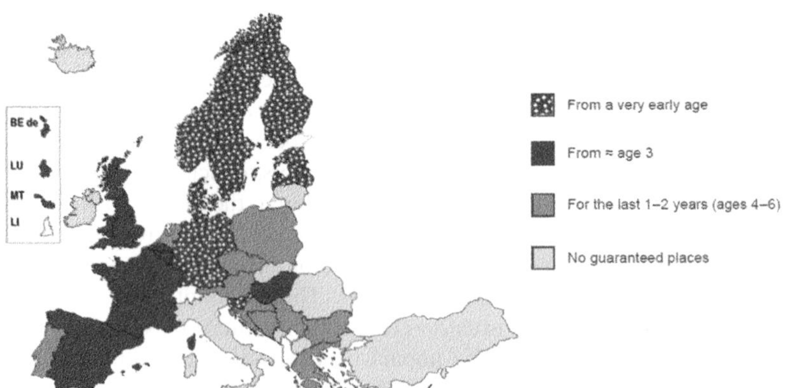

Fig. 2. Age from Which a Place in ECCE is Guaranteed, 2015–2016. *Source*: Eurydice.

Table 5. Interprovincial Fragmentation of Access to EE.

Jurisdiction (Provinces and Regions)	Households with NBI (%)	Urban Population (%)	Population of Three-year-olds	Population of Three-year-olds Attending the Kindergarten	
				Absolute	Percentage
Buenos Aires (Pampa)	14	96	238.813	159.287	67
Chaco (NEA)	27	79	24.454	2.102	8
Formosa (NEA)	28	77	11.787	760	6
Chubut (Patagonia)	13	89	8.127	2.925	36
Misiones (NEA)	23	70	24.496	897	4

Source: Losso (2008) after analysing data of the Annual Survey DiNIEE (2008).

more difficult both in the quantity of coverage and in quality. The rural area and the social sectors with the highest NBI indexes have the lowest attendance figures for Kindergarten and the Maternal Cycle is practically non-existent. The following table shows some variables that account for interprovincial fragmentation (Table 5).

The jurisdictions with the highest percentage of households with unsatisfied basic needs and more rural population have the lowest coverage in the three-year section of the EE. We can appreciate the extreme data that indicate a 67% attendance to the three-year section in the city of Buenos Aires and a 4% attendance of the population of that age in the province of Misiones.

According to the socio-economic level of the population, children are grouped according to their household belonging to one of the five categories or quintiles of monetary income that households receive. Thus, it is possible to note the differences in the attendance rate for each of the income quintiles, from the first, which brings together 20% of the poorest or lowest-income households, where the attendance rate is 65, up to the fifth and last, which brings together 20% of households with higher incomes, and in which the numbers of school attendance reach 84% (DiNIEE, 2016).

If we consider the two variables: territorial location and economic situation, the main causes of inequality are synthesized. Children who live in the North or North East of Argentina (NOA and NEA)[10] and in families with the lowest incomes have a rate of access to EE significantly lower than the child population of the rest of the country and of families with the highest income (Fig. 3).

Children Aged 45 days – 2½ Years

On the Maternal Cycle of the Initial Level, the differences are even more obvious, children from 45 days to 2½ years. In Argentina, the majority of these ages are not attending state educational institutions. According to official censuses, only eight Argentine provinces have educational units of Maternal Cycle. Of the total enrolment in the Maternal Cycle of the country (67,641 children), 27,326

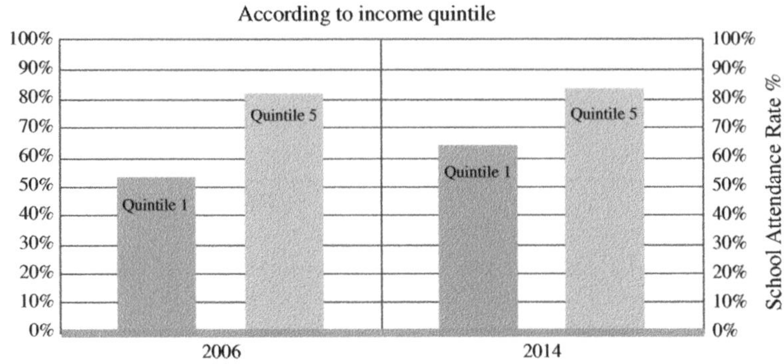

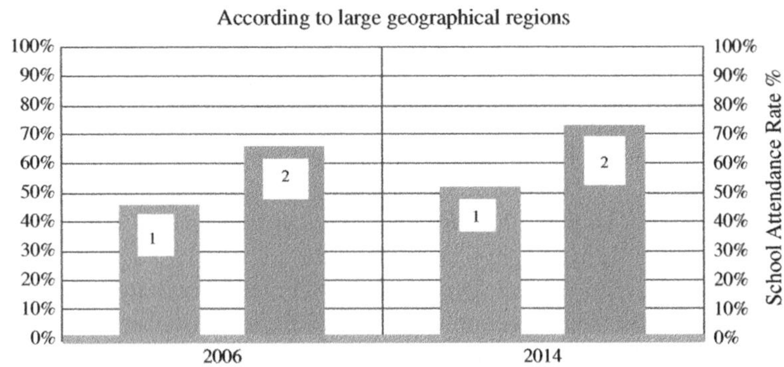

Fig. 3. Development of the Rates of School Attendance Between 2006 and 2014 According to Family Income and Regions of Argentina. *Source*: EPH-INDEC (2016).

students attend state-run institutions (41%) and 39,815 children (59%) attend institutions in the private sector.

The data analyzed shows that the private sector responds to the needs of early childhood education and attention of vast sectors of the population. This trend is historical and could already be perceived in the first decades of the twentieth century and has been sustained – with some variations – up to the present. It is a sector that has grown notably since the 1990s, especially in the social sectors most favored economically in the urban area. In the rural area, the private sector isn't available, the population live far and have not the economical possibilities to pay the education or care for children.

The concentration of Maternity institutions in the Province of Buenos Aires is notable, especially in the state sector. As we move away from the main urban areas, coverage decreases. You can see greater coverage of private management, which, although scarce, has a presence in different provinces.

When the State does not cover the needs and the private sector is inaccessible, civil society has generated some alternatives. There are still no specific studies that explain and describe with certain rigour the reality of the non-formal system of childcare. It is difficult to gather all the information necessary to prepare a study of this type at a national level since there is no official and systematized data on these institutions. Some research advances made in the province of Río Negro (Losso, 2007, 2008) have served as a basis for comparing the situation of other jurisdictions.

The origins of children's centres share some features and differ in others. Some have emerged as restructuring of municipal 'day-care centres', others began to function in community centres and soup kitchens based on social demand and the organization of mothers. In some cases they were self-managed by the community and in others they were managed by initiatives of private organizations and foundations. The origin of the infantile centres was giving rise to the formation of provisional networks institutions (municipalities, programs of assistance, members of the community, churches, etc.) that were involved in the process of constitution of the new institutions.

The names of non-formal institutions of Child Care are diverse and are linked to their origin and to the programs or agencies that assisted them for their emergence and development. We found Nursing Care Centers, Child Care Centers, Recreation Centers, Child Development Centers. Their basic functions are similar and they are diversified in the features that have to do with the identities that they are building in relation to the community that shelters them. These identities are also linked to the needs they must meet and the demands they receive.

The data about EE in Europe, previously described in section 'Examples from Europe', show a fragmentation the level of institutionalization and the role of the states in accessing the EE. In addition, other studies show differences within each state between the services of each region. As in Latin America, there are differences between the urban and rural areas, and in rural areas we find the lowest number of EE institutions and the lowest level of education for the child population.

THE CONCEPT OF EDUCARE

Educare, combining education and care, stands for a model of early childhood education starting in the 1970s in Sweden and other Nordic welfare states (Walch, 1993). The idea is for EE to organize preschools characterized by a good playful environment meeting the needs of the children and at the same time meeting the parents' needs by taking good care of the children and thus contributing to the society, by enabling parents to go to work (Engdahl, 2011). According to Hammarström-Lewenhagen (2013), the Educare model is a pragmatic result of negotiations regarding societal needs; democratic values, equality, social equalization, the youngest children's upbringing and education, within a system of life-long learning (Delors, 1996). The Swedish Educare model is also within international studies described as an Educare model, and recognized for its unique characteristics (OECD, 2006). An international survey of early childhood education and care (UNICEF, 2008) looking at parental leave systems, plans and resources for expansion of ECCE, enrolment of children, training of staff, child/teacher ratio, and child health initiatives placed Sweden as the top of the 25 participating nations.

There are some significant patterns related to the Educare concept. First, *the holistic approach* given by integrating care, nurture, play, development and learning. This aspect is often referred to as the Nordic model, in comparison with other countries (Broström & Wagner, 2003). The holistic perspective perceives the child as one entity and integrates knowledge, sensations and feelings. It looks at the child as one whole person, not to be divided into binary and dualistic views linked to reasonings about body and soul, mind and heart, cognitive and motoric et cetera. 'Play is the foundation for development, learning and well-being. For children, playing is an important activity in its own right' (NAFE, 2018b, p. 8). This holistic approach has implications for how to organize the preschool (Engdahl, 2011).

Secondly, a recurrent pattern has to do with *child care*, i.e. taking care of children when their guardians work or study. Educare strives for only one additional environment to the family home, not multiple. Thus, the opening hours are set to cover the needs for most parents.

Thirdly, *quality and quantity are interrelated*, and in Educare you strive for high quality in all institutions, as a 'preschool-for-all'. In Sweden, there are very few separate institutions for children with different kinds of special needs. The universal right to qualitative education with a conscious social purpose is highly important.

Fourthly, within Educare, there is a struggle to define and further *develop the pedagogy*, while at the same time keeping the core of early childhood education. A new view on children, where children are citizens, with competencies and agentic rights, has paved the way for a more child-oriented pedagogy. The children have the right to express their ideas, to be listened to and to participate in decision makings in their daily lives, including in EE (CRC, 2009; UN, 1989).

Additionally, the process of care, as one part in Educare, is seen as a learning process, a two-way directed communicative act, based on relationships. Trust, close relationships and care are by some researchers looked upon as preconditions for growing and learning. Turning to education, the edu-part in Educare, research shows that learning is related to relationships and to context. Early childhood education is about learning to be human (not to become a human). It is about learning the fundamental values in society and how to build relationships (Engdahl, 2015)

Paraphrasing Loris Malaguzzi and his metaphor of the 100 languages, quality in preschools is linked to the ability to listen to what the children are telling us and to act accordingly. Sylva et al. (2010) suggests an approach signified by *shared sustainable thinking*, where the initiative may come from either the children or the teachers, and in a balanced way. Teaching is about showing something for someone (Pramling Samuelsson & Pramling, 2014) and to create meeting-points and challenges for the children. Children prefer to play and learn together, the child is a playing learning child, and the teachers should use a collaborative approach with child participation at the core. Characteristically, the Educare pedagogy use children's everyday lives and their shown interests while working cross-subjects with projects and themes. By using integrated curriculum approaches and authentic topics, the teachers are leaning on child participation and listening to the children's voices.

The preschools' primary task is to ascertain the best opportunities for every child's learning and development within the framework of secure care (Engdahl, 2004; UN, 1989). In the Swedish national curriculum, the task is founded in the Educare model and described in the following words:

> Education in the preschool should lay the foundations for life-long learning. It should be enjoyable, secure and rich in learning for all children. Education should be based on a holistic approach to children and the needs of children, in which care, development and learning form a whole. In cooperation with the home, the preschool should promote the development of children to become active, creative, competent and responsible people and members of society. (NAFE, 2018b, p. 7)

FINAL THOUGHTS

The data shows that the process to democratize Early Education (EE) has begun, guaranteeing all children the right to care and education from birth in EE institutions specially created to fulfill that function. However, data also shows that the children of the popular sectors, the children who live in the periphery of the cities, the rural areas, whether due to geographical, social or economic marginalization, are being 'left out' of the educational actions. The realization of the public policies indicate a continued coexisting diversity of modalities of attention to EE. Considering this context, it is essential to additionally invite alternatives to improve the quality of existing institutions, paying special attention to those that correspond to the non-formal sector and for the youngest children.

Furthermore, to follow the expansion of EE, it is necessary to demand from the relevant organizations up-to-date surveys of national coverage, on children from birth to three years old as well as from three to five years, specified by age. Data on the childcare and education system should include the formal programs supervised by the ministries of education, are also necessary, and include private institutions operating without dependence on the educational area and with municipal authorization. Data from non-formal institutions such as Children's Centers, Child Development Centers, Child Care Centers, Mother Care Centers, etc. should also be collected. The surveys should cover both urban and rural areas, reaching the entire population.

Having a clearer picture of the reality of the complex Early Childhood Care and Education system, it is essential to design actions that aim to improve the conditions of these institutions, in order to expand the reception and permanence of young children with a child-oriented perspective and from the logic of children's rights (See e.g. Engdahl, 2011; Pramling Samuelsson & Asplund Carlsson, 2008).

In this line of work, now is the time when the political agenda should emphasize the state guarantee of access and permanence also for the youngest children in the

Maternal Cycle. Just as a decade ago the extension of the coverage of the five-year section was proposed, and the data show significant advances, by initiating systematic actions for younger children, in a decade, encouraging results could achieved, replacing today's worrisome panorama. To put it short, multiple efforts and collaboration between many different organizations and stake holders are necessary to meet the UN Global goal 4.2 about EE for all children.

NOTES

1. We say "new" in the sense that Arendt (1998[1958]) proposes.
2. Concept from Cullen (2009).
3. The World Conference "Education for All". (1990). Jomtien, Thailand.
4. Emilia Velázquez Hernández (2006) refers to this as a concept that covers all geographic regions, community, social group that inhabits a social space produced on unequal material bases with respect to the most favored sectors of a state.
5. In this section a detailed review of the case of Argentina is presented as a punctual reference of what is described in the article. The research is part of a doctoral thesis project by Losso (ongoing).
6. NBI (Unsatisfied Basic Needs) defined according to the methodology used in Poverty in Argentina (Estudios INDEC series, No. 1, Buenos Aires, 1984). Households with unsatisfied basic needs are households that present at least one of the following deprivation indicators:

   - Overcrowding: households with more than three people per room.
   - Housing: households that live in a dwelling of the inconvenient type (piece of tenancy, piece of hotel or boarding house, square, room not built for a room or mobile home, excluding house, apartment and ranch).
   - Sanitary conditions: homes that do not have any type of toilet.
   - School attendance: households that have at least one child of school age (6 to 12 years) who does not attend school.
   - Subsistence capacity: households with four or more persons per occupied member whose head has not completed the third grade of primary school.

7. This concept does not have a direct translation into English.
8. This concept does not have a direct translation into English.
9. "Censo Nacional de Población, Hogares y Viviendas 2001" and "Censo Nacional de Población, Hogares y Viviendas 2010", Argentina.
10. NOA: Northwest Argentina, includes the provinces of the provinces of Jujuy, Salta, Tucumán, Catamarca, La Rioja and Santiago del Estero. This region is prone to climate changes due to its geography and deforestation, social vulnerability to disasters (mainly floods) reaches critical levels, especially in the provinces of Santiago del Estero and Salta, Catamarca and La Rioja being in better conditions. NEA: The Argentine northeast includes the provinces of Formosa, Chaco, Corrientes and Misiones.

REFERENCES

Arendt, H. (1998 [1958]). *The human condition*. Chicago, IL: University of Chicago Press.

Bárcena, F. (1997). *El oficio de la ciudadanía: Introducción a la educación política*. Barcelona: Paidós.

Broström, S., & Wagner, J. T. (2003). *Early childhood education in five Nordic countries. Perspectives on the transition from preschool to school*. Århus: Systime Academic.

Carli, S. (Ed.). (2006). *La cuestión de la infancia: Entre la escuela, la calle y el shopping*. Buenos Aires: Paidós.

Coraggio, J. (1995). *Desarrollo humano, economía popular y educación*. Buenos Aires: Editorial AIQUE-IDEAS.

CRC. Committee on the rights of the child. (2009). *General comment no. 12: The right of the child to be heard.* Geneva: Human Rights, office of the high commissioner.

Cullen, C. (2009). *Entrañas éticas de la identidad docente.* Buenos Aires: La Crujía.

Dahlberg, G., Moss, P., & Pence, A. (1999). *Beyond quality in early childhood education and care: Postmodern perspectives.* London: Falmer.

Delors, J. (Ed.). (1996). *Learning: The treasure within.* (Report to U N E S C O of the International Commission on Education for the Twenty-first Century). Paris: UNESCO.

Denzin, N. K., & Lincoln, Y. S. (1994). Introduction: Entering the field of qualitative research. In N. K. Denzin & Y. S. Lincoln (Eds.), *Handbook of qualitative research.* Thousand Oaks, CA: SAGE.

DiNIEE. (2008). *Mapa educativo nacional.* Retrieved from http://www.mapaeducativo.edu.ar/Atlas/inicial

DiNIEE. (2016). *Dirección nacional de información y estadística educativa.* Ministerio de Educación y Deportes, Argentina. Retrieved from http://ceadel.org.ar/centrodoc/?page_id=1232

Eidevald, C., & Engdahl, I. (2018). *Utbildning och undervisning i förskolan: Omsorgsfullt och lekfullt stöd för lärande och utveckling.* Stockholm: Liber.

Engdahl, I. (2004). Implementing a national curriculum in the Swedish preschool. *International Journal of Early Childhood Education, 10*(2), 53–78. Seoul: Korean Society for Early Childhood Education.

Engdahl, I. (2011). *Toddlers as social actors in the Swedish preschool.* (Doctoral thesis). Stockholm: Stockholm University, Department of Child and Youth Studies.

Engdahl, I. (2015). Early childhood education for sustainability: The OMEP world project. *International Journal of Early Childhood, 47*, 347–366. doi:10.1007/s13158-015-0149-6

European Commission/EACEA/Eurydice. (2015). *Description of national education systems Sweden.* Luxemburg: Publications Office of the European Union.

Eurydice/European Commission/EACEA. (2016). *Structural indicators on early childhood education and care in Europe* (Eurydice report). Luxembourg: Publications Office of the European Union.

European Commission/EACEA Eurydice. (2017). *The structure of the European education systems 2017/18: Schematic diagrams* (Eurydice Facts and Figures). Luxemburg: Publications Office of the European Union.

Fernández, M., Lemos, M., & Wiñar, L. (1997). *La Argentina fragmentada: El caso de la educación.* Buenos Aires: I.I.C.E. Miño y Dávila.

Freire, P. (1972). *Pedagogy of the oppressed.* New York, NY: Herder & Herder.

Fujimoto, G. (2006). Conference presentation at the *Innovation in Pedagogical Practice: A challenge for the 21st century.*

Giroux, H. (2000). *Stealing innocence: Corporate culture's war on children.* London: Palgrave Macmillan.

Hammarström-Lewenhagen, B. (2013). *Den unika möjligheten: En studie av den svenska förskolemodellen 1968–1998.* [The unique possibility: A study of the Swedish preschool-model 1968-1998]. (Doctoral thesis). Stockholm: Stockholm University.

Hammersley, M., & Atkinson, P. (2007). *What is ethnography?* (3rd ed.). New York, NY: Routledge.

INDEC. (2016). *Censo Nacional de Población, Hogares y Viviendas 2010.* Retrieved from https://www.indec.gov.ar/nivel4_default.asp?id_tema_1=4&id_tema_2=33&id_tema_3=98

InfoLEG. (2018). *Información Legislativa y Documental.* Ministerio de Justicia y Derechos Humanos, Argentina. Retrieved from http://www.infoleg.gob.ar/

Law No. 24195 Federal of Education. Published in the Official Gazette of the Argentine Republic on May 5, 1993, N ° 27632, p. 1. Argentine Congress, Buenos Aires.

Law No. 26075 Educational Financing. Published in the Official Gazette of the Argentine Republic on January 12, 2006, N ° 30822, p. 1. Argentine Congress, Buenos Aires.

Law No. 26206 National Education. Published in the Official Gazette of the Argentine Republic on December 28, 2006, N ° 31062, p. 1. Argentine Congress, Buenos Aires.

Law No. 26075 Initial Education, amends Law No. 26206. Published in the Official Gazette of the Republic of Argentina on January 7, 2015, No. 33044, p. 1. Argentine Congress, Buenos Aires.

Losso, M. (2007). *Políticas públicas y derecho a la Educación Infantil en la provincia de Río Negro. Estudio de caso: Departamentos Pilcaniyeu, 25 de Mayo y 9 de Julio.* (Thesis). UNCPBA, Tandil.

Losso, M. (2008). *Derecho a la Educación de la Primera Infancia: Un estudio en la Región Sur de Río Negro.* Presentada en el X Congreso Nacional y II Internacional: "Repensar la niñez en el siglo XXI", REDUEI. Mendoza.

Losso, M. (2009a). *Infantia.* Paper presented at the III Coloquio Interdisciplinario Internacional Educación, sexualidades y relaciones de género. Investigaciones y experiencias. Facultad de Ciencias de la Educación, UN Comahue.

Losso, M. (2009b). *Language and socialization in preschool education.* Paper presented at the OMEP World Congress *Learning to Listen, Listening to Learn*, Lagos, Nigeria.

Losso, M. (2016). Lo público y el derecho a la educación de la Primera Infancia. Un estudio en la provincia de Río Negro, Argentina.*@rquivo Brasileiro de Educação, Revista, PUC Minas*, *4*(8).

Lyotard, J. ([1991] 1997). *Lecturas de infancia.* Buenos Aires: EUDEBA.

Maxwell, J. (1996). *Qualitative research design: An interactive approach.* Thousand Oaks, CA: Sage.

Myers, R. (2000). Atención y desarrollo de la primera infancia en Latinoamérica y el Caribe: una revisión de los diez últimos años y una mirada hacia el futuro. *Revista Iberoamericana de Educación*, *22*, 17–39.

NAFE National Agency for Education. (2011). *Curriculum for the Preschool - Lpfö 98* (Revised ed.). Retrieved from https://www.skolverket.se/publikationer?id=2704

NAFE National Agency for Education. (2018a). *PM: Barn och personal i förskolan 2017.* (Statistical data, only in Swedish). Stockholm: Skolverket.

NAFE National Agency for Education. (2018b). *Curriculum for the Preschool - Lpfö 18* (Revised ed.). Retrieved from https://www.skolverket.se/publikationer?id=4049

OECD. (2006). *Starting Strong II.* Paris: OECD. Retrieved from http://www.SourceOECD.org

Pramling Samuelsson, I., & Asplund Carlsson, M. (2008). The playing learning child: Towards a pedagogy of early childhood. *Scandinavian Journal of Educational Research*, *52*(6), 623–641.

Pramling Samuelsson, I., & Pramling, N. (2014). Children's play and learning and developmental pedagogy. I L. Brooker, M. Blaise, & S. Edwards (Eds.), *The Sage handbook of play and learning in early childhood* (pp. 169–179). London: Sage.

Sylva, K., Melhuish, E., Sammons, P., Siraj-Blatchford, I., & Taggart, B. (Eds.). (2010). *Early childhood matters: Evidence from the effective pre-school and primary education project.* Abingdon: Routledge.

UN. (1989). *The UN convention on the rights of the child.* New York, NY: United Nations. Retrieved from http://www2.ohchr.org/english/law/crc.htm

UN. (2015). *The sustainable development goals.* Retrieved from https://sustainabledevelopment.un.org/sdgs

UNESCO. (1990/1994). *World declaration on education for all and the framework for action to meet basic learning needs.* approved by the world conference on education for all, Jomtien, 1990. Paris: UNESCO.

UNICEF. (2008). *The child care transition: A league table of early childhood education and care in economically advanced countries.* (Innocenti Report Card 8). Retrieved from http://www.unicef-irc.org/cgi-bin/unicef/Lunga.sql?productID=507

Velázquez Hernández, E. (2006). *Territorios fragmentados: Estado y comunidad indígena en el Istmo veracruzano.* Centro de Investigaciones y Estudios Superiores en Antropología Social/ Publicaciones de la Casa Chata, México.

Walch, J. (1993). *The commotion of a social good: The case of Swedish Educare.* Stockholm: HLS förlag.

THE CONVENTION ON THE RIGHTS OF THE CHILDREN (CRC), THE GLOBAL DEVELOPMENTAL AGENDA AND CHILDREN IN SMALL ISLAND DEVELOPING STATES (SIDS)

Aldrie Henry-Lee and Yhanore Johnson-Coke

ABSTRACT

The members of the United Nations celebrate 30 years of the adoption of the Convention of the Rights of the Child (CRC) in 2019. This milestone has added significance in a context in which we are about a decade away from fulfilling the targeted goals of the UN 2030 Agenda with its pledge to leave no country or no-one behind. This is an opportune moment to assess the status of children in Small Island Developing States (SIDS). Using primary and secondary data, the chapter assesses the status of children after 30 years of the CRC in four Caribbean SIDs; Barbados, Jamaica, Haiti and St Lucia. The focus is on poverty, education, health and climate change related CRC articles and Sustainable Development Goals (SDGs). Data analysis reveals that the vulnerabilities of SIDS impede adherence to Child Rights for large proportions of children who are at risk of being left behind. *Climate Change increases their vulnerabilities and disparities persist in access to basic social services. As with the CRC and the Millennium Development Goals (MDGs), the implementation of the SDGs is plagued with a lack of timely and disaggregated data to inform the policy process; inadequate programmatic coordination; insufficient financial support; limited accountability and political*

Human Rights for Children and Youth: Sociocultural Differentiation, Resistance and Unity
Sociological Studies of Children and Youth, Volume 24, 35–58

ISSN: 1537-4661/doi:10.1108/S1537-466120190000024003

will. Cultural perceptions of children and inadequate recognition of the importance of children to any the Developmental Agenda also thwart progress for children in SIDs. Urgent action is needed if we are to fulfil all the commitments that we made to our children since 1989 with the adoption of the CRC.

Keywords: Child Rights; CRC; SDGS; UN2030 Agenda; SIDS; Caribbean

INTRODUCTION

In 1989, with the adoption of the Convention on the Rights of the Child (CRC), members of the United Nations pledged to provide for and protect all children everywhere. The UN2030 Agenda advocates that no country or individual should be left behind in the fulfilment of the Sustainable Development Goals (SDGS). However, even before 1989, a group of countries (SIDS) existed on the periphery of developmental process; their vulnerabilities persist even today and threaten to inhibit the fulfilment of the CRC and the SDGs.

SIDs are characterized by significant susceptibility to economic and environmental shocks; small labour markets compounded by limited skilled labour and high unemployment; limited productive sectors and heavy reliance on imports; an impending large increase in the size of the elderly population and high levels of poverty and inequality (Williams, Cheston, & Coudouel, 2013, p. 9). Given the characteristics of SIDs, adequate and sustained investment in children has been problematic.

Research has shown that social investment in children is essential for sustainable development (e.g. Gertler et al., 2014). Good quality pre-primary education produced significant economic benefits, including high rates of primary and secondary completion, higher earning in adulthood and lower crime (Heckman, Moon, Pinto, Savelyev, & Yavitz, 2010). Raising pre-school enrolment to 50% in low- and middle-income countries has been estimated to result in benefits of over US $33 billion (Engle et al., 2011). Improving nutrition and parental stimulation for infants and toddlers have resulted 20 years later in raising IQ, reducing anxiety, depression and violence, and increasing earnings by 50% (Gertler et al., 2014). It is difficult to argue against the case for investment in children.

However, given the vulnerabilities of SIDS, it is difficult to attain full adherence to children's rights or achieve the goals set by Developmental Agenda. The constant exposure to external and environmental shocks retards progress in meeting the targets and commitments set by the CRC and the UN2030. Insignificant economic growth and high levels of debt pose challenges to the adherence of the rights of all children. There is growing evidence that 'children in SIDS' are being left behind in the fulfilment of the CRC and the SDGS.

The discussion focuses on children's right to a decent quality of life: health, education and adequate protection from the impact of climate change, SDGs (1, 3, 4 and 13) These SDGs and related Millennium Development Goals (MDGs) and CRC Articles were specifically chosen because if they are fulfilled, there is an increased likelihood that the goals of the other SDGs would be attained. This chapter seeks to answer the following research questions:

(1) What are the synergies in the goals and targets among the CRC, the MDGs and the SDGs?
(2) What is the current status of the children in Caribbean SIDs in the fulfilment of the SDGs (1, 3, 4, and 13) and their relevant CRC articles and MDGs?
(3) What are some of the policies needed to increase adherence to the CRC and leave no child behind in the fulfilment of the UN2030 Agenda?

The chapter concludes that putting children's rights at the centre of any Developmental Agenda is key to sustainable development.

METHODOLOGY

Given the indisputable value of children to any attempt at sustainable development, we need to focus on the inputs necessary to ensure that children grow into productive adults. Ideally, adequate investment is needed from birth to adulthood. However, the quality of childhood that a child enjoys depends on several factors (Fig. 1). Apart from the immediate agents of socialization (e.g., the family, the school, the community) with which they interact, the national environment can determine their quality of life. The quality of childhood that children experience will shape their adulthood and ultimately, their contribution to their societies (Fig. 1).

The chapter examines the status of children in four SIDs; Barbados, Jamaica, Haiti and St Lucia, 30 years after the implementation of the CRC. These

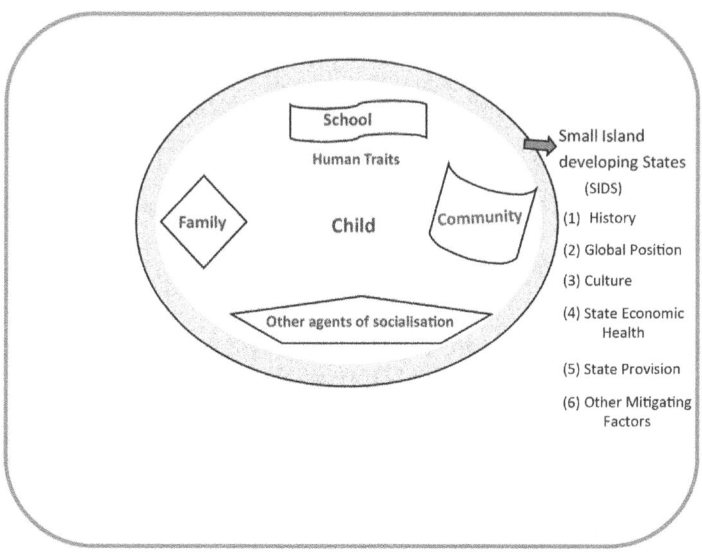

Fig. 1. Conceptual Framework. *Source*: Adapted from Bronfenbrenner (1947).

countries were chosen as they represent varying cultural and economic circumstances. In spite of their differences, all four countries face similar challenges in the implementation of any Development Agenda for children. To examine the progress made for children since 1989, secondary data was collected from previous research and statistical reports from local, regional and international agencies. Much of the secondary data was from national statistical institutes and international agencies, for example World Bank (WB), International Monetary Fund (IMF) and the World Health Organization (WHO).

Primary data from a survey among 103 children in Jamaica in 2013–2014 were also analyzed to present the views of children in that country. Similar studies have not yet been completed for the other countries given time and cost constraints. Invitations were sent to four public urban schools but only two allowed access. It was easier to access the children at school, and the researcher believed that children would be able to speak more freely at school than at home. Only the students whose parents granted written consent were interviewed. There were 82 girls and 31 boys from the upper schools and they were enrolled in grades 11 and 12.

The study among the 103 students sought to determine the perceptions of children on:

- the quality of life in Jamaica;
- parents' treatment of children;
- teachers' treatment of children;
- levels of violence in Jamaica; and
- the problems that children face in Jamaica.

While the sample is too small to generalize to the national population, the data does indicate the perceptions of some children in an urban setting. The analysis of the status of children in the other countries depends heavily on secondary data. Data from the 2014 national Jamaica Survey of Living Conditions (JSLC) also enhanced the analysis by examining the disparities among children living in poverty and those who do not. The other countries under discussions do not have an annual survey of living conditions. Generally, research on children in Caribbean SIDS is hampered by the paucity of current and representative data.

THE INTERNATIONAL DEVELOPMENTAL AGENDA AND CHILDREN

Children were only universally accepted as rights holders with the adoption of the Convention on the Rights of the Child (CRC) in 1989. Before that, their concerns were peripheral to International Development Agenda. However, child-related goals were included in the MDGs, adopted in 2000 at the Millennium Summit. The SDGS which replaced the MDGs also gave children some policy attention.

The Convention on the Rights of the Child (CRC) is the main legally binding international instrument for the guarantee and the protection of children's rights. Adopted in 1989, its objective is to protect the rights of all children in the world. The Convention comprises of 54 articles that established the body of all children's civil, political, economic, social and cultural rights (Humanium, 2012).

However, Humanium (2012) put forward some deficiencies of the CRC:

(1) *The CRC presents children as burdens rather than responsible individuals* – it is often the parents who are held financially responsible for their child's misdemeanours while they are under 18 years of age. The child, therefore, can be seen as more of a burden than a responsible individual.
(2) *Universal age (18) is still left up to subjectivity* – the universal age of a child as defined by the Convention makes it difficult to determine the precise age at which a child becomes an adult since each person develops at a different pace. As such this fixed age limit is determined by opinion and can prove very inappropriate in some countries where individuals are legally held responsible for their actions before the age of 18 years.
(3) *Rights do not exist without their counterpart responsibilities* – the rights regarding the child suggest only moral obligations such as respect towards parents and therefore are often seen as irrelevant and not as important as other rights that dictate the treatment of children.

However, despite these criticisms, the CRC is used as an appropriate international framework for the implementation of Child Rights.

The MDGs were comprised of 8 main goals. Each goal had measurable targets and clear deadlines for improving the lives of the world's poorest people. The MDGs were adopted by 189 country leaders in 2000. The MDGs included the provision of universal primary education and reduction of child and maternal mortality. The goals were set out to be achieved in 2015.

The MDGs were credited for the bold move to transform the planet into a safe haven not just for children but for all the world's inhabitants. However, some writers have pointed to some of their deficiencies:

(1) *Top–down approach* – The MDGs were considered as donor-led, that is, little attention was paid to local context and as a result, they penalized and stigmatized the poorest countries where achieving the goals was a greater challenge (Easterly, 2009 in Melamed & Scott, 2011, p. 2).
(2) *Failed to take into account the initial conditions of the various regions and countries* – The MDGs failed to take into account the initial conditions of the various regions and countries, that is, the difference in effort countries would have needed to make in order to make the same relative degree of progress (United Nations, 2012, p. 8).
(3) *Neglected the poorest and most vulnerable* – The MDGs neglected the poorest and most vulnerable since they were based on average progress at a national or global level (Holmes, Jones, & Espey in Melamed & Scott, 2011, p. 2).

(4) *Missed out on some critical dimensions of development* – The MDGs missed out on critical dimensions of development such as climate change, the quality of education, human rights, economic growth, good governance and security (Vandemoortele & Delamonica, 2010 in Melamed & Scott, 2011, p. 2).
(5) *MDGs were difficult to implement because of paucity of data* – the absence of timely and reliable disaggregated data made it very difficult to have implemented the MDGs and subsequently, track their progress (Dar & Khan, 2011; Easterly, 2009; Sachs, 2012).

However, the MDGs can be credited for increasing international focus on issues of poverty and human development. They harnessed resources towards efforts at the implementation of one global development agenda.

The final international framework under discussion involves the SDGs. Also known as the Global Goals, they call for an end to poverty, protection of the plane, peace and prosperity. The SDGs consist of 17 Goals that build on the successes of the MDGs along with some new inclusions such as climate change and sustainable consumption. They provide clear guidelines and targets for all countries to adopt in accordance with their own priorities and the environmental challenges of the world at large. The goals are set to be achieved by 2030.

Some writers have highlighted shortcomings of the SDGs:

(1) *The poverty targets require further specification* – The issue of provision of basic income and social protection to eliminate extreme poverty, promotion of effective and equitable processes of wealth creation and distribution; employment and insurance in the present and the future have not been given adequate attention (Deacon and St Claire in International Council for Science, 2015, p. 18).
(2) *Outcome statements are needed for the goal on gender equality* – The targets regarding gender equality and the empowering of women and girls need to have outcome statements; they need to be time-specific, and there needs to be the inclusion of a number of key economic and social targets on employment, pay, education, and mental and physical health (Nyasimi and Peake in International Council for Science, 2015, p. 30).
(3) *Additional dimensions to SDG 4 are needed* – To address the problem that most educational policies and programmes are not linked to the purposes and goals of sustainable development. A new target is recommended for life-long learning (Sterling in International Council for Science, 2015, p. 30).

In spite of all the gaps identified, these three international frameworks serve as global aspirations and guidelines for the Development Agenda of the members of the United Nations. There are several synergies among these frameworks and they re-emphasize and complement each other (Table 1).

There are many synergies among the CRC, MDGS and SDGs; they complement and re-emphasize each other's goals. The articles of the CRC and the SDGS have provided more holistic and multi-dimensional perspectives on development than the MDGS. If the CRC and the SDGS are successfully

Table 1. Synergies among the SDGs, MDGs and the CRC.

SDGs	MDGs	CRC (Articles)
1. No poverty	Eradicate extreme poverty and hunger	1, 2, 4, 6, 19, 20, 22, 23, 24, 26, 27, 28, 29
2. Zero hunger	Eradicate extreme poverty and hunger	1, 2, 4, 6, 19, 20, 22, 23, 24, 26, 27, 28, 29
3. Good health and well-Being	Combat HIV/AIDS, Malaria and other diseases	1, 2, 3, 4, 6, 7, 13, 17, 19, 23, 24, 25, 27, 29, 31, 32, 33
4. Quality education	Achieve universal primary education	1, 2, 3, 4, 6, 13, 14, 17, 19, 22, 23, 28, 29, 30, 31, 32, 33, 34, 36, 37, 38, 40, 42
5. Gender equality	Promote gender equality and empower women	1, 2, 4, 5, 9, 10, 18, 19, 22, 24, 26, 27, 28, 29, 32, 34, 35, 36, 37, 38, 39
6. Clean water and Sanitation	Ensure environmental sustainability	1, 2, 3, 4, 6, 12, 13, 15, 16, 17, 22, 23, 24, 27, 28, 29, 32, 34, 36, 38
7. Affordable and clean Energy	Ensure environmental sustainability	2, 4, 17, 24, 27, 28, 29
8. Decent work and Economic Growth		1, 2, 4, 15, 18, 19, 23, 24, 28, 29, 32, 34, 35, 36, 37, 38, 39
9. Industry, innovation and infrastructure	Ensure environmental sustainability	2, 4, 13, 17, 28, 29
10. Reduced Inequality		2, 4, 8, 9, 10, 11, 12, 13, 17, 22, 23, 26, 27, 30
11. Sustainable cities and communities	Ensure environmental sustainability	1, 2, 4, 6, 12, 13, 15, 16, 17, 19, 22, 12, 24, 27, 28, 29, 30, 31, 33, 34, 35, 36, 37
12. Responsible consumption and production		13, 17, 24, 28, 29
13. Climate Action	Ensure environmental sustainability	4, 6, 12, 13, 15, 17, 23, 29, 30
14. Life Below water		4, 13, 17, 24, 28, 29
15. Life on Land		2, 4, 13, 17, 28, 29
16. Peace, Justice and Strong Institution	Global partnership for development	1, 2, 4, 6, 7, 8, 12, 13, 14, 15, 16, 17, 19, 21, 23, 24, 29, 30, 31, 32, 33, 34, 35, 36, 37, 38, 39, 40, 42
17. Partnership for the Goals	Global partnership for development	4, 12, 13, 17, 28

Source: Modified version of 'mapping the global goals for sustainable development and the Convention on the Rights of the Child', UNICEF (2016).

implemented, there will be increased adherence to children's rights and ultimately an improvement in the quality of life for children everywhere.

THE CARIBBEAN CONTEXT

In the absence of an enabling environment, the rights of children will never be given the attention and focus that are deemed adequate to realize their full potential and enable them to effectively contribute to their societies. The chapter examines child well-being in Barbados, Jamaica, Haiti and St Lucia. As discussed earlier, the characteristics of SIDS impede their progress in the fulfilment of the CRC and SDGs for children. Economic growth in these four countries has been less than impressive ranging from 1.4% growth rate in Haiti and Jamaica to 2% in Barbados (Table 2). In spite of this dismal economic progress, social indicators are fairly reasonable. Life expectancy rates on the islands averaged 76 years old with the exception of Haiti where a person is expected to live on average up to 63 years old (Table 2). Inequality is high (as measured by the gini coefficient) and ranges from 0.61 in Haiti to 0.38 in Jamaica (Table 2).

Children (aged under 15 years) make up a significant portion of the population in these Caribbean countries, as much as 36% in Haiti (Table 3). All the four countries under review ratified the Convention of the Rights of the Child (CRC), the latest being Haiti in 1995 (Table 3). Legislative and policy attention has increased in these countries since the ratification of the CRC. Some examples are provided in Table 4.

In Jamaica, agencies have been established to focus on the delivery of services to children. The main State agency with the responsibility to protect the nation's children is the Child Protection and Family Services Agency (CPFSA). The CPFSA is a merger between the Office of the Children's Registry (OCR) and the Child Development Agency (CDA). The mantra of the CPFSA is 'Protecting children, empowering families, securing the future'.[1] One of the main social protection programmes in Jamaica is the Programme of Advancement through Health and Education (PATH). In December 2016, there were 251,592 registered children on PATH. The Health category (0–under 6 years) reported 45,181 registered children and the Education category (6–17 years) recorded 206,411 registered children (Planning Institute of Jamaica, 2017).

The Child Care Board (CCB) is the leading child protection agency and the main investigative body for reports about child neglect in Barbados. One of the agency's thrusts is to better understand the nature and complexity of child abuse and neglect, and to develop a public sensitization campaign about the various forms of child abuse and neglect (Child Care Board and UNICEF, 2012). In 2010–2011, there were 321 cases of new or reassigned and/or reclassified neglected cases for investigation (Child Care Board and UNICEF, 2012). Another child-centred initiative in Barbados is the PAREDOS[2] (Parent Education for Development in Barbados). PAREDOS is a non-profit organization formed in 1965 in response to needs identified by parents and concerned professionals in the community for parenting skills.

The Division of Human Services and Family Affairs in St Lucia has the primary responsibility to protect, support and improve the status of children and families from violence and abuse in any form (UNICEF, 2015). There are three main residential care facilities in St Lucia. There is also the Saint Lucia Family Court Act which was revised in 1994. The Family Court has introduced a parenting programme targeting parents with children who are victims of family violence (UNICEF, 2015). Equally important is the implementation of the child

Table 2. Some Socio-economic Indicators for Selected Caribbean Islands.

Country	GDP Growth[a] (2016)	Gross Public Debt as a % of GDP (2015)[b]	HDI (2015)[c]	Life Expectancy (2015)[c]	Total external debt as percentage of GDP[l] (2016)	Unemployment (2016)[a]	Poverty	Gini Coefficient	Homicide rate (Intentional) 2015[d]
Barbados	2.0	103.9	0.795	75.8	34.0	9.7	15.0 (2012)[e]	0.47 (2010)[e]	10.9
Jamaica	1.4	131.5	0.730	75.8	73.0	9.0	21.2 (2015)[f]	0.38 (2015)[f]	43.2
Haiti	1.4	29.9	0.493	63.1	26.4	13.2[g]	58.5 (2012)[h]	0.61 (2014)[i]	10 (2012)
St Lucia	1.7	89.0	0.735	75.2	31.7	24.1 (2015)[j]	21.4 (2007)[e]	0.42 (2007)[e]	21.6 (2012)

Sources: [a]http://estadisticas.cepal.org/cepalstat/PerfilesNacionales.html?idioma=English (retrieved January 25, 2018); [b]https://www.gfmag.com/global-data/economic-data/public-debt-percentage-gdp?page=3 (retrieved January 25, 2018); [c]http://hdr.undp.org/sites/default/files/hdr_2016_statistical_annex.pdf (retrieved January 25, 2018); [d]https://data.worldbank.org/indicator/VC.IHR.PSRC.P5?locations=JM-HT-BB-LC (retrieved January 29, 2018); [e]http://www.caribank.org/uploads/2012/12/Barbados-CALC-Volume-1-MainReport-FINAL-Dec-2012.pdf; [f]PIOJ, JSLC (2017); [g]https://www.ceicdata.com/en/blog/haiti-employment-2016 (retrieved January 25, 2018); [h]http://data.worldbank.org/country/haiti; [i]http://www.worldbank.org/en/news/opinion/2014/07/16/haiti-2030-un-pays-sans-pauvrete-extreme-catastrophes-naturelles; [j]Central Statistics Office http://192.147.231.244:9090/stats/

Table 3. Some Indicators on the Status of Children in Selected Caribbean Islands.

Country	Population ('000)[a] (2018)	Children (under 15) as a % of population (2018)[a]	Date of Ratification of CRC [b]	Infant Mortality Rate (2016)[c]	Child Poverty [d]	Registration at birth (%) 2012[e]	Immunization (DPT %) 2016[f]	Children 0-14 years living with HIV[g]
Barbados	286	18.9	09 Oct 1990	11.4	29.2	98.7	97	...
Jamaica	2 819	30.1	14 May 1991	13.2	26.5 (2015)[2]	99.5	99	<500
Haiti	11 085	35.9	8 June 1995	50.9	25.0	79.7	58	7600
St Lucia	189	22.8	16 June 1993	11.8	38.7	92	95	...

Sources: [a]http://countrymeters.info/en/ (retrieved May 17, 2018); [b]https://treaties.un.org/Pages/ViewDetails.aspx?src=IND&mtdsg_no=IV-11&chapter=4&lang=en; [c]https://data.worldbank.org/indicator/SP.DYN.IMRT.IN?locations=JM-LC-BB-HT (retrieved May 17, 2018); [d]JSLC 2015, 2005/6-http://www.caribank.org/uploads/publications-reports/economics-statistics/country-poverty-assessment-reports/SLUCPAVolIIIQuantitative.pdf; [e]http://data.worldbank.org/indicator/SP.REG.BRTH.ZS?locations=JM-BB-HT-LC (retrieved May 17, 2018); [f]http://data.worldbank.org/indicator/SH.IMM.IDPT?locations=BB-JM-HT-LC (retrieved May 17, 2018); [g]http://www.unaids.org/en/regionscountries/countries (retrieved August 29, 2018)

Table 4. Examples of Legislation and Policies Put in Place since the Ratification of the CRC.

Barbados	Haiti	Jamaica	St Lucia
Child Care Board Act 1997 Prevention of Cruelty to Children Act 1904 Registration of Private Child Care Centres 1997 Minors Act 1985 The Domestic Violence (Protection Orders) Act 1994 amended 2006	Prohibiting the corporal punishment of children 2001 Prohibition and elimination of all forms of abuse, violence, ill-treatment or inhumane treatment against children 2003 Amendments to the rules on sexual assault and eliminating discrimination against women (Decree)2005 Establishment and organization of the National Office for Partnerships in Education 2007 Abduction, kidnapping and hostage-taking of persons 2009 The integration of persons with Disabilities Act 2012 Taking measures to ensure the integrity of procedures for the international adoption of children of Haitians (Decree) 2012	Child Care and Protection Act 2004 The Adoption of Children Act 1958 The Sexual Offences Act 2009 The Cybercrime Act 2010 Trafficking in Persons Act 2007 The Child Pornography Act 2009 The Corrections Act 2005 The Judicature Act 1999 Larceny Act 2002 Offences against the Person Act 2011	Domestic Violence Act 1995 Attachment of Earning Act 1996 The Saint Lucia Criminal Code 1957 reviewed 2004, came into effect on January 1, 2005 The draft Labour Code of 2006 addresses the Committee's concerns about child labour, and also seeks to harmonize the domestic law with the ILO Convention No. 138. The draft Building Code of 1999 addresses the issues of accessibility for persons with disabilities including children. The Counter Trafficking Act of January 2010 makes provision for trafficking of children. The adoption of the Prevention of Misuse Drug Act in 1988 and its Amendment of 1993 which promotes 'drug-free zone' in schools The ratification in 2000 of ILO Convention No. 182 concerning the Prohibition and Immediate Action for the Elimination of the Worst Forms of Child Labour The establishment of the Legislative and Monitoring Committee -mandated to examine and monitor the extent to which existing laws, policies and services are matching the needs of children within the context of child protection The adoption of the Education Act No. 41 in 1999 -this makes provision for the promotion of universal access to primary and secondary education services to children between the ages of 5–15 years;

Source: JSLC 2014 dataset (data for children under 18 years old), analysis by authors using SPSS v. 21.

victim witness programme. This programme prepares children for their role in court. There is also the Boys Training Centre (BTC), which was established in 1960. To date, it is the only residential centre for troubled boys in St Lucia (UNICEF, 2015). A total of 140 boys were admitted to the BTC between 2009 and 2013 for care and protection or as offenders. There is the Court Diversion Programme in St Lucia which targets young persons aged from 12 to 19 years old and who are admitted to the centre as probationers, juveniles, chronic school suspenders or school dropouts. The total number of referrals to the programme between 2011 and 2014 recorded was 63 (UNICEF, 2015).

In Haiti, there is the National School Canteens Programme (PNCS) created in 1997. The PNCS's mission is primarily the management of canteens in public schools and the coordination of all the interventions by donors and NGOs (ECLAC, 2013). The programme provides a hot meal per day for students. Its coverage increased from a little over 150,000 students in 2007–2008 to just over 330,000 students in 2010–2011. In 2012, the PNCS and its partners (World Bank, PMA and USAID) achieved a nationwide coverage of 1.1 million students from 3,200 schools (ECLAC, 2013).

There are several other policies and programmes that target children in these SIDS. Since the ratification of the CRC, there has been an intensification of legislative, policy and programmatic attention on children (Table 4). However, as data analysis shows, inequities and disparities persist. Even though, one accepts that resources are scarce, there appears to be a lack of political will to prioritize investment in children in these SIDS. There is insufficient evidence of long-term planning and programming. Research has highlighted that a lack of political will and limited focus on sustainability issues hinder the successful implementation of any Developmental Agenda. (DESA and UNDP, 2012). These factors impede the attainment of sustainable development in developing countries and the implementation of the CRC and SDGs for children in SIDs.

THE RIGHT TO A GOOD QUALITY OF LIFE

UNICEF reports that almost 385 million children worldwide survive on less than $1.90 (£1.50) a day, the World Bank international poverty line.[3] Despite the advances in the last decades, children, their childhood and ultimately sustainable development remain at risk in Small Island Developing States (SIDs).

Breaking the intergenerational cycle of poverty can only be achieved through the eradication of child poverty. There are at least 13 CRC articles that underscore the importance of poverty reduction. Eradication of poverty is seen as so critical to development that it is listed as MDG 1 and SDG 1.

> Children living in poverty experience deprivation of the material, spiritual and emotional resources needed to survive, develop and thrive, leaving them unable to enjoy their rights, achieve their full potential or participate as full and equal members of society. (UNICEF, 2005 p. 18)

After 30 years of the CRC and about a decade away from the UN 2030 deadline, in Latin America and the Caribbean, one in five children still lives in conditions of extreme poverty; that is a total of 32 million children.[4] Child poverty rates in the countries under review remain higher than their national levels. Haiti recorded the highest rate of child poverty (38.7%) followed by the 29% as reported in Barbados (Fig. 2). The eradication of poverty, which remains number one in the list of SDGs is critical for the fulfilment of any Development Agenda for children. Without the eradication of child poverty, there cannot be full adherence to the 54 rights listed in the CRC or the fulfilment of the SDGs.

Table 5 examines the disparities between children living in poverty and those who are not using the 2015 Jamaica Survey of Living Conditions (JSLC). The analyses found that the mean age of children living in poor and non-poor households differed. The difference in the mean age observed between the two groups was statistically significantly ($p = 0.04$) (Table 5). The age of the average child in a poor household was approximately 9.1 years when compared with a non-poor household where the child was approximately 8.6 years. The number of children living in poor households were more likely to be greater than those living in non-poor households. The average number of children living in poor households was 2.6, this fell to 1.9 for non-poor households. The differences observed in the number of children living in the household between the groups were statistically different ($p = 0.00$). For the general population, the mean household size was estimated to be 4.4 persons. The difference in the mean

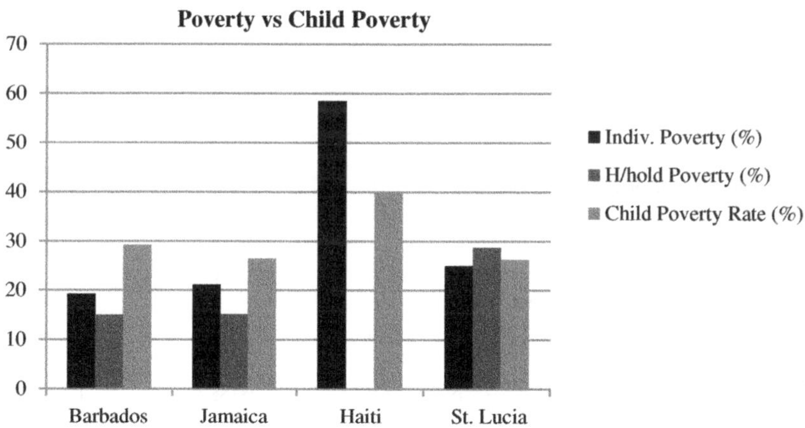

Fig. 2. National Poverty vs Child Poverty in Selected Caribbean Countries. *Sources*: http://www.caribank.org/uploads/2012/12/Barbados-CALC-Volume-1-MainReport-FINAL-Dec-2012.pdf; Planning Institute of Jamaica 2015 Survey of Living Conditions (Kingston: Planning Institute of Jamaica) http://data.worldbank.org/country/haiti; http://www.caribank.org/uploads/2012/12/Barbados-CALC-Volume-1-MainReport-FINAL-Dec-2012.pdf; https://www.unicef.org/easterncaribbean/ECAO_St._Lucia__Child_Protection_Statistical_Digest_2015.pdf;[2] Sir Arthur Lewis Institute of Social and Economic Studies, 2012:29

household size between the poor and non-poor households was statistically significant ($p = 0.00$). The mean household size for non-poor households was approximately 4.1 persons, this increased to 5.5 for poor household. From the reference period of 20 days, nationally children attended school an average of 19.2 of those days. Children in poor households attended school for 18.9 of those days when compared with children of non-poor households who attended school for 19.3 of those 20 days. The difference observed were statistically different ($p = 0.04$). The percentage of individuals in poor and non-poor households who had access to health insurance differed significantly. Approximately, 16% of the individuals in non-poor households had access to health insurance. This fell to 3.7% in poor households. The difference observed between the two groups were statistically significant ($p = 0.00$). The mean annual consumption expenditure for households and expenditure on education by households varied between the groups. Poor households spent $512,955 on consumption expenses, on average. This increased to $1,146,429 for non-poor households. Average education expenditure by non-poor households were $155,103, this fell to $129,539 for poor households. The differences observed in the spending patterns of poor and non-poor household on consumption expenditure and education expenses were statistically significant ($p = 0.000$ and p = 0.001 respectively). A total of 65.8% of the total population reported to have received PATH benefits. The differences observed between the poor and non-poor households differed and was significant (p = 0.000). For non-poor households, 59.4% reported receiving PATH benefits. This amount increased to 80.4% for poor households (Table 5).

Table 5. Some Indicators on Disparities between Poor and Non-poor Children in Jamaica.

	Poor	Non-poor	National
Mean age (years)* $N = 2837$	9.09	8.64	8.76
Mean number of children in household** $N = 1419$	2.6	1.9	2.0
Mean household size** $N = 1419$	5.5	4.1	4.4
Mean Total Annual consumption expenditure by household** $N = 1419$	J$512,955.38	J$1,146,429.86	J$1,017,313.09
Mean days of school attendance (20 day period)* $N = 2277$	18.9	19.3	19.2
Mean Total education expenditure by household** $N = 1275$	J$129,538.90	J$155.103.49	J$149,904.56
% with health insurance** $N = 2837$	3.7	15.9	12.7
% of household receiving/have received benefit from PATH** $N = 767$	80.4	59.4	65.8

Source: JSLC 2015 dataset (data for children under 18 years old), analysis by authors using SPSS v. 21. Also in Henry-Lee (2019, forthcoming).
*$p < .05$
**$p < .01$

> The child shall be registered immediately after birth and shall have the right from birth to a name, the right to acquire a nationality and as far as possible, the right to know and be cared for by his or her parents. (Article 7, CRC)

Violation of Rights may begin as early as birth. Those living in poverty are more likely not to have their birth registered (Adi et al., 2015; Humanium, 2018). Birth registration establishes nationality and is a right to access basic social services, for example, medical care, education, and housing. Birth registration facilitates the fulfilment of most of the MDGs and SDGs, especially MDGs 1–6 and especially, SDGS 1–8 and 10.

All children have a right to have their birth registered. Yet in Haiti only approximately 80% of children were registered at birth (Table 3). Birth registration was higher in the other countries; Jamaica was the closest to the 100% target as it reported 99.5% registration at birth, whereas Barbados and St Lucia reported 98.7% and 92% birth registration in 2012 (Table 3).

As the data analysis showed, child poverty inhibits the full adherence of Child Rights.

THE RIGHT TO HEALTH

Access to good quality health is the focus of 17 CRC articles, SDG 3 and MDG 2. The countries under review spent approximately 6–7% on health care with the exception of Jamaica which spent 5.4% of its GDP on health (Table 6). This is consistent with the spending of other countries in the Latin American and Caribbean region. However, this is some 2–3 percentage points lower when compared with Norway who spends approximately 10% on health (Table 6). Norway recorded the highest HDI (0.9753) in 2017.[5]

Child safety is essential for child well-being. Primary data collected from 103 secondary school students in Jamaica revealed that violence in the home is high or very high. When asked about their perception of violence in the home, of all the children interviewed, 62% of them thought that the violence that children face at home in Jamaica was high or very high. Another 32% of them deemed the violence in communities that children experienced to be high or very high. Direct violence against children is a major problem as 80% of them perceived that the violence against children in Jamaica was high or very high.

Child immunization is essential for child development and growth. However, immunization (DPT) was at only 58% in Haiti in 2016. The other countries recorded over 95% with Jamaica reporting the highest immunization diphtheria, pertussis (or whooping cough), and tetanus (DPT) in 2016 – 99% (Table 6).

In terms of health outcomes for children, Haiti had the highest infant mortality rate (53.9) in 2017 when compared with Jamaica (13.1) and St Lucia (14.7). However, mortality is trending downwards (Table 7).

Sexual abuse is a major problem in these SIDS and there are many children whose rights are violated. In Jamaica, there were 3,386 reported cases of sexual abuse against children in 2012–2013.[6] This increased to 3403 in the 2013–2014 reporting period.[7] Barbados and St Lucia also experience sexual violence against children. There were 203 reported cases in Barbados in 2011–2012 compared

Table 6. Some Education & Health Indicators (Children) in selected Caribbean Islands.

Country	Gross Enrolment rates in education 2008-2014 (Pre-Primary School age children)[a]	% of country Budget spent on Education (% of GDP) (2015)[b]	% of country Budget spend on Health (All levels) (% of GDP) (2014)[c]	Immunization (DPT %) 2016[f]	Children 0-14 years living with HIV[g]
Barbados	79	6.6 (2014)	7.5	97	...
Jamaica	82	5.5	5.4	99	<500
Haiti	92		7.6	58	7600
St Lucia	78	4.9	6.7	95	...
Latin America and the Caribbean		4.9	7.2		
Norway		7.4 (2013)	9.7		

Sources: [a]Caribbean Human Development Report, 2016 p. 117; [b]https://data.worldbank.org/indicator/SE.XPD.TOTL.GD.ZS?view=chart; [c]http://data.worldbank.org/indicator/SH.XPD.TOTL.ZS?end=2014&locations=BB-JM-HT-LC&start=1995&view=chart

Table 7. Infant Mortality Rates.

	Jamaica	St Lucia	Haiti
2011	15.6	16.3	59.6
2013	14.8	16	57.9
2015	13.9	15.5	56.1
2017	13.1	14.9	53.9

Source: https://data.worldbank.org/indicator/SP.DYN.IMRT.IN?locations=JM-HT-LC

with the 158 cases in 2012–2013.[8] St Lucia received 87 reports of sexual violence against children in 2011–2012.[9]

While all children are at risk of non-adherence of their rights, children living in poverty and those children with disabilities face higher levels of vulnerabilities because of their limited voice and agency. For example, in Haiti, persons with disabilities have very limited mobility: lack of ramps in schools, churches, shops, government buildings and foreign embassies. Very few children have wheel chairs, crutches or even a simple white cane for the blind. Cultural stigma impedes development of children as many caregivers consider children with disabilities as 'burdens' for the family and they are often neglected as families focus on the healthiest of the family for economic survival.[10]

Another extremely vulnerable group of children is those who are infected with and affected by HIV/AIDs. There were an estimated 16,000 children under 15 years in the Caribbean living with HIV in 2012.[11] Children infected with and affected by HIV/AIDS face many challenges. Poverty intensifies their vulnerability. In Haiti, there were 7600 children living with HIV/AIDs (Table 3).

Research has shown that in Jamaica, children living with HIV/AIDS suffer from inadequate access to health – major problems with the supply, distribution and dispensing of ARV drugs, and long waiting hours for prescriptions to be filled. Few pharmacies stock antiretroviral (ARV) drugs and basic drugs for related conditions such as sexually transmitted infections (STIs) are frequently not available in the public sector and are too expensive for most patients in the private sector.[12]

THE RIGHT TO EDUCATION

About 24 CRC-related articles and SDG 4 and MDG 2 focus on access to good quality education. Education and health are the most important areas of focus in the development of human capital.

This is supported by Becker (1994) who underscored that education and training are important investment for human capital development. Olaniyan and Okemakinde (2008) emphasized the role of education in the development of the productive capacity of a nation. Norway, the highest ranked country in terms of HDI spends on average 7.4% of its GDP on education (Table 6). The average spending in Latin America on education in 2015 was 4.9% (Table 6). The countries under review spend on average approximately 5%–6% of their GDP on education which is close to their regional counterparts but approximately two percentage points lower than the leading country in the world in terms of HDI, Norway.

Good teacher–student relations promote environments conducive to learning. Yet, in Jamaica, some students claimed that their relations with their teachers are less than desirable. Primary data collected from 103 secondary school students in the urban areas revealed that generally, students gave their teachers fairly good ratings. Of the children interviewed, 75% of them gave their teachers ratings from 4 to 5 (5 being the highest). The other 25% rated their teachers from 3 to 1. The reasons they provided for the low ratings included: paid little attention to me/disrespect me (51%); they don't like me (35%) and they like to punish students (14%).

Gross enrolment in early childhood (pre-primary) institutions was relatively high over the period for three countries (Table 6). In Jamaica, approximately 82% of the pre-primary school-aged children were enrolled in early childhood and approximately 92% and 78% in Haiti and St Lucia respectively (Table 6).

An examination of the main secondary exit programme for the Caribbean, (CXC) showed that over the last three years, the percentage of passes recorded in the core subjects (English Language, Mathematics and Information Technology) fluctuated greatly. Jamaica for example, in the area of Mathematics showed a 14.3 percentage point drop from 2015 to 2016. However, performance improved

Table 8. CXC Passes.

Jamaica					St Lucia				Barbados
Percentage Passes Subjects	2015	2016	2017	2018[a]	Percentage Passes Subjects	2015	2016	2017	2015–2016
English Language	65	71.2	70.8	68.7	English Language	66.2	n.a	n.a.	79
Mathematics	62	47.7	50.2	46.5	Mathematics	55.2	45.8	n.a	56
Information Technology	85.5	75.2	82.6	–	Information Technology	n.a	n.a.	n.a	–

Sources: Jamaica-Planning Institute of Jamaica-ESSJ report 2017; St Lucia- https://www.stlucianewsonline.com/csec-results-continue-to-improve-in-saint-lucia/, https://thevoiceslu.com/2016/08/s-j-c-tops-csec-exams/; Barbados – 2015-2016 STATISTICS_ON_EDUCATION_IN_BARBADOS_AT_A_GLANCE.pdf; [a]https://jis.gov.jm/increase-in-csec-passes/; Also in Henry-Lee (2019, forthcoming).

Table 9. Educational Outcomes.

	Jamaica	St Lucia	Barbados
CSEC pass rate – Overall[a]	68.4 (2018)	73.3 (2017)	68 (2015/16)[b]
Dropout rates-to the last grade of secondary (2016)[c]	3.98	3.17	
Persistence to Grade 5 (2013)[d]	95.39	92.14	94.46 (2010)
Primary to secondary Transition rate (2016)[c]	94.52	96.81	

Sources: [a]https://jis.gov.jm/increase-in-csec-passes, https://www.htsstlucia.org/saint-lucia-cxc-results-show-1-increase-in-pass-rates/; [b]2015-2016_STATISTICS_ON_EDUCATION_IN_BARBADOS_AT_A_GLANCE.pdf; [c]http://data.uis.unesco.org/index.aspx?queryid=150; [d]https://data.worldbank.org/indicator/SE.PRM.PRS5.ZS?locations=BB-JM-LC; Also in Henry-Lee (2019, forthcoming).

slightly to 50.2% in 2017 (Table 8). In St Lucia, core subject passes did not exceed 70% (Table 8).

Overall, CXC passes for Jamaica and St Lucia were recorded at 68.4% and 73.3% respectively (Table 9). Barbados CSEC results indicated a 68% pass rate in 2015–2016 (Table 9). Primary to Secondary transition rates were relatively high. Jamaica recorded a transition rate of 95.39 and St Lucia 96.81 (Table 9). However, dropout rates (secondary) were highest for Jamaica (4%). Persistence to Grade 5 measured by share of children enrolled in the first grade of primary school who eventually reach grade 5 were equally high in the three countries. For St Lucia, the persistent rate in 2013 was 92.14% and in Jamaica it was 95.39%. Barbados recorded a 94.46 persistence rate in 2010 (Table 9). Data on the number of students eligible to sit for the exams and the number who actually sit for the exams are not available for all countries.

Approximately 11,000 pupils across the region who wrote the Caribbean Secondary Education Certificate (CSEC) Exam in May/June of 2018 got no passes (grades 1–3). It should be noted that only 20% of the eligible population cohort in the Caribbean has an opportunity to write the CSEC Examination. Of this cohort, some 13% passed no subjects.[13]

THE RIGHT TO PROTECTION AT ALL TIMES

Nine CRC articles, SDG 13 and MDG 7 relate to climate change issues and its impact. The focus by the SDGs on climate change is key to the fulfilment of the CRC as children are the most negatively impacted by climate change. During natural disasters, children are physically less able to fend for themselves and are more exposed to abuse and exploitation both during and after these occurrences. They usually suffer more trauma, attend school less and become more vulnerable to infectious diseases. Women and children are particularly vulnerable as they are more exposed to physical harm and injury during and after natural disasters. Children are particularly sensitive to climatic changes as they are less able physiologically and metabolically to adapt (Akachi, Goodman, & Parker, 2009). Natural disasters disrupt childhood and may have long-term negative effects.

SIDS are especially susceptible to the impact of climate change as hundreds of poor households live in poorly constructed buildings made of inferior material and located in flood-prone areas. There has been some progress on climate action since the adoption of the MDGs. As of 20 April 2017, seven developing countries successfully completed draft national adaptation plans in response to climate change.[14] Developed countries have promised to jointly mobilize USD $100 billion per year by 2020 to address the climate-related needs of developing countries through to 2025.[15]

The Caribbean islands, because of their geology, location and geography, are prone to several natural hazards. The major threats include hurricanes, floods, landslides, droughts and earthquakes. The economic impact of natural disasters has been enormous (Table 10). Two of the most recent hurricanes to make landfall in the Caribbean were Hurricanes Irma and Maria. Puerto Rico was left devastated after the passing of Hurricane Maria in 2017. At least 10 people were killed as a result of the hurricane's direct hit.[16] Although Puerto Rico was spared the worst of Irma's wrath, at least three people were killed.[17] As a result of the passage of Hurricane Irma (2017), more than 36 people were killed in the affected Caribbean countries. The worst affected countries were Anguilla, Barbuda, the British Virgin Islands, St Martin, the US Virgin Islands and Turks and Caicos.[18] The damages in St Martin alone totalled US $1.4 billion meanwhile, in Cuba; ten people died as a result of Irma.[19]

Before, during and after a natural disaster, the safety of all children is of paramount importance. Focussing on Haiti, the impact of natural disasters on children has been tremendous. Henry-Lee (2010, p. 86) noted that before, during and after the several hurricanes in 2008, Haiti was not able to adequately provide for, and protect, its children. After the 2010 hurricane, some 369 child-friendly spaces have opened up offering more than 94,800 children daily opportunities to engage in recreational activities, access psychosocial support, and

Table 10. Countries Experiencing Severe Natural Disasters, 2000–2017.

Country Economic	Year	Disaster	Cost ($)	Damage % of GDP
Jamaica[a]	2017	Rainfall	J$ 4 Billion	0.2
Haiti	2010	Earthquake	US$ 8 Billion	121
St Lucia	2011	Hurricane		34

Sources: Extracted from IMF Policy paper available at https://www.imf.org/external/np/pp/eng/2016/110416.pdf. Accessed September 15, 2017 and Caribbean Human Development report, 2016; [a]http://www.pioj.gov.jm/Portals/0/Sustainable_Development/Macro%20Socio-economic%20and%20Environmental%20Impact%20Assessment%20of%20the%20Damage%20and%20Loss%20caused%20by%20the%20March%20to%20June%202017%20Rains.i.pdf

reclaim their childhood (United Nations Children's Fund, 2011). However, there is still much to be done to provide adequate protection for all children before, during and after a natural disaster in the Caribbean.

CONCLUSION

Thirty years ago, through the adoption of the CRC, governments promised to protect children's rights, everywhere. Adherence to the rights of all children everywhere is key to sustainable development. Children whose rights are violated will be *left behind* in the fulfilment of any Developmental Agenda. Social investment in children is critical to the adherence of Child Rights and the attainment of sustainable development. The level of social investment made in children and the quality of childhood they enjoy, is dependent on internal and external factors (Fig. 1). Internal factors include human and personality traits while external ones include agents of socialization and the characteristics of the small island developing states (SIDs) in which children live. The latter (the characteristics of SIDs) constrain the amount and quality of social investment made in children.

The members of the United Nations have recently been guided by two main Development Agendas, namely the MDGs and the SDGs. Before that, in 1989, the UN adopted the Convention on the Rights of the Child (CRC) whose 54 articles focus exclusively on children.

This chapter examined the synergies among the three main international frameworks – the CRC, MDGs and SDGs – and assessed the current situation of children in the Caribbean SIDS in the fulfilment of the poverty, education, health and climate change-related articles and goals in Barbados, Jamaica, Haiti and St Lucia. These areas of focus were specifically chosen as they were felt to be critical to child development and sustainable development. These countries were chosen as they represent various stages of regional socio-economic advancements. The authors utilized secondary data from Barbados, Haiti and St Lucia. For Jamaica, primary data from 103 secondary school children were also analyzed. This was also complemented with an analysis of the 2014 Jamaica Survey of Living Conditions (JSLC).

Data analysis revealed that there are many synergies among the CRC, MDGs and SDGs. The commonality is greater between the CRC and the SDGs. The latter is more comprehensive and they provide a more holistic prescriptive developmental model than the MDGs. The CRC with its 54 articles focuses exclusively on children. The chapter provided a critique of the three developmental agendas and noted that in spite of all their deficiencies, the three models provide guidelines and consensus for the members of the United Nations.

An analysis of both secondary and primary data showed that thirty years after the adoption of the CRC, there remain large proportions of children whose rights are violated. High levels of child poverty pose a risk to sustainable development in these countries. While there is universal access to education, there are some groups of children whose needs are not met; for example, children with disabilities. Analysis of primary data from interviews with 103 secondary school children in Jamaica revealed that teacher–student relations are less than desirable for 25% of them.

While there is generally good access to health facilities, children with disabilities and those who are infected with or affected by HIV/AIDS receive inadequate policy attention. Our children live in unsafe environments and sexual abuse remains a serious problem. Data analysis of primary data from 103 secondary school students revealed that children live in 'violent circumstances' with 80% of them stating that violence against children is high or very high in Jamaica.

Perhaps the most critical of all goals are those related to climate change. Research has shown that during a natural disaster, there is a higher risk of children's rights being violated. Data analysis revealed that there is insufficient attention paid to reduce the adverse effects of climate change on the citizens in these SIDs, especially, the children. Haiti remains the most vulnerable of all the countries under discussion.

POLICY RECOMMENDATIONS

Children's rights are of central importance to the attainment of sustainable development. No international Development Agenda will be fulfilled if children's rights are violated and social investment in children remains peripheral to the policy implementation process. The State, agents of socialization and all citizens must see children as a priority for the attainment of sustainable development for all.

Eradication of child poverty, improved access to good quality education and health facilities will be difficult because of financial constraints as evident by the low economic growth experienced by the four countries under review. However, for any Development Agenda to succeed, some immediate policy imperatives are necessary. Policy formulation and implementation must be informed by adequate and timely data. Micro analysis of various groups of children was difficult because of the lack of recent and disaggregated data. Monitoring of progress for children continues to be constrained by the lack of data.

At the global level, in the same way that the United Nations can unanimously adopt the SDGs, there must be increased effort at addressing the vulnerabilities of SIDs. SIDs remain trapped in the abysses of debt and insignificant growth. Debt forgiveness is the first step to the improvement in the economic health of SIDS and increased investment in children.

Within the SIDS themselves, without efficient re-allocation and reassignment of existing resources, the more vulnerable groups will receive much needed attention. The 54 articles of the CRC are not only for the more abled children; they are for all children with different abilities. However, children with special needs continue to have their rights violated.

Poverty reduction, increased access to good quality education and health and effective climate action for all children may be achieved through effective partnership and effective targeting. This would require a cultural shift which sees the 'child' as the most important human asset that needs significant investment and policy attention.

It is only through political will, accountability and effective targeting and partnership at the global, regional and local levels that the CRC, MDGs, SDGs or any other future Development Agenda can be comprehensively fulfilled for all children in the Caribbean.

NOTES

1. Retrieved from http://childprotection.gov.jm/. Accessed on July 4, 2018
2. Retrieved from http://paredos.net/documents/about_us.html. Accessed on September 4, 2018.
3. Retrieved from https://www.theguardian.com/global-development/2016/oct/05/nearly-half-all-children-sub-saharan-africa-extreme-poverty-unicef-world-bank-report-warns. Accessed on September 12, 2018.
4. Retrieved from http://www.unicef.org/socialpolicy/index_46984.html. Accessed on September 3, 2018.
5. Retrieved from https://countryeconomy.com/hdi/norway. Accessed on September 17, 2018.
6. Retrieved from http://www.unicef.org/easterncaribbean/ECAO_St._Lucia__Child_Protection_Statistical_Digest_2015.pdf. Accessed on September 17, 2018.
7. Retrieved from http://www.ocr.gov.jm/index.php/statistics/2014-statistics/sexual-abuse-2014. Accessed on September 17, 2018.
8. Retrieved from http://www.unicef.org/easterncaribbean/ECAO_BARBADOS_Child_Protection_Statistical_Digest_2015.pdf. Accessed on September 17, 2018.
9. Retrieved from http://www.unicef.org/easterncaribbean/ECAO_St._Lucia__Child_Protection_Statistical_Digest_2015.pdf. Accessed on September 17, 2018.
10. Retrieved from https://www.theguardian.com/journalismcompetition/haiti-disabled-children. Accessed on July 1, 2019.
11. Retrieved from http://www.unaids.org/en/media/unaids/contentassets/documents/epidemiology/2013/gr2013/201309_epi_core_en.pdf. Accessed on August 4, 2016.
12. Retrieved from http://www.vision2030.gov.jm/Portals/0/Workshops_Reports/JAMAICA%20COUNTRY%20ASSESSMENT%20-%20PRELIMINARY%20DRAFT%20Revised%20%20APRIL2012.pdf. Accessed on August 4, 2016.

13. Retrieved from https://newsday.co.tt/2018/08/12/cxc-11000-pupils-got-zero-passes/. Accessed on November 26, 2018.
14. Retrieved from https://sustainabledevelopment.un.org/sdg13. Accessed on September 15, 2017.
15. Retrieved from https://sustainabledevelopment.un.org/sdg13. Accessed on September 15, 2017.
16. Retrieved from https://gizmodo.com/hurricane-maria-left-puerto-rico-absolutely-devastated-1818706517.
17. Retrieved from http://www.express.co.uk/news/weather/853576/Hurricane-Irma-damage-aftermath-death-toll-caribbean-florida-usa
18. Retrieved from https://weather.com/storms/hurricane/news/irma-aftermath-keys-caribbean-florida
19. Retrieved from http://www.express.co.uk/news/weather/853576/Hurricane-Irma-damage-aftermath-death-toll-caribbean-florida-usa

REFERENCES

Adi, A. E., Abdu, T., Khan, A., Rashid, M. H., Ebri, U. E., Cockcroft, A., & Andersson, N. (2015). Understanding whose births get registered: a cross sectional study in Bauchi and Cross River states, Nigeria. *BMC Research Notes*, *8*(1), 79.

Akachi, Y., D. Goodman, & D. Parker. (2009). Global climate change and child health: A review of pathways, impacts and measures to improve the evidence base. Innocenti Discussion Paper No. IDP 2009-03. Florence: UNICEF Innocenti Research Centre: 2.

Becker, G. S. (1994). Human capital revisited. In *Human capital: A theoretical and empirical analysis with special reference to education* (3rd ed., pp. 15–28). Chicago, IL: The University of Chicago Press.

Caribbean Human Development Report. (2016). United Nations Development Programme. Multidimensional progress: Human resilience beyond income. Retrieved from http://hdr.undp.org/sites/default/files/undp_bb_chdr_2016.pdf. Accessed on July 18, 2019.

Child Care Board and UNICEF. (2012). Child neglect in Barbados. Retrieved from https://www.unicef.org/easterncaribbean/ECAO__Child_Neglect_in_Barbados.pdf

Dar, O. A., & Khan, M. S. (2011). Millennium development goals and the water target: Details, definitions and debate. *Tropical Medicine & International Health*, *16*(5), 540–544.

DESA and UNDP. (2012). Synthesis of National Reports for Rio + 20.

Easterly, W. (2009). How the millennium development goals are unfair to Africa. *World development*, *37*(1), 26–35.

ECLAC. (2013). Social protection systems in Latin America and the Caribbean: Haiti. Retrieved from http://archivo.cepal.org/pdfs/2013/S2013068.pdf

Engle, P. L., Fernald, L. C., Alderman, H., Behrman, J., O'Gara, C., Yousafzai, A., & Iltus, S. (2011). Strategies for reducing inequalities and improving developmental outcomes for young children in low-income and middle-income countries. *The Lancet*, *378*(9799), 1339–1353.

Gertler, P., Heckman, J., Pinto, R., Zanolini, A., Vermeersch, C., Walker, S., & Grantham-McGregor, S. (2014). Labor market returns to an early childhood stimulation intervention in Jamaica. *Science*, *344*(6187), 998–1001.

Heckman, J. J., Moon, S. H., Pinto, R., Savelyev, P. A., & Yavitz, A. (2010). The rate of return to the HighScope Perry Preschool Program. *Journal of public Economics*, *94*(1–2), 114–128.

Henry-Lee, A. (2010). Natural Disasters and Child Rights in Haiti. Promoting Child Rights through Research. In A. Henry-Lee and J. Meeks-Gardner (Eds.), Selected Papers from the Caribbean Child Research Conference 2007-2008 (Vol. 2, pp. 75–90). Kingston: Sir Arthur Lewis Institute of Social and Economic Studies, Mona Campus.

Henry-Lee, A. (2019, forthcoming). *Endangered and transformative childhood in Caribbean small island developing states*. London: Palgrave.

Holmes, R., Jones, N., & Espey, J. (2010). *The MDGs and gender*. ODI policy brief. June. London: ODI.

Humanium. (2012). Criticisms of children's rights. Available at https://www.humanium.org/en/criticisms-of-childrens-rights/

Humanium. (2018). Right to an identity around the globe. Available at https://www.humanium.org/en/world/right-to-identity/

International Council for Science. (2015). *Review of the sustainable development goals: The science perspective*. Paris: International Council for Science (ICSU).

Melamed, C., & Scott, L. (2011). *After 2015: Progress and challenges for development*. London: Overseas Development Institute.

Olaniyan, D. A., & Okemakinde, T. (2008). Human capital theory: Implications for educational development. *Pakistan Journal of Social Sciences*, *5*(5), 479–483.

Planning Institute of Jamaica. (2017). Economic and Social Survey Jamaica 2016. Planning Institute of Jamaica 330.97292'06'05 ISSN 0256-5013.

Sachs, J. D. (2012). From millennium development goals to sustainable development goals. *The Lancet*, *379*(9832), 2206–2211.

UNICEF. (2011). Children in Haiti one year after- The long road from relief to recovery. Retrieved from https://www.unicef.org/media/files/Children_in_Haiti_-_One_Year_After_-_The_Long_Road_from_Relief_to_Recovery.pdf

UNICEF. (2015). Saint Lucia 2015 Child Protection Statistical Digest. Retrieved from https://www.unicef.org/easterncaribbean/ECAO_St._Lucia__Child_Protection_Statistical_Digest_2015.pdf. Accessed on December 20, 2018.

UNICEF. (2016). Mapping the global goals for sustainable development and the convention on the rights of the child. Retrieved from https://www.unicef.org/agenda2030/files/SDG-CRC_mapping_FINAL.pdf

United Nations. (2012). Review of the contributions of the MDG Agenda to foster development: Lessons for the post-2015 UN development agenda. Retrieved from http://www.un.org/millenniumgoals/pdf/mdg_assessment_Aug.pdf

Vandemoortele, J., & Delamonica, E. (2010). Taking the MDGs beyond 2015: Hasten slowly. *IDS Bulletin*, *41*(1), 60–69.

Williams, A., Cheston, T., Coudouel, A. et al. (2013). Tailoring social protection to small island developing states: Lessons learned from the Caribbean (English). Social Protection and labor discussion paper; no. SP 1306.

BRAZILIAN CHILDHOOD STUDIES AND RELATIONS TO CHILDREN'S RIGHTS

Anete Abramowicz, Gabriela Guarnieri de C. Tebet and Tatiane Cosentino Rodrigues

ABSTRACT

This text is the result of an extensive bibliographical research on the development of Childhood Studies in various regions of Brazil based on the understanding that childhood is a social discursive construction, as well as human rights, and both concepts are interlinked when the subject in focus is the children's rights. According to research data while advances in the concept of childhood have supported specific child protection policies, the issue of marginalization and inequalities affecting children is some of the central matters developed within childhood studies in Brazil. In this article, we map the advances of childhood studies in Brazil and its relation to children's rights. However, we may state that neither childhood nor children's rights are still a reality for all Brazilian children, especially when considering other markers that have challenged the rights of our children, such as race, ethnicity, social class, and gender.

Keywords: Brazilian Childhood Studies; Brazilian Children's Rights; sociology of childhood; education; race; South America

INTRODUCTION: ON CHILDHOOD AND HUMAN RIGHTS

We begin this text based on the idea that the way modernity is related to children is a social construction that is overlapped with two important concepts:

Human Rights for Children and Youth: Sociocultural Differentiation, Resistance and Unity
Sociological Studies of Children and Youth, Volume 24, 59–77

ISSN: 1537-4661/doi:10.1108/S1537-466120190000024004

Childhood and Human/Children Rights. If, during the Middle Ages in Europe, we may say that children (treated as 'mini-adults', according to Ariès, 1960, 1981) and adults had mixed worlds, then it is also that true the way we understand children and childhood nowadays is a modern construction, and there are many laws and institutions acting to guarantee this modern model of childhood for every child as much as possible.

In other words, we can also state that Childhood and Human/Children Rights consist in a social discursive construction that constrains people's actions in modernity. This perspective is supported by authors, such as Jenks (1982), and James and Prout (1997), in studies on Childhood and also by Santos (2013) and Žižek (2005), on Human Rights.

According to Jenks (1982), our understanding of children and the way they relate among themselves are social constructions crystallized by institutional discourses. In this sense, we can state that there are many and diverse discourses about what childhood is or what it should be, which allow us to think about multiple childhoods and multiple discourses about childhood. The same applies to Human Rights. For James and Prout (1997), the understanding of childhood as a discursive construction is part of Foucault's (2004) ideas about 'regimes of truth', which instigates us to reflect on the way a certain truth about childhood is constructed and the way such truths, coupled with a set of institutionalized practices of subject production, contribute to the validation of the truth initially affirmed. Hence, considering that scientific production of universities plays an important role in the production of truths on specific themes, we understand that an important perspective for the debate on Human Rights for Children is to understand what truths have been produced and how these truths have contributed to debates on Children's Rights. What theoretical perspectives of childhoods are being constructed in this debate?

When the United Nations (UN) promulgated the International Declaration of Human Rights, there was an idea, a discourse about human beings and a discourse about rights that supported this declaration. From this period, many laws and national programs for children and for childhood were approved in Brazil, based on some specifics ideas of what a child is, what childhood should be and what rights children must have. Of course, scientists often play an important role in such programs.

A Brazilian researcher, Fulvia Rosemberg, in discussing the action of scientists, social movements and politicians in the process of public policy-making (for early childhood education), states that:

> In this interplay of conflicts, tensions, coalitions and negotiations, scientists, their corporations, and their knowledge also play a role. [...] It is not the knowledge that must determine, directly, the priorities in public policies. In this determination, the knowledge must instrumentalize the actors, because these options are political, resulting from the game of interests and pressure. (Rosemberg, 2001, p. 21 – free translation)

Therefore, our focus in this study will be to draw a genealogy of Brazilian childhood studies from the 1940s, highlighting the main themes and ideas in each period of Brazilian history. As we will observe throughout the text, many ideas from Childhood Studies were closely connected to discussions related to Children's Rights.

Although, we should also suspect Human Rights discourses and assume it as a social discursive construction that reflect ideas, conflicts, economic, and political interests of a specific society and period, according to Santos (2013). The author emphasizes how the discourse on human rights has achieved an undeniable breadth and hegemony. However, he leads us to think that, despite a hegemonic discourse, the vast majority of the world's population does not really constitute itself as a subject of human rights. They are at most 'objects of human rights discourses'. The author instigates us to assume '[...] a hermeneutic of the suspicion of human rights as they are conventionally understood and defended', and points out that even the discourse on human rights is not homogeneous. He states that:

> The liberal matrix conceives human rights as individual rights and privileges civil and political rights. On this matrix, other concepts of human rights were developed, namely those of Marxist and socialist inspiration, which recognize collective rights and privilege economic and social rights. (Santos, 2013, p. 43 – free translation)

However, this discourse is not as incontestable as it may seem. In 2005, the Slovenian sociologist Slavoj Žižek published a text titled 'Against human rights!' In this text, Žižek contests grounds on which human rights rests, and instigates us to think: what are the human rights of those who are not comprehended in their humanity? We could think today of children and families who die every day trying to enter Europe illegally. We could think of black children and young people who suffer with the greatest genocide of young population, and think of children from Brazilian indigenous communities who live in danger of being victims of the overwhelming desire for rural lands and Brazilian agribusiness, in the constant struggle for land and against indigenous peoples. What are the rights of children murdered by their parents after the end of their marriage, or children whose mothers have been murdered by their ex-husbands, victims of the highest rates of femicide Brazil has registered? Or what about black children who are victims of constant 'stray bullets' in the Brazilian slums? And what about thousands of children in Brazil with no school to study, due to insufficient vacancies in the public education system? What humanity is attributed to these people? What human rights are guaranteed to them?

Considering such situations, it seems appropriate to think of what Žižek proposed:

> What, then, happens to human rights when they are the rights of *homo sacer*, of those excluded from the political community; that is, when they are of no use, since they are the rights of those who, precisely, have no rights, and are treated as inhuman? Jacques Rancière proposes a salient dialectical reversal: 'When they are of no use, one does the same as charitable persons do with their old clothes. One gives them to the poor'. (Žižek, 2005, pp. 162–163)

The author still highlights that:

> [...] 'Man', the bearer of human rights, is generated by a set of political practices that materialize citizenship; 'human rights' are, as such, a false ideological universality, which masks and legitimizes a concrete politics of Western imperialism, military interventions and neocolonialism. (Žižek, 2005, p. 164)

That is what it looks like when we see scenes such as those previously described. Somehow, from the expressed ideas and based on a Foucauldian perspective, we can say that 'truth itself has a history' and that the subject 'is constituted in the very interior of history, and that is at every moment founded and refounded by history' (VEYNE, 2009, p. 10). That is, society itself can also be understood as a construction, or as 'that which in every epoch makes all the discourses and devices of which it constitutes itself as receptacle' (VEYNE, 2009, p. 29 – free translation).

Thus, we need to recognize that the university and its research have been contributing to construct an idea of childhood and of Human/Children's Rights. Understanding how childhood has been constructed in Brazil will allow us to better understand how it has delimited a kind of life for children, and also how children have changed from an idea of vulnerability to a perspective of a protagonist and subject of rights. To do so, we analyzed the intellectual production about childhood of Virgínia Bicudo and Florestan Fernandes in the 1940s, and of some of the most important Brazilian childhood researchers who started publishing since the 1970s: Fulvia Rosemberg, Maria Malta Campos, Ethel Kosminsky, Ana Lúcia Goulart de Faria, Sônia Bramer and Tizuko Kishimoto. The full results of this research are available in a book organized by Anete Abramowicz (2015a), titled *Estudos da Infância no Brasil: encontros e memórias* [Childhood Studies in Brazil: meetings and memories]. Here, we bring a brief view of four findings related to the discussion on Human/Children's Rights.

THE 1940s: THE INITIAL LANDMARK IN THE SOCIOLOGY OF CHILDHOOD IN BRAZIL

We consider the 1940s as the ground zero of our genealogy of Brazilian Childhood Studies from a sociological perspective of Childhood. We started with the work of two authors: Virgínia Leone Bicudo, with her doctoral thesis defended in 1945 on racial attitudes of blacks and mixed-race people in São Paulo, and Florestan Fernandes, with his articles published between 1942 and 1947 from the study on children's groups in a neighbourhood of the city of São Paulo, denominated *Trocinhas do Bom Retiro* [*Trocinhas* of Bom Retiro]. In these articles, Fernandes focused on the process formation of children's groups, the role of children and folklores in the education of children, and the role of folklore in social changes. Somehow, all these discussions are present in the 1947 article, which ended up gaining more repercussion.

Bicudo's (1945) research evidenced the anticipation of thinking about race relationships in childhood and what would become central to contemporary childhood studies: the agency of the child and, in particular, the specificity of this agency in terms of race relationships. Bicudo was a precursor to the articulating categories of analysis such as race, gender, nationality, age group and social class. The results articulated from a theoretical emphasis between sociology and social psychology were analyzed by the author, who verified the existence of a colour prejudice independent of class prejudice. Despite the importance of Bicudo's work, she lived in a certain invisibility in the theoretical field, whether in Social Sciences, or in the field of childhood and education; thus, it is the work of Florestan Fernandes that has been constantly indicated as a landmark in the Brazilian Sociology of Childhood due to the numerous quotations made by those that theoretically compose this field.

The Florestan Fernandes study during decade of 1940 about folklorical and sociological studies on children's culture and groups becomes very famous in Brazil, and is usually pointed out as the starting point of a Brazilian Sociology of Childhood, due to its repercussion. It introduces us either into the debate it creates or into the detailed description of the *trocinhas* – games, folklore and revelry – the pressing issues that are in the current debate among those who want to work in line with what has been called the sociology of childhood. The monograph Fernandes developed in 1944 sought to highlight processes of children's socialization through what he called children's culture, which is both an inflection and a relative autonomy regarding adult culture. In fact, it is sociology as a science that was formulated from the concept of children's culture, which is the key by which Fernandes highlights processes of children's socialization. Florestan Fernandes researched the social base, social support of culture and of children's folklore, and socialization processes within the same group; thus, we could say that what he produced was a sociology that can be called 'pure'. However, this sociology, by taking the elements present in childhood's universe in detailed descriptions of games, songs and merrymaking, has brought all the elements of a sociology that we might call of childhood, which was constituted as a field in Brazil in the 1990s.

As we read the monograph considering the assumptions already made about the sociology of childhood, we can observe the relevance and fruitfulness of Fernandes's work. In his ethnographic descriptions of the childhood universe, current and contemporary issues were already addressed somehow, even though Florestan Fernandes did not explore them. Issues, such as gender, sexuality, ethnicity, race, social class and foreign people composed the nature of children's culture as central themes. All current concepts created by the sociology of childhood had already been addressed in the author's analyses of the rituals of children: merrymaking, amusements, symbolic games, etc. By seeking to identify children's socialization processes rather than building a sociology of culture and folklore studies, Fernandes developed a sociology of childhood that is today often ignored by sociologists, who somehow abandoned the issue of children's socialization. This issue is much considered by those who work with sociology of childhood because there is an understanding in the field against a type of 'school centrism,' that is, the assumption that the central processes of children's socialization occur at school. With this work by Fernandes, the debate on singular childhood, in the sense that childhood could be observed as a social environment for children's socialization, could be reopened. If we consider the contemporary debate in our text, Fernandes' work fits more into a sociology of childhood than it does into studies on children, although there are also elements of this approach. Fernandes was interested in culture and in socialization process. In order to discuss this subject, he conducted a study with children's groups that are formed in the streets. Children involved in his study was over 7 years of age with a certain group consciousness. So, in children's peer group (named by Fernandes as "trocinhas"), they usually reproduces and evidence cultural background from their previously socialization processes, that are already internalized. What is needed for cultural formation and socialization processes? According to Florestan Fernandes (1979), first, a *geography*. You need a shared territory, the neighbourhood and spatial contiguity. With geography, adult culture can be linked to childhood because the latter does not autonomously create territories; it binds them to the adult's will. Moreover, it is noteworthy that there is still a debate about the nature of children's culture.

However, geography is insufficient for constituting a group and the social realm: recreation, games and the goal of addressing individuals who Fernandes (1979) referred to as 'immature' are needed. *Play*, at first is a bonding point, which, according to the author, deepens from the activities we now call 'make-believe'. These are the activities that form a group and manifest intolerance to foreign and different people. These playful activities and others, such as 'Barra Manteiga', a Brazilian kind of tag, are referred to by Fernandes as folkloric activities, and show that girls are closer than boys to such activities because boys flee from them in exchange for physical activities such as football, swimming, etc., which, according to Florestan Fernandes, are not folkloric.

In descriptions of group organization, *sexuality and gender* issues appear overwhelmingly. Florestan Fernandes does not work with these topics, but it is evident that they emerge and are relevant to children. Even if these issues are completely subsumed in Florestan Fernandes's work, since he intended to constitute sociology or the social bases of group formation and culture, sexuality comes up through what we would now call the initiation into heteronormativity on the part of children themselves. That is, Fernandes's descriptions in his monograph are detailed enough to make us realize that sexuality scholars have as a basis a line of analysis that is totally focused on children. That is, the principles of sexual normativity are established by children's groups 'formed in the streets', in a relatively autonomous space and away from adult control. In the monograph, there is a full description of the *division between sexes and gender formation* in which the author notes that the 'misfit' girl has a higher disapproval rate than do 'misfit' boys, so she is called names such as 'tomboy', and the boys are called 'sissy', 'fag', 'fagot', and others. That is, boys who play with girls have their reputations enhanced, whereas girls can be segregated. Still on the subject matter of sexuality and the group, Fernandes says that 'girls have a less intense group mind' and boys have a collective spirit and a division of labour more intense than those of girls (Fernandes, 1979). We need to verify the current literature regarding how the debate on games for girls and boys has developed.

Another topic that was not further developed in this work is *power relations*, in which Florestan Fernandes shows that girls' leadership is exercised in a more active way than boys' leadership. The issue of *social class* is also present, showing that in groups of girls this is more important than it is in groups of boys. In fact, the social basis of any cultural constitution is crossed by social class, sexuality and gender, ethnicity and race, and religion. This is the description of what constitutes the notion of social that Fernandes has in the first phase of his research.

All of Fernandes's descriptions – boy or girl, social class, ethnicity, race, leadership style – are for him the support or the social basis of what he coined as children's culture and/or children's folklore, whose difference for him 'is not subtle'. Children's culture is defined as a subculture and more 'inclusive than children's folklore' (Fernandes, 1979). Children's culture is the result of social relations and socialization processes experienced and practiced among children. Folklore is a social phenomenon resulting from the shocks of the structure and social dynamics. He notes that there is a children's culture, almost exclusively composed of children, of a ludic nature that is acquired 'on the streets', that is, among the very group of children.

At this point, Florestan Fernandes relied on Piaget (1932) to argue that unlike the common interpretation given by the folklorists of the time, according to which merrymaking was an aspect of the imitation of adults on the part of children, merrymaking belongs to the cultural heritage of the group and 'is sufficiently depersonalized, given the duration in time and by successive transfers among the groups, to the point of not personally appointing anyone. It is rather an acquisition of the functions than an imitation' (Fernandes, 1979, p. 175). The degree of autonomy of children's culture in relation to adults' culture – the existence or not of a genuine children's culture, its characteristics, the genealogy of the games, the way children use what they experience – remains in dispute among sociology, psychology and anthropology; even children's geography is discussed. According to Fernandes (1979), children play with social functions, for example, the father's, rather than with the father's figure specifically, which means that children are socially constituted; there is a social way of being a parent and a child, and this is also learned on the streets in an informal manner and among peers.

For Florestan Fernandes, the existence of a culture properly to children (of a ludic nature), established among peers, comes from the adult culture, which is learned by groups of children not as an imitation, but as an accepting process. For him, this children's culture is formed from the 'leftovers' of adult culture, recreated by the children. What he says is that children draw from elements of adult's and children's culture. We can say that even with the intense theoretical study among authors who think about culture, the debate initiated by Fernandes[2] is of unprecedented modernity. The issues posed by the sociology of childhood – such as what is children's culture? Does it exist? What is its autonomy in relation to the culture of adults? What is it composed of? What is its social basis? How is it seized by children? – are present in Fernandes's work because they constitute the field of sociology, since it is related to the creation of social beings and to the socialization processes of children within their own social groups. The analysis of these social groups, as well as children's education, culture and social bases, results in the possibility that the author was able to analyze a society that he called 'in chrysalis'. (Fernandes, 1979) How much are the children willing to group? What rules do they obey? How do they recreate what they have learned? Why do they accept social rules? Is that an imposition from adults? Why is accepting the rules among peers easier? By showing the ways in which children are socialized (either among themselves or not), we can perceive that socialization permeates all the lines into which the Brazilian sociology of childhood has been constituted: gender, sexuality, race, religion, social class and ethnicity. In a text written before this monograph, in 1942, Florestan Fernandes said: 'The children's groups are a gentle introduction to society, humanizing and nationalizing the child' (Fernandes, 1979, pp. 377–386). That is to say, children learn to be children, to have childhood and to be Brazilian. The sociology of childhood intends to scrutinize the lines of what constitutes children, childhood and their rituals through the perspective of race, gender, social class and so on.

French childhood sociologists chose a smaller and unfinished text written in 1937 by Mauss as the text to ground the debate on the sociology of childhood. In this text, the author clearly coined the term 'sociology of childhood'. Florestan Fernandes most likely did not know this text because it was recovered later than the monograph he wrote, but both shared the theoretical atmosphere proposed by Durkheim regarding what was forged as the field of sociology, in particular concerning the social formation of individuals, groups, etc. In the text *Three Observations on the Sociology of Childhood*, Mauss (2010) discusses childhood as a social environment for the child, the generation issue, body techniques (in their social dimension), and children's education. In Brazil, the extensive and dense work of Fernandes is what clearly introduces the issue and the existence of a children's culture, which will later be extensively discussed in the sociology of childhood. Mauss's and Fernandes's efforts were to create a sociological perspective on children's manifestations that was both opposed and related to psychology, because Fernandes describes children as still psychologically immature. There is an effort to introduce a sociological gaze into children's media, including media themselves. Florestan Fernandes (1979) incorporated Durkheim's concept of 'social being' to contrast with the 'individual being', suggesting that groups of children socialize the child, acting in the same manner as the parish, the school and the family in the formation of social beings and in the development of personality in the children. Informal education, the one on the streets, plays the role that Durkheim attributed to education of developing the individual's 'social being', proposing ways for children to see, to feel, to act, in ways they would never spontaneously learn.

In Brazilian children's folklore, the contribution and decisive influence are distinctly Portuguese and not black, as one might suppose. Additionally, Fernandes shows how tradition promotes and organizes children's socialization. The starting point is to take folklore facts as association factors, directing the analysis to groups of children, the social basis of recreational activities, and their relation to sociocultural tradition.

A final point to consider in relation to the issues currently raised about children and childhood is on the mediating role that children play in social relations overall. There are studies in the fields of history and sociology who have shown the importance of children during slavery in Brazil whereby children played a socializing function in the relationship between society and the enslaved families. Children facilitated their families' learning of the language, customs, culture, etc. In this monograph, Fernandes is aware of one of the key functions performed by children – he describes how the migrant child facilitates the acculturation of his or her family in Brazilian society.

Florestan Fernandes shows that groups of children are initiating groups and that through the path of children's culture (which is not an imitation of adult culture but part of a more general sociocultural system), children acquire standards of conduct and the community values through which they constitute themselves as children and as Brazilian people. On the social phenomena of the analytical path of Mauss and Durkheim, Fernandes develops a social science using folklore as a method of research, seeking the roots of what could become the Brazilian sociology, and we could say that this work opens the doors to the constitution of the sociology of childhood in Brazil.

After these first works produced in the 1940s, whether from Virgínia Bicudo and/or Florestan Fernandes, we noticed that publications became more frequent after 1970, a fact that may had emerged from some episodes in the history of Brazil, such as the creation of the first graduate programs at the end of 1965, the creation of the Educational Research Department of Carlos Chagas Foundation (FCC) in 1971 and, finally, the creation of the National Association of Education Research (ANPED) in 1978, when there were already 20 graduate programs in education in the country.

BRAZILIAN CHILDHOOD STUDIES, FROM THE 1970s TO THE 1990s

In Brazil, during the 1970s and 1980s, the field that would later be referred to as social studies of childhood and/or the sociology of childhood vehemently criticized Piaget's theory, because of the creation of other epistemological vectors that contributed to the formation of the theoretical field as defined by Bourdieu. Piaget especially, but also on a smaller scale Jerome Bruner, had theoretically influenced Brazilian researchers.

In the 1970s, psychology in Brazil was a strong area that, we can say, conducted early studies on children and childhood, both within the group of Ana Maria Poppovic, who founded Carlos Chagas Foundation Research Department, and also within the Experimental Schools of São Paulo, influenced at the same time, as aforementioned, by sociologists' abandonment of the topic of children. An interview with the researcher Maria Machado Malta Campos is instructive in this regard:

> The pedagogy course had a high demand at the time; not for pedagogy itself, but because it was the gateway to the course of psychology who was Mother Cristina's figure, at the time, an important figure, who was a nun but had significant intellectual production on psychology and was also a political leader of a line one can call the Catholic Left, the Catholic Action linked to JUC[3], JEC[4]. There, everyone was back, and was linked to leftist movements closely connected to the Catholic Church that opposed the more Communist secular tradition, which was the tradition of Maria Antonia, and then there was this rivalry and the Catholic Church was placed as to become a third way, neither communism nor capitalism. The pedagogy course, then, was the gateway to psychology, because you could only get into the psychology course after finishing pedagogy, that

course called clinical psychology; and that clinic exists today linked to the Pontifical Catholic University. (Interview with Maria Malta Campos in Abramowicz, 2015b)

The theoretical atmosphere in the 1970s, in which interest in the issue of children and childhood was being developed, was growing in the debate on the theory of cultural deprivation in the North American line of thought on psychology and sociology from the theory of reproduction, which did not focus especially on children (Bourdieu & Passeron, 1970).

According to Maria Malta:

> Ana Maria Poppovic, who was very intelligent, very educated, soon realized that the word "deprivation" had a negative connotation in the sense that it could mean that children were defective. So she changed the word and called it "marginalization," because with the name marginalization she meant that it was recognized as a process that was causing certain effects in children because of their economic and social marginalization and such. She recognized this when she changed the name, and when she presented the research, there was a joke she liked to use – it was a cartoon that should be found somewhere – it was a joke where there was a very poor person and all, and then this person said, "Well, before they called me miserable, then they called me needy, then called me deprived and now they call me marginalized." You know, a joke as if we were all saying the same thing, but each time different. But the fact is that Ana Maria Poppovic began to relativize a little this thing about a strictly psychological theory. (Interview with Maria Malta Campos, in Abramowicz, 2015b)

Therefore, between 1970 and 1980 the debate on Brazilian children took place from the perspective of cultural deprivation, and later, marginalization. It is important to highlight that the issue of social inequality in Brazil has always been the social substratum understood by most researchers as the key to consider children and childhood as subjects for research and academic and political militancy. Brazilian social inequality places children as the focus of the topic (since there are many inequalities), and beyond that, it focuses on children as subjects of a more perverse social inequality. Children in Brazil allow for the possibility of a debate on social inequality. In this sense, at the same time childhood was being thought as a structure, childhood was evidently very distinct for children from different social groups[5]. Fulvia Rosemberg is one scholar who highlights the structural approach when studying childhood, understood as an inequality in relation to adults. She is categorical in this statement:

> I think what mobilizes me is to fight social inequality, and in the children's case, to fight injustice against children. And in the children's regard is the injustice, which is something I realized very early in life; I think this is the point, if I went down there and looked inside. So, I have always been thrilled with children, always felt an intrinsic pity for children, because of injustice, and I always strongly felt that in my personal life and the lives of others. (Interview with Fulvia Rosemberg, 2012 in Abramowicz, 2015b)

Therefore, the intrinsic link between children and social inequality intertwines militancy, research, and the left social movements, particularly the feminist social movement and women fighting for children against social inequality. It is as if children in Brazil denounced the crude social inequality. Additionally, concerning children, some issues about women and social inequality were interwoven; reacting against the inequality experienced by children was also a reaction in favour of equality for women. In 1970, there was the women's movement for day care, and in 1980 there was the debate over children's right to day care, which was finally embodied in the 1988 constitution.

Thus, in 1970, the majority of studies on children were grounded in the debate on the theory of cultural deprivation, and there was also criticism on the existing conceptions of children from naturalistic to genetic approaches and developmental psychology. These studies resumed the social perspective of studies on children from some of the interdisciplinary elements of history, psychology and sociology (among them, we can mention Rosemberg, 1976). Within this context, authors of these studies highlighted the limits of the compensatory education perspective, rejecting the hegemonic view of the theory of cultural deprivation and reproduction.

Then, there is a movement in which the theory of cultural deprivation gives way to a new perspective that discusses children as marginalized. Gradually, children cease to be studied using psychological theories, and begin to be studied from a more sociological analysis according to which the impact of economic and social marginalization, and of social inequality on children is recognized.

Therefore, cultural and social marginalization and social inequality are the bases on which much of the research is structured, starting in the 1970s. The theoretical key, social inequality, came to be the main theoretical framework of research on children and childhood in Brazil for many years.

Among the main topics discussed in the 1970s were social inequalities promoted by gender and race. We can find research involving issues of gender and comparative analyses between men and women and boys and girls used as indicators of school performance. In 1976, another issue that was discussed about children and that gradually began to appear as an important issue referred to the hierarchies of power between adults and children; today, this subject is the central point of debate in the sociology of childhood. An adult-centric character is present in social representations in which children and adults appear, in the literature, and even in the philosophical and educational concepts of children. The negative concept of children present in philosophy and education was an impacted and subsequently refuted subject in Brazilian research.

In 1980, although few researchers had considered the racial issue as a topic, young children's race appeared to be an axis 'forgotten' by researchers and by women's and black people's social movements. Research on race and young children deemed social inequality as an underlying issue. The intensification of social inequality among black children greatly increased.

Another axis of research that focused on children and childhood in Brazil at the time was the debate about the social function of preschool and/or day care. This schooling was associated with the phenomenon of working women and was therefore linked to working mothers, in addition to being a preventive and palliative measure for the huge rates of school failure that Brazil experienced between the 1970s and the 1980s. This debate was primarily based on documentary and bibliographic research.

Regarding the concept of children in this period, in the late 1970s, prevailed perspectives founded at theories of cultural and nutritional deprivation which represented children as culturally deprived and malnourished, understood as people who had nothing, and who therefore should receive compensatory education. Children were then described in some texts (Rosemberg, 1977, 1979) as a 'social category', not considering the perspective of their intervention in social dynamics, but in the sense that there was an investment in children as consumers for whom it was necessary to produce specific products.

From the theoretical reference that recognized the process of marginalization that affects children, a new discourse emerged, according to which, overall, a set of rights was claimed for children, supposedly to protect them from exploitation and poor living conditions. This discourse was shaped at the international level with the Geneva Declaration of the Rights of the Child of 1924and was strengthened by the adoption of Declaration of the Rights of the Child, proclaimed by the UN (1959); this was effectively consolidated in 1989, with the adoption of the Convention on the Rights of the Child.

In Brazil, this discourse gained strength and intensity throughout the 1980s, when the country experienced a period of great political unrest around the drafting of a new federal constitution. Thus, the theoretical production of the 1980s was marked by pro-constitutional debates in which the child was claimed as a subject of rights. This new conception of the child and childhood was consolidated in the Brazilian legislation in the late 1980s, after 21 years of military dictatorship, through the 1988 Federal Constitution and the 1990 Statute of Children and Adolescent.

In the context of the redemocratization of Brazilian society, the reorganization of social movements and the possibility of creating another educational project brought to light the debate on the right to education, especially kindergarten and preschool as a child's right. This debate took place in the academic sphere, particularly given the discussion of issues such as literacy (among children of preschool age), public policies for children and early childhood education.

Overall, the emphasis of the analyzed studies was on a proposal for quality day care and preschool that could overcome the hitherto dominant conception of 'poor schools for the poor'. (Rosemberg, 1986) The need for investing in this level of education, as well as guaranteeing the exclusive application of public resources to public education, aimed at ensuring the implementation of this proposal.

Negativity, before inherent among children, was replaced with a discourse that assigned a positive hue to children and childhood. Children, from that moment on, gained the status of deserving rights, ensuring a place also in the legal discourse.

In the academic sphere, after the final draft of the Federal Constitution, emphasis on research turned to the integration of gender and race, especially regarding ethnic and racial discrimination. This period coincided with the reorganization of the Black Movement and started to guide complaints regarding racism and racial discrimination in education.

However, since the early 1990s, studies on child development have failed to investigate isolated aspects (especially those of cognitive domain), focusing their concerns on the development process and its determinants from a socio-historical approach. Vygotsky's[6] and Wallon's theories strongly influenced the debate in Brazil, and despite the social character of their works, the influence of the field of psychology still remains.

In this same period, the social studies of childhood, that is, sociology, geography and anthropology, attempted to address something that apparently was subsumed in research: the child. Thus, we may observe among the works of the main Brazilian researcher of childhood the way concepts of children and childhood were discussed within the topics previously described.

In summary, we may indicate that from the 1970s to the 1990s, research has mainly concentrated the following themes:

- Social Inequality and Cultural Marginality.
- Gender, performance indicators, and social inequality.
- Concepts of children and childhood.
- Children's education – curriculum design, history, and public policies, games and playful activities.
- Race and Childhood.

BRAZILIAN CHILDHOOD STUDIES, FROM THE 2000s

It is only in the beginning of the 2000s that the term 'sociology of childhood' was effectively incorporated into Brazilian academic production, which until that time had studied children and childhood from a sociological perspective, and even an anthropological one, without taking the time to ground this research within this field of knowledge.

Research conducted by Silva, Luz, and Faria Filho (2010) indicates that among a set of 150 research groups that were dedicated to the topics of childhood, children and early childhood education in 2008 and 2009, only three indicated sociology of childhood as a keyword. In 2011, we found that the number had increased to 24, which indicates the popularization of sociology of childhood among researchers on children and childhood.

The dialogue of Brazilian research on the sociology of childhood with Francophone and Anglo-Saxon traditions was observed especially after the publication (in 2001) of two articles on the sociology of childhood in the issue 112 of the journal *Cadernos de Pesquisa*. The two articles are 'The emergence of a sociology of childhood: The evolution of the object and the vision', by Régine Sirota (2001), and 'The sociology of childhood: A balance of works in the English language', by Cléopâtre Montandon (2001). Four years later, the magazine *Educação e Sociedade* issue 91 published a dossier titled *Sociology of childhood: Research with children*, with articles by Manuel Sarmento, Claude Javeau, Suzanne Mollo-Bouvier, Eric Plaisance, Priscilla Alderson, William Corsaro, Patrick Rayou, Cléopâtre Montandon and Régine Sirota.

Among the topics covered by Brazilian research published during the 2000s, a significant number of studies addressed the issue of research in children and research methodologies relevant to such studies. Following this topic, research on issues, such as race, gender, public policy, and the social role of day care and preschool was still being conducted.

Among the production of Rosemberg, for example, there is a set of articles (Rosemberg, Bazilli, & Silva, 2003; Rosemberg, 1999, 2002) that discussed the negative impact of multilateral organizations, such as the UN, UNICEF, UNESCO, the World Bank, and the IMF, which define public policy guidelines for children and early childhood education for underdeveloped countries based on their interests. According to the author, black children are mostly harmed by such guidelines, which overall see early childhood education as a measure to fight poverty and support their proposals for 'informal' care for children in a movement contrary to what the social movements gained in Brazilian legislation. That is, they perceived early childhood education as a right of all children, becoming the first stage of primary education and not a mere palliative measure for social issues.

From this discussion, we can share some thoughts on the reconfiguration of the concept of childhood promoted by neoliberals and modernity. This reconfiguration removed the image of the 'dangerous child', the 'child at risk', social threats and also the child 'in danger', and set the focus of attention on children as the 'bearers of rights'; the restructuring also placed the same emphasis on children as human capital, a concept that renews ancient alliances between capital, hygiene, medicine and pedagogy.

These discourses attempted to reveal an important role played by children, who as the targets of provision and protection policies earned rights relative to participation. However, this concept of the child is not exempt from the influence of multilateral organizations and capital interests.

The policy proposals for children's assistance in developing countries by organizations, such as the World Bank, rely on a proposal titled Early Child Development (ECD). This model is based on the theory of social capital and aims to intervene with children who are still very young, starting with proposals to stimulate child development. Children are seen as 'future human capital', and the objective of policies for children is 'to increase the social capital of a person, their ability to bind to social networking and sharing risks', enabling the development of a 'fully productive adult' as if that were enough to counterbalance the effects of poverty (Penn, 2002).

Regarding the impact of such policies in Brazil, the Brazilian researchers Rossetti-Ferreira and Rosemberg argue that:

> The World Bank's and partner institutions' investments aimed at redeeming poverty promote models of early childhood education far inferior to those acceptable to more prosperous people. They do little to help the poor, especially insofar as they endorse the exploitation of women, early childhood education professionals in occupations with low wages. In fact, evidence suggests that the promotion of these "programs at low cost" has been cynically used to reduce investment in children education. (Rossetti-Ferreira and Rosemberg quoted by Penn, 2002, p. 19)

Overall, we can say that the 2000s bring to the theme of childhood the issue of quality in Early Childhood Education, reaffirming the concerns with public policies, the rights of children and women, and the fight against social inequalities as well as training policies for childhood teachers.

The research also sought to understand children in Early Childhood Education (institutions) and in other contexts, that is, in the time, space and childhood in which they are inserted. Hence, some studies emerged on other spaces such as toy libraries.

Culture, contemporaneity, and technology are also subjects of research. Children, their creations, situations in life and culture are the focus of several studies. Working with childhood memories of indigenous children, assisted children, children of prisoners, working children, among others reconstitutes the universe of research on childhood, children, early childhood education and culture, bringing new meanings to references, contributions and inquiries within this field. These themes are associated with the aforementioned studies, and there is an increasingly great concern: research in children, emphasizing the ethical issue.

We may observe a movement that follows the course of sociology itself, at first a debate about the functioning of what we could call generically of 'the system', for a debate on these subjects. In the research on children and childhood, we also found a shift that analyzed the way in which the 'system' focused on children, towards a research that aims at listening to the subjects: children themselves.

FINAL CONSIDERATIONS: ON CHILDREN'S RIGHT IN BRAZILIAN STUDIES ON CHILDHOOD

The research enables relevant considerations for how children's right has constantly been a point of interest of Brazilian Childhood Studies. Overall, we observed that Brazilian Studies on Childhood emerged based on the theme of inequalities. We have also perceived that in the early 2000s, a new approach was developed based on authors of research and articles who sought to settle the issues of children and childhood in the substrate of difference, and not inequality; this new research is based on post-structural and post-colonialist theories. The perspectives are discordant, however, as long as race, for example, can constitute the substratum of social inequality as well as of differences. The gender issue remains core to the debate because kindergarten and preschool are female conquests in Brazil as well as feminine careers. Currently, there are studies whose authors attempt to discuss the role of early childhood education, studying its history, measuring access, and highlighting the inequalities of care and residence. Academic research and political action go together and seek public policies to improve these structures. School, early childhood education, child literacy, children's production and their cultures are reevaluated. A 'concrete' child's concept, that of the Brazilian child, became evident and was immersed in the context from which emerged a Brazilian sociology of Childhood.

Among reports analyzed so far, which nowadays could be grouped under the subject of the sociology of childhood in Brazil, the discussion is emphasized on the contemporary neoliberal proposals that are present especially in articles about early childhood education and public policy as well as those involving debates on social class, race, ethnicity and gender. Thus, from our data, we may assert that the Brazilian sociology of childhood is constituted in opposition to all forms of colonialism and recognizes the plurality of childhood in Brazil as its specificity.

There are no illusions: children's rights are not for everyone! The very emergence of the child in the Western scientific sphere has emerged with colour, with aesthetics, with 'natural' attributes, such as playing, for example, what child is this? The idea of a child is under dispute. We need to be part of this dispute!

Something has changed in history in such a way children emerged in a certain way. In line with this thought, a form does not have an origin, but has an emergence, and if the forces change, the shape changes. If there is no immutable form, that means children always change and may even disappear. Philippe Ariès said that this child 'form' was changing (Abramowicz & Henriques, 2018).

Foucault is interested in the problem of what differentiates itself in history, children emerge because a difference was produced. In this epistemological course, therefore, everything is historical, since everything emerges. There is no form that does not emerge, in such a way research means to identify the historical forces that converge to the constitution of a particular body, and our focus of interest is on the child.

If this form is constructed by relations of force, it is disputed. Therefore, when the black movement affirms that it is necessary to represent black children, it is because the idea of a child emerges in a certain form, with a colour, with certain habits, etc., a form that excludes the black child. This was evident in 2016 when, for the first time, there was an opening of an exhibition on the history of childhood in Brazil. The Museum of Art of São Paulo (MASP) presented two images for the opening of the exhibition: a painting by Renoir and a photo of two black boys. The museum had to use a photo because there is no picture of black children made by a classic Impressionist or Post-impressionist painter (Abramowicz & Henriques, 2018).

Childhood, early childhood education and children's rights have not been excluded from a Power-knowledge movement to determine what it is like to be a child and what is to have a childhood. This movement aims to "educate" poor children from zero to three years old majority in religious philanthropic institutions, and to understand children as a human investment that should provide economic returns. First, we must say that children's rights and the defence of a childhood have always been grounds for disputes. There is no territory and body more disputed than that of the children to attribute to them essence and subjectivity. Foucault (1998) forged the term 'biopolitics' to designate one of the modalities of exercise of power over life, since the eighteenth century. Biopolitics is conjugated as an active methodology whose object is the population. In this sense, children are permanent objects of biopolitics, because there are no territories more fugitive than those of children; we must ceaselessly address them, and effectively do it so, all the time, addressing the bodies of the children and their territories.

Therefore, biopolitics acts incessantly on it to attribute forms of being, forms of life, processes of socialization and schooling. When we talk about rights and the childhood, it means thinking about what apparatuses and devices we can create to protect children from racism, discrimination, poverty, war and misery created by the very capital that expropriates children and forges rights.

This whole plot is complicated, because all the ideas established in the protection of the child, such as humanism and the rights under the basis of capitalism, according to Mbembe (2018), show us that the constitution of European thought, established in opposition to Africa as the darkness of the world. From the eighteenth century, the combination of humanism and racism have been the complex core from the modern project diffusion, which has the 'principle of race' as an important basis for techniques of domination of Europe over Africa that marks the period and produces the transnationalization of the black condition. And that was the black condition: a state of ontological nature's degradation. According to the author, the notion of race allows non-European humanities to be represented as if they were a minor being, one who is possible to be explored by capital. In Mbembe's words:

> The term "Black" was the product of a social and technological machine tightly linked to the emergence and globalization of capitalism. It was invented to signify exclusion, brutalization, and degradation, to point to a limit constantly conjured and abhorred. The Black Man, despised and profoundly dishonored, is the only human in the modern order whose skin has been transformed into the form and spirit of merchandise – the living crypt of capital. (Mbembe, 2018, p. 6)

Racism, colonialism, Europe and capitalism are parts of the same gear of which we are direct heirs. Capitalism is founded on the racial logic. Hence, when we say that racism is structural and structuring, we mean that there is no capitalism without the production of the black as a racial figure. Brazil is one of the cruelest countries in relation to the black condition; we constantly watch what has been called the genocide of young blacks, every 23 minutes a young black man is murdered according to UNICEF. And that is why when talking about children's rights, we must do it so from the perspective of the black, of difference, which was never 'universal'.

NOTES

1. The theme of folklore is regarded by his followers as a "warm topic" of the first phase of his intellectual trajectory, compared with topics of great impact, linked to the theorization of class society in Brazil, specific to a period whose beginning is identified, overall, during the 1960s. However, during the 1940s and 1950s, especially in São Paulo, folklore was a "hot" topic, overflowing with political and cultural meanings that circulated through the different ways of interpreting popular culture (Garcia, 2001).
2. Although nothing indicates that Florestan was a reader of Walter Benjamin, there is something about his perception of the leftovers and remains of culture in children's play: "They recognize in the remains the face that the world of things shows them [...]" (Benjamin, 1992, p. 46). *Selected Works. About Art, Technology, Language and Politics.* Lisbon: Relógio D'Água, 1992.
3. Juventude Universitária Católica.
4. Youth Catholic Student (aimed at high school students).
5. To better understand this discussion about different ways to understand childhood within the Sociology of Childhood (as structure, discourses, group of peers etc.), see Alanen (2012) or Tebet and Abramowicz (2014).

6. Vygotsky outside the USSR has been known in the West since 1960 as the responsible for recasting psychology on the basis of Marxism.

ACKNOWLEDGEMENTS

This study uses data from a Research Project supported by the Fundação de Amparo à Pesquisa de São Paulo – FAPESP [grant no. 2010/05187-3].

REFERENCES

Abramowicz, A. (Ed.) (2015a). *Estudos da infância no Brasil: encontros e memórias*. São Carlos: Editora da UFSCar.

Abramowicz, A. (Ed.). (2015b). Interviews [CD]. In. *Estudos da infância no Brasil: encontros e memórias*. São Carlos: Editora da UFSCar.

Abramowicz, A., & Henriques, A. (Eds.). (2018). *Educação Infantil: A luta pela infância*. Campinas: Papirus, 2018.

Alanen, L. (2012). L'infanzia come concetto generacionale. In: HENGST, Heinz; ZEIHER, Helga (Orgs.). *Per uma Sociologia dell'infanzia*. Milão: Franco Angeli.

Ariès, P. (1960). *L'Enfant et la vie familiale sous l'Ancien Régime*, Plon.

Ariès, P. (1981). *História social da família e da criança*. Rio de Janeiro: LTC.

Benjamin, W. (1992). *Selected works. About art, technology, language and politics*. Lisbon: Relógio D'Água.

Bicudo, V. L. (1945). *Estudo de atitudes raciais de pretos e mulatos em São Paulo* (Doctoral dissertation, Escola Livre de Sociologia e Politica de São Paulo(Instituição complementar da Universidade de São Paulo).

Bourdieu, P., & Passeron, J. (1970). *La reproduction : Éléments d'une théorie du système d'enseignement*, Les Éditions de Minuit, coll. "Le sens commun", p. 284.

Fernandes, F. (1979). *Folclore e Mudança Social na Cidade de São Paulo* (2nd ed., pp.153–258). Petrópolis: Vozes, 1979.

Foucault, M. (1998). *História da sexualidade 1*. A vontade de saber. Translated by Maria Thereza da Costa Guilhon Albuquerque. São Paulo: Graal.

Foucault, M. (2004). *Vigiar e Punir*. Petrópolis: Vozes.

Garcia, S. G. (2001). Folclore e sociologia em Florestan Fernandes. *Tempo Social: Revista de Sociologia da USP*, *13*(2), 143–167.

James, A., & Prout, A. (1997). *Constructing and reconstructing childhood: contemporary issues in the sociological study of childhood*. London: RoutledgeFalmer.

Jenks, C. (org.). (1982). *The Sociology of childhood*. Essential readings. Brookfield, VT: Gregg Revivals.

Mauss, M. (2010). Três observações sobre a sociologia da infância. *Pro-Posições*, Campinas, *21*(3). doi:10.1590/S0103–73072010000300014

Mbembe, A. (2018). *Crítica da razão negra*. São Paulo: N-1 edições.

Montandon, C. (2001). Sociologia da infância: balanço dos trabalhos em língua inglesa. *Cadernos de Pesquisa*, (112), 33–60.

Penn, H. (2002). Primeira infância: a visão do Banco Mundial. *Cadernos de Pesquisa*, São Paulo, (115), 7–24, mar.

Piaget, J. (1932). *Le jugement moral chez l'Enfant*, Paris.

Rosemberg, F. (1976). Educação para quem? *Ciência e Cultura (SBPC)*, *28*(12), 66–71.

Rosemberg, F. (1977). O adulto, a criança e a literatura. *Revista brasileira de estudos pedagógicos*, *62*(141), 7–15.

Rosemberg, F. (1979). *Eu consumo, tu me consomes* (Vol. 31, pp. 41–48). São Paulo: Cadernos de Pesquisa (Fundação Carlos Chagas).

Rosemberg, F. (1986). Creches domiciliares: argumentos ou falácias. *Cadernos de pesquisa*, *56*, 73–81.

Rosemberg, F. (1999). O estado dos dados para avaliar políticas de educação infantil. *Estudos em Avaliação Educacional*, São Paulo, (20), 5–58.

Rosemberg, F. (2001). Avaliação de programas, indicadores e projetos em educação infantil. *Revista Brasileira de Educação*, (16).

Rosemberg, F. (2002). Organizações multilaterais, estado e políticas de educação infantil. *Cadernos de Pesquisa*, (Fundação Carlos Chagas), São Paulo, (115), 25–64.

Rosemberg, Bazilli, C., & Silva, P. (2003). Racismo em livros didáticos brasileiros e seu combate. *Educação em Revista (UFMG)*, São Paulo, *29*(1), 109–124.

Santos, B. (2013). Direitos Humanos, Democracia e Desenvolvimento in: Chauí, M; Santos, B. *Direitos Humanos, democracia e Desenvolvimento*, pp. 41–133.

Silva, I., Luz, I., & Faria Filho, L. (2010). Grupos de pesquisa sobre infância, criança e educação infantil no Brasil: primeiras aproximações. *Revista Brasileira de Educação*, *15(*43), jan./abr. 2010.

Sirota, R. (2001). Emergência de uma sociologia da infância: evolução do objeto e do olhar. In: *Cadernos de Pesquisa*. n. 112. São Paulo.

Tebet, G., & Abramowicz, A. (2014). O bebê interroga a sociologia da infância. *Linhas Críticas*, *20*(41). Retrieved from https://www.redalyc.org/html/1935/193530606004/

Veyne, P. (2009). *Foucault, o pensamento, a pessoa*. Lisboa: Ed. Texto e Grafia.

Žižek, S. (2005). *Against human rights*. New Left Review 34, July–August. Retrieved from https://newleftreview.org/issues/II34/articles/slavoj-zizek-against-human-rights

EARLY CHILDREN'S EDUCATION: INSTITUTIONALITY AND THE RIGHT TO EDUCATION

Marle Aparecida Fidéles de Oliveira Vieira and Valdete Côco

ABSTRACT

In this article, we discuss the issue of the right to education of young children, focusing on the Institution of Early Childhood Education (EIC in Portuguese), of views with legal markers and educational indicators of a Brazilian State. From a research that approached Early Childhood Education (EI in Portuguese) in settlements of the Landless Rural Workers Movement (MST in Portuguese) and making use of the Bakhtinian framework we highlight the processes of inequality that devastate childhood in the rural settings. The data reiterate the need to not only combat the logics of precariousness that affect the service given but also to guide the specificity of Children's education field, within a framework of the effectiveness of primary school attendance. Hence, we call one's attention to the debate of the ways of setting up institutions, with a view to serving children, urging the regulations related to the right to education, particularly, the right to Early Childhood Education in the peasant's context, particularly in settlements.

Keywords: Early Childhood Education; institutionality; right to education; landless workers movement; settlements; service

INTRODUCTION

In the context of the ideas on the relations between human rights and socio-cultural differentiation, in this text we revisit the issue of the right to education

Human Rights for Children and Youth: Sociocultural Differentiation, Resistance and Unity
Sociological Studies of Children and Youth, Volume 24, 79–95

ISSN: 1537-4661/doi:10.1108/S1537-466120190000024005

of children, in the meeting of the premises of the Early Childhood Education with the assertions of Rural Education. Starting from this meeting, echoing in the proposition of a Children's Early Childhood Education, it implies considering the historical constitution of the two fields, with their accumulations, very sustained in the actions of social movements. Both Early Childhood Education and Children's Education have, in a marked way, a social movement in the struggle with a group of social movements that have been working to defend the right to education of the young children and the rural people. Then, it also means proposing dialogues among its own premises, which, without tension, has been contributing to make peasant children visible, marking their right to Early Childhood Education, in their specificity as dwellers of Brazilian rural territories.

In this connection, the discussion presented here includes a Master's research that aimed to understand how the continuous training of educators working in settlements coordinated by the Landless Rural Workers Movement in a state in the Southeast region is effective. For this article, we highlight data concerning the right of children to Early Childhood Education focusing on the configuration of institutions, and more specifically, the service performed in Agrarian Reform settlement areas in the context researched.

In this agenda, we concentrate on the social negotiation of Early Childhood Education configuration, with attention to the production of institutionalization in Brazilian society. We work with the idea that its institutionalization is formed from a set of elements, both formal and informal, involved with the production of its social recognition. In this context, we cut the materiality of institutions as one of the elements of recognition of the right of rural children to education. It is important to emphasize that we do not locate in the scope of the State researched its own institution of EI, in areas of settlements. Still, the data report a quantitative care of young children. Then, it is necessary to consider the strategies directed in the local contexts to direct the attendance, implicated with the configuration of the institutionality of Children's Education in the area of the right to education.

In the meetings with the subjects that promote the educational actions with small children, in particular the ones of the settlements, a set of questions emerged that investigate the processes of construction of the institutionalization of Early Childhood Education, especially in the proposition of Early Childhood Rural Education. We are urged to consider that Rural Children Education's institutionality has been built through care issues, in several strategies of materiality that do not seem to imply the configuration of Children's Education own institutions for this service, as recommended in the infrastructure standards that guide the service of young children (Brasil, 2006a, 2006b).

With the Bakhtinian referential (Bakhtin, 2011), we emphasize that there are many voices that inform – and dispute – the ways of defining and, consequently, of forwarding Rural Children Education. Accordingly, the equality of the right to education, in the diversity related to the rural peoples – especially the rural peoples linked to the Landless Rural Workers Movement settlements and, more particularly, children – are moving to consider the processes of inequality that devastate the childhood, focusing the institutionalization of Children's Education in the cut of the configuration of the institutions.

We propose to ponder on the structuring of social inequality in the right to education of young children, considering the problem of the constitution of the institutionality of Children's Education, through the expectation of guaranteeing its own institutions of Childhood Education in the peasant context, and with that, young children's service referred to the margin of this expectation.

In this proposition, we dialogue with the discussions about (dis) equality, considering that it is "precisely where problems are more intractable and less resolvable than politics matters most" (Scott, 2005, p. 29). With a view to reaffirming the equality of the right to education of young children, we investigate a possible social differentiation of Childhood Education when materialized in the context of the Brazilian field. Without suggesting dualisms, we propose the possibility that the richness of nuances present in the forms of care may have in the diversity of signs not yet recognized, being careful not to ignore the denunciations necessary to the precariousnesses, especially those that seek to conceal themselves, respect to diversity.

With the purpose of developing this thematic architectural, we organize this text in three topics, in addition to this introduction and final considerations. To what concerns to the legal markers on the right to education, in the first topic we aim to synthesize problematizations about Childhood Education service to the small children living in rural areas. Considering the indicators of precariousness in the educational service, in the second topic we explore the indicators referring to the service in settlements, from the setting researched. From the data, in the third topic, we reaffirm the legal frameworks seeking to move considerations on the institutionality of Childhood Education. Finally, we advance to the thoughts marking the procedural character of the construction/negotiation of the structure of the first stage of basic education. Noting the importance of recognizing Childhood Education processuality, we went on to the first topic, focusing on educational assistance to rural children.

ACCUMULATIONS IN THE DISCUSSIONS ABOUT EARLY CHILDHOOD EDUCATION

In the focus of Childhood Education institutionality in articulation with the defence of the educational service located in the children's home scenarios, it is important to highlight our recognition of the many voices that participate in this discussion. In this sense, although it is not possible to review the literature within the limits of this theme, it is worth noting that we are included in the debate on the Rural Education along with Caldart (2000); Caldart, Paludo, & Doll (2006), Reforma Agráfia em Dados Website (2006) and others, in the part of EIC Gonçalves (2013), Côco (2011), Pamphylio (2010), Conde and Farias (2011), Silva and Pasuch (2010), Vieira (2016), Vieira and Côco (2016), Vieira e Côco (2017) and others. In this insertion, observing a not very visited issue, we emphasize the importance of fomenting this dialogical network, investing in making it visible, discussing and thematizing the right to education, in the partnering life children, especially peasant children.

From the productions on the theme, as we indicated in the architectural presentation of the text, in this first topic we aim to synthesize problematizations about Children's Education service offered to the small children living in the Brazilian rural areas. Initially, we underline the consensus – based on legal bases (Brasil, 1988, 1990, 1996) – that regardless of their place of residence, all children have recognized their right to education and that this right is not separated from other rights of 'very young citizens' (Nunes, Corsino, & Didonet, 2011, p. 73). Yet, by cutting indicators for rural children, there is an 'uneven distribution of the benefits of social policies [...]' (Rosemberg & Artes, 2012, p. 18).

Therefore, to reiterate that even the rural children have the right to education might seem redundant, since they are inserted in the educational children's collective, but this (although redundant) statement has been very pertinent and necessary. The evaluation data of the Childhood Education service reveals the denial of this right to the children living in the field, especially if the indicators of the range of care in the day care centre are taken (Brasil, 2013). In this observation, it is seen that 'in the countryside, children, when they have not guaranteed the right to school, usually they accompany families in the work done in the country or stay at home in the company of older brothers', indicating the relevance of EIC (Conde & Farias, 2011; n/p).

With this finding, a second problematization present in the accumulations refers to the need for recognition of diversity in the context of Rural Education. In this sense, Arroyo asks and proposes a perspective:

> Why to give attention and centrality to diversity in the construction of a Rural Education project? Because the struggles for the construction of Rural Education carry the historical marks of the diversity of collective subjects, of social movements that are in the struggles for another education in another project of field and society. Recognizing this diversity enriches the Field Education project. (Arroyo, 2012, p. 229)

In this sense, some studies (Barbosa et al., 2012; Freitas, 2006; Rocha & Hage, 2010) have shown a denial of the recognition of this diversity, and may also lead to the negation of the spaces in which children in the countryside have been attended. They are studies that move us to invest in keeping the dialogical chain of this discussion alive, in order to encourage the ongoing debate and make children aware of the spaces they are offered for educational services.

We place ourselves in this discussion in a relationship of otherness, recognizing our belonging to the theme, in an entrance resulting from our unique and singular being, in the encounter with so many others who, in this movement of existing together, constitute us. Under our terms of reference:

> At the basis of the unity of a responsible consciousness there is no principle as a starting point, but the fact of the actual recognition of my own participation in existing as a singular event, something which cannot be adequately expressed in theoretical terms, but only described and experienced with the participation [...]. (Bakhtin, 2012, p. 96)

Having explained our commitments, in the dialogue with several interlocutors who have been thematicalizing Rural Education, we continue to explore the problematizations present in the accumulations on the institutionality of Rural Childhood Education, with special attention to the materiality of the institutions. A third important question concerns the analysis of the (dis) encounters between advances in legal frameworks and the concreteness of the living conditions of children, their families and the community.

In this issue, the recognition of the importance of integrating Children Education into education systems is highlighted, constituting the first stage of basic education (Brasil, 2006a, 2006b). Nevertheless, the negotiation of this organicity has demonstrated that we need to move forward so that this legal framework does indeed constitute a public policy for all children. Among the obstacles, it is observed that '[...] in the process of regulation and implementation of early childhood education, there has been a difficulty (or even rejection) of incorporating kindergartens into the education system, which is reflected in several indicators [...]' (Rosemberg & Artes, 2012, p. 18). Among these indicators, it is also important to remark another denial of rights that social movements are continually facing: the closure of rural schools.

If this issue seems to plague the whole of Childhood Education regardless of its particularity of linkage to the context of the rural areas, other issues gain distinctions in ways of affecting children's collectives. For instance, the advances in the past 30 years in the education of young children are evident, assuming an educational identity in a process of institutionalization that has promoted a considerable expansion of the service. Even so, the vast majority of children, specifically the 'poorest [...] of the black and the brown population, children under the age of three, as well as those living in rural areas' have not benefited from the achievements of legislation (Barbosa, Gehlen, & Fernandes, 2012, p. 74). In this confrontation between the legal and the real, there is a logic of '[...] insufficient service and with sequels with respect to its quality' (Rosemberg & Artes, 2012, p. 20).

In this logic, the analysis of the conditions in which the service given to the children residing in rural settings of the country is commonly reported that:

> [...] we have repeatedly observed that the conditions of educational provision for children up to 6 years of age living in rural areas are more precarious than those observed in urban areas [...]. In fact, the perverse logic of the production and support of inequalities converges, for children from 0 to 6 years old in rural areas, particularly if they live in a differentiated location (settlement or quilombo), a reduced supply associated with their low quality. (Rosemberg & Artes, 2012, p. 54)

In view of this configuration, it does not seem redundant to reiterate that children in the countryside are also subject to rights and, as such, have the right to education. It is also not a question of disqualifying the legal achievements, though its concreteness shows great weaknesses, since:

> The violation of social rights calls into question advanced legislation, which is even more ineffective. This legislation, however, serves as a tool to fight children as subjects of law, and has materialized in the field from various perspectives. (Silva, Felipe, & Ramos, 2012, p. 418)

We propose an understanding of the legal bases of the right to education in the social struggle movement, representing a significant part of this path, because on the one hand, they inform the insertion of achievements in the legislating apparatus of the education systems, and on the other hand, they are important for the continuity of the fight, since the concreteness of the laws does not effective along the social game of negotiation of investment priorities.

With this understanding, we look at the construction of the Rural Childhood Education's institutionality, with attention to spaces linked to child care, noting that municipalities – which are placed in the relationship with other federated entities as direct responsible for the provision of Childhood Education – should construct and maintain spaces that respect the specificities of children. In this respect, we observe that the right of access to the Childhood Education institution must be guaranteed in the community in which they live (Silva & Luz, 2012). It is understood that

> [...] the location, physical structures and organization of the educational institutions' environments constitute an important dimension of the quality of Early Childhood Education [...]. Its configuration may favor or disempower the sense of security, the development of children's autonomy and child-child interactions, and between children and adults. (Silva & Luz, 2012, p. 189)

In this regard, Pasuch and Santos (2012, p. 117) ask: 'What does it mean to care for children and the children of the countryside, respecting their spaces, times, organization of social life? Which school organization can host children of the countryside?' These are questions placed on the observation of the various forms proposed for the care of children. In this guideline we understand that:

> These and other questions will be necessary so that, within the scope of public policies, we can fulfill the duty of the State to guarantee the right of children in the countryside to have quality access to Early Childhood institutions in places close to their homes. These relations of proximity are quite significant for the guarantee of rights of constitution of subject subjectivities of rural areas. We must fight for the guarantee of equality of opportunity, of access that allows children in the countryside to become beings of meaningful relationships with their spaces of social and cultural life. To deny this right is to deny the possibility of being a subject of rural areas, incorporating their struggles, their memories, their valuations of identity. (Pasuch & Santos, 2012, pp. 148–149)

With regard to the recognition of the right to educational services, we have seen that children living in rural areas of the country, in addition to having access to institutions, have access in a precarious and often decontextualized ways, due to transportation to another community, usually in an urban area, which ends up guaranteeing the right to access, but not guaranteeing the quality of service, in terms of recognizing the specificity of the Rural Children Education.

With this synthesis, we bring to light the accumulations of the research in the (dis) encounter with the legal assertions, informing deficiencies and precariousness in the educational attendance to the children living in the rural areas. With this, we are investigating the legal recognition of Children Rural Education, suggesting the possibility of indications that may bring other elements to this logic of deficiency, taking as a reference of study the experiences underway in the scope of the state researched. In this attempt, we move on to the second topic, aiming at exploring indicators related to educational assistance in settlements coordinated by the Landless Rural Workers Movement.

EARLY CHILDHOOD EDUCATION IN AGRARIAN REFORM SETTLEMENTS

In order to understand how care has been configured in the specificity of small children residing in settlements, we compose a data production itinerary with three movements, considering all the municipalities in the context of the state studied, aiming at mapping the configuration of the systems municipalities, identifying the presence of the settlements and the educational assistance to children in this specific context.

These movements were directed considering that the settlements of Agrarian Reform are territories originating from the struggles of the rural social movements that, through land occupations, seek to put pressure on the State so that people who are encamped happen to have a piece of land to plant, harvest and live with their families. Currently, in the context of the study, Landless Rural Workers Movement is organized in 13 camps with approximately 1,000 families who are fighting permanently to achieve the dream of obtaining land to lay the foundations and give continuity to the process of living in the countryside and with 2,750 settled families where they produce food for subsistence and for society as a whole (Movimento dos Trabalhadores Rurais Sem Terra, 2018). Families understand that 'conquering the land, a fraction of the territory, and territorialising itself is an effective way of reacting and demonstrating its form of organization' (Fernandes, 1999, p. 238).

In this organization, the struggle for public policies takes place in a space that embraces children, youngsters and adults who give continuity to life in this conquered territory, where 'dealing with politics implies working with movement, considering a complexity of involved elements' (Côco, 2013, p. 188). Hence, to move studies articulated with the process of the Agrarian reform, implies to consider '[…] the fundamental aspects that characterize the peasant existence in the reality of the *latifundio* (landlordism)' (Freire, 2013, p. 80). Observing the diverse elements involved in the struggle for public policies for the countryside, fruits of resistance and the collective organization of social movements, Landless Rural Workers Movement in the context of the study is organized in 29 municipalities (37,17% of the total), with a total of 62 settlements (Movimento dos Trabalhadores Rurais Sem Terra, 2018).

With this context (field of study), in our research itinerary, as a first movement, we mapped the municipalities with their own educational system, accounting for a total of 30 municipalities (38.46%) with their own education systems (UNCME, 2015). The choice of municipalities with their own education systems is justified by the possibility that the discussions about the referrals concerning the service in the Rural Children Education are also based at the local level. Then, from this first set, we identify those who have Agrarian Reform settlements coordinated by Landless Rural Workers Movement, in which we have a total of nine municipalities. Finally, among these municipalities, we sought to select settlements that have educational services for children in their own institutions (considering own building for the institution and attendance in the nursery and preschool). Since we have zeroed the quantitative in the last criterion, we repositioned it to select settlements with Childhood Education service. With this adjustment, we reached a total of five municipalities, totalling 10 settlements with offer of assistance in the Rural Children Education. Therefore, it was possible to advance in the research, arriving at an institution for the continuity of the study.

In this experience, the (dis) encounter with the local indicators makes us react in our ideological and life-related positions (Bakhtin, 2014), proposing these reflections in the dialogue with the constitution of the Childhood Education in the Countryside. From this perspective, we present the verified data, summarized in the Table 1.

The remarks of the indicators make it possible to inquire about this service, referring the questions to the discussion of Children Rural Education's legal recognition, within the framework of legal markers for the educational assistance of young children. Considering the legal markers (Brasil, 2006a, 2006b; 2009, 2011), the question of the configuration of institutions is complex. Although we can point out that Childhood Education institutions cover (jointly or separately) the care of children in the nursery (0 to 3 years) and preschool (4 to 6 years[1]) (Brasil, 2009), which is observed is the extended spectrum composition of institution identification references. This set of forms of identification of institutions may indicate that this configuration suggests to be confined to the first stage of Basic Education – with the Municipal Centers of Early Childhood Education (CMEI or CEIM) – or associate with the next stage – with the Municipal Schools of Early Childhood Education and Elementary Education (EMEIEF). On the other hand, the fact that we have not located an exclusive institution of Childhood

Table 1. Indicators of the Attendance of Childhood Education in the Study Outline.

Early Childhood Education Assistance In Settlements					
Municipality	Settlement	Ways to Identify the Institution	Number of Children in EIC	Age	Number of Rooms for Early Childhood Education
1	A	EMP	9	3, 5	1
2	B	EMEIEF	4	3, 5	1
3	C	UPEM	26	3, 4, 5	2
	D	UPEM	17	3, 4, 5	1
	E	UPEM	37	3, 4, 5	2
4	F	CMEI	21	4, 5	1
5	G	CEIM	17	4, 5	1
	H	CEIM	15	4, 5	1
	I	EMEIEF	35	4, 5, 6	2
	J	PEM	17	4; 5	1

Source: Vieira (2016, p. 125).

Education indicates that, in spite of the forms of naming it, its structuring is coupled to the Elementary School (EF) in the researched context (Vieira, 2016).

Approaching this context we highlight the example of an institution identified as Municipal Education Center whose materiality is constituted as a room attached to Elementary School. Therefore, it is necessary to mark the approach of the Childhood Education to Elementary School, taking the analysis of the forms of identification. We investigate three compositional forms of this proximity, implicated in the discussion of the institutionalization of Childhood Education.

In the first one, we point out an invisibility of the Childhood Education, so that the unidocent[2] or pluridocent [3]teaching unit also serves children in the Childhood Education age group. In the second, it marks the presence of Childhood Education, having its own room (although part of an Elementary School institution), earning the proper name of Child Education Center. In this case it is suggested the existence of two institutions, even if they are coupled, dividing walls. In the third, there is a single institution, the EMEIEF, recognizing its internal distribution to attend the different age groups.

Accordingly, the observation of the number of rooms, the number of children and the age group, informs many other questions. Among them, the attendance to the day care center (0 to 3) seems to be restricted to the age group of 3 years, often composing a care in common with the preschool band.

It is also important to reinforce that in this debate Goal 1 of the National Education Plan in relation to the care of children from 0 to 6 years of age points out the expansion of service. In this scope, Côco and Salgado (2018) report that:

> It is also important to combine the quantitative objectives of the expansion of supply with the observation of the qualitative indicators, affirming the specificity of the EI within the public education systems, in order to strengthen the unity between day care and preschool, the physical and materials (according to national quality parameters), qualification (initial and continuing training) and the valorization of professional staff (integrated into the teaching profession), the implementation of pedagogical proposals that favor the integral development of the children, as well as the observance of the other (without submission) to the next stage of the educational process and the promotion of articulated policies, in order to recognize the various demands of children and their families (Côco & Salgado, 2018, pp. 8–9).

In this direction, the various forms of naming evidence and/or denouncing the different forms of directing the care of children affects the configuration of the institutionality of IE. In this movement, we do not disregard the importance and recognition of the articulations that guarantee this service, often resulting from a persistent struggle of social movements. Without disqualifying the energies dispensed to mobilize the presence, even if with precariousness, of Childhood Education in the context of rural areas, it is important to problematize the ways of directing the agenda of children's education in this context. On this agenda,

> We must also research and theorize in a more depth way the historical determinants of the persistent precariousness of the rural school, especially the historical determinants of the conformation of others as nonexistent in intellectual and cultural history. If we do not analyze in depth the history of the production of these non-existences of the diverse peoples of the countryside, it will be difficult to understand the denial of the rural school and the construction of another school. (Arroyo, 2012, p. 235)

From this analysis, we can infer that the debates that address the institutionality of the educational service 'constitute stages of meetings/confrontations of different conceptions, produced in different places and attending to diverse interests' (Padilha & Oliveira, 2013, p. 127). The diverse possibilities in which this right to access to education, 'indicative of different options that have repercussions on the impact of care and the organization of educational networks' (Côco, 2015, p. 151), constitute to stimulate this debate, which seems to have been:

> [...] built on the clash between the generally unequal plural reality and the legal instruments conquered and available to the daughters of family farmers, extractivists, artisanal fishermen, river dwellers, settlers and campesinos of agrarian reform, landless workers, quilombolas and caiçaras. (Silva et al., 2012, p. 418)

For rural children, what we have perceived is that 'inequality is one facet of this common that they share; the equality of rights is the ethico-social horizon of transformation' they aim for (Silva et al., 2012, p. 422). Thus, when looking at the specificity of rural children, care must be taken not to 'value only diversity, but the universality of culture, which does not nullify diversity nor is it limited to it' (Padilha & Oliveira, 2013, p. 128).

In this context, the discussion of the Children Education's institutionality, focusing on the materiality of care in confronting the configuration of institutions, is implicated in the affirmation of its identity, as highlighted, in which:

> [...] it carries possibilities of structural conditions that, in turn, are inhabited by the subjects - adults and children - who daily produce EI. It should be noted that this daily production of EI is effective in the different communities. Here, I open a parenthesis to recall the variety of local contexts. This variety of differentiated conditions of investment, [and attendance] in function of the different positions of the municipalities in the capture and distribution of resources. It is also associated with the typical characterization of each municipality, such as the organization of local politics, the region's outstanding cultural elements, the activities of social movements, etc. The variety of local contexts obviously echoes in the diversity of EI. (Côco, 2013, p. 191)

In this complexity, the emergence of different initiatives in response to commitments to the education of young children entails two simultaneous challenges. In the nuances of the context, to recognize the efforts and the composition of alternatives in dialogue with their own demands, though they are distinguished from the more stabilized understandings of what is the service and the institutional configuration, especially the references carried with the observation of Childhood Education in the urban zone. One example is the reorganization of the age groups, within Childhood Education, in order to form groups with groups of children of various ages. Without losing the commitment to the promotion of qualified educational processes, these experiences can provide important information about the possibilities of moving the children's interactions in the development of institutional educational processes. In this way, all experiences in the discursiveness of precariousness should not be confined, making other propositions invisible in the negotiation of possibilities in the delineation of the legal recognition of Rural Children Education, and at the same time care must be taken not to gather in the diversity the experiences that mark the precariousness to which are submitted to small peasant children (Vieira, 2016).

The assertions regarding the observation of precariousness must be constituted as components of the struggle for better conditions, having in mind not to lend themselves to the weakening of alternative proposals that respond, with consistency, to the own demands of certain communities. After all, the very timid service indicators reveal themselves as a place that demands attention in the search for ways that can respond to the right to education of children. From the data shown here, a question arises as to whether it is necessary, pertinent and/or possible to advocate a Childhood Education institution for the care of rural children.

In observing a context that has responded with a negative to this question, it is necessary to question the proposed alternatives, noting in particular their dialogue with the elements that constitute the identity of Childhood Education (Cerisara., Rocha, & Silva Filho, 2007). In this dialogue, it is also necessary to ask whether the Childhood Education's institutionality depends on a partnership with Rural Children Education and Elementary School, and particularly how this partnership is being formed in the local scenarios. It is worth noting the assumptions made in the legal basis of the right to education of young children, in articulation between Childhood Education and Elementary School, guaranteeing the continuity of the children's development process aiming to respect the specifics of the age group (Brasil, 2009). Thus, reflections on the institutional structure of the Rural Childhood Education should consider the importance of marking its identity, being careful not to succumb to schooling logics, so that, with its presence, to inform its identity markers located in the axes of interactions and games as guiding educational work with small children.

Finally, with this data we bring complex questions which summon the consideration of several other actors, allowing us to compose several ways for the reflections. In this debate, with several informative inputs, different interlocutors and different strategies of action, we have the legal frameworks as fundamental guides in this dialogue. In this perspective, in the third topic, we revise the legal and guiding instruments that emphasize delineating elements for the institutionality of Rural Childhood Education.

WITH THE LEGAL MARKERS, THE INSTITUTIONALITY OF RURAL EARLY CHILDHOOD EDUCATION

When we are discussing the different ways in which Rural Childhood Education has been going in the different contexts of its service, with a Bakhtinian framework, let us emphasize that we do not objectify one last word, considering that it is always possible to say something else. In the investment in this dialogical network, we intend that many new/other reflections can be thought, said and addressed in the struggle for the expansion of the service in Childhood Education, especially in the context of rural settings and, in particular, in the peasant context linked to the settlements. In this sense, we affirm that rural children, 'like all Brazilian children, are subjects of rights! They have guaranteed the right to attend kindergartens and preschools with quality! The Right to early childhood education *in the* countryside, offered near their home, in their community' (Silva & Pasuch, 2010, p. 2, emphasis added). Also, 'they have all the human rights, fundamental to any person, which must be recognized and enforced by society and by the State' (Silva et al., 2012, p. 418).

With a view to reaffirming the recognition of children as citizens of law, with regard to care, we recover legal assertions to remember that:

> It is necessary to identify more precisely the existing structure conditions; to verify the possibilities / conditions of service of the EI in the field in order to enable the most practical and gradual form of care; a more in-depth debate is needed; this discussion must be taken to the state poles. To review the standard physical structures - build schools compatible with the field characteristics. (Brasil, 2011a, p. 13)

It is important to emphasize that the recognition of the right to quality concerning Childhood Education has been marked in many documents, in which, besides recognizing the right, Childhood Education is affirmed as *loci* that allow children to:

- play;
- move in large open spaces;
- express feelings and thoughts;
- develop imagination, curiosity and capacity for expression;
- permanently expand knowledge about the world of nature and culture supported by appropriate pedagogical strategies; and
- diversify activities, choices and interaction partners in kindergartens, preschools and Early Childhood Centers (BRASIL, 2006a, 2006b, p. 19).

With these markers we reiterate the questions that ask if the children who live in the rural areas have had this quality care when we look at the institutions. Thus, it is important to investigate the conditions under which this care has been given, how they respond to the guarantee of the specificities and the diversities in which the area is inserted, as the configuration of the own institution of Childhood Education, focused on the singularities of young children. These issues invite the State to a commitment, those responsible for Education and society in general. They cannot be separated from child participation as subjects of the educational process, they, inside, analyze their context, noting that 'to get to my school, I walk very, very, very […] In my room, there is a big child and a small child' (Brasil, 2011b, p. 24). With this, they need to be included, increasingly consistently, in the spaces of this discussion. In these referrals, it should be noted that:

> With the design of the spaces for children, I point out new nuances in the ways of understanding institutional settings, pointing in particular to the importance of interactions, play and play the inherent elements of the school configuration and the educational process developed there. (Côco, 2013, p. 186)

Thus, when we emphasize the right to an education with quality, and that respects the diversity of the subjects of rural areas, we are reaffirming, according to the official documents, that, beyond the physical structure, we must think that:

> [...] in the Brazilian context, discussing the quality of education in the perspective of respect for diversity necessarily implies confronting and finding ways to overcome inequalities in access to good quality programs that respect the basic rights of children and their families, regardless of their origin or social status, without forgetting that these basic rights include the right to respect for their diverse cultural, ethnic and gender identities. (Brasil, 2006a, 2006b, p. 23)

In looking at the specificities of the subjects of rural settings, we understand that they are part of a broad context in which social and collective histories are divided, of peoples that are marked by cultural, social and economic difference, but having the understanding that:

> [...] the politics of difference produces a depoliticizing discourse when it fails to recognize that material inequalities create differences, just as cultural differences legitimize inequalities and hide their production process. The essentialist idea of difference, which removes from its problematic its historical and social dimension, is an obstacle to the transformation of the asymmetrical and hierarchical conditions in which the different ones live. (Silva et al., 2012, p. 422)

In recognition of the diversity that populate the countryside, we affirm that institutions are also demarcated by the pedagogical proposals articulated to this environment and the target audience. Thus, with the advancement in the guidelines for children in the field, the National Curriculum Guidelines for Early Childhood Education have reaffirmed that:

> The pedagogical proposals of the Children's Education of the children, the daughter of family farmers, extractivists, artisanal fishermen, riverine dwellers, settlers and campesinos of agrarian reform, quilombolas, caiçaras, forest peoples must:
>
> - recognize the proper ways of life in the countryside as fundamental for the constitution of the identity of children living in rural territories;
> - have inherent links to the reality of these populations, their cultures, traditions and identities, as well as environmentally sustainable practices;
> - be flexible, if necessary, the calendar, routines and activities respecting the differences regarding the economic activity of these populations;
> - value and highlight the knowledge and role of these populations in the production of knowledge about the world and the natural environment;
> - predict the supply of toys and equipment that respect the environmental and socio-cultural characteristics of the community. (Brasil, 2009, p. 13)

Also added to these documents there are many others that discuss the question of the specificities of young children, such as the Quality Indicators in Early Childhood Education (Brasil, 2009), which in a number of aspects address how they should be articulated to the EI institution with regard to dimensions of:

> 1 - institutional planning; 2 - multiplicity of experiences and languages; 3 - interactions; 4 - health promotion; 5 - spaces, materials and furniture; 6 - training and working conditions of teachers and other professionals; 7 - cooperation and exchange with families and participation in the social protection network. (Brasil, 2009, p. 16)

Hence, we understand with the legal and guiding principles of Rural Childhood Education, 'it is therefore a question of guaranteeing a quality of school attendance in rural settings equivalent to that of other localities: different, but not inferior' (Brasil, 2006a, 2006b, p. 38). Therefore, it is also a matter of affirming the difference, intertwined with the movement to enrich the identity of Rural Childhood Education. Then, in this third topic, we repeat the legal assertions in order to reaffirm the right to education of children, integrated with the recognition of the singularities present in the peasant context and in articulation with the strengthening of Children Education calling for the negotiation of its institutionality.

FINAL CONSIDERATIONS

In the possibilities of approaching the relations between human rights and sociocultural differentiation, we revisit the issue of the right to education of young children, moving ideas on the institutionality of Childhood Education, considering in particular the configuration of institutions in answering the demands for care, especially, of peasant children.

In the dialogue with the studies, with the legal basis of the theme, with the educational guidelines and also with the data of the local context, we inform that, in observing the specificities of the children of the rural areas, a panorama of inequalities with regard to the guarantee of the right to education. In this observation, we discuss the ways of care in the Rural Children Education, specifically when offered to children living in settlement areas. With these problematizations we aim to keep the discussions on this agenda alive, advocating the need to advance the indicators of care and, in the expansion of Rural Children Education, to associate the quantitative indicators with the qualitative ones with a view to recognizing, in the possible diversities, the guarantee of the rights to the education of the children. Therefore, we can combat the logics of precariousness that have been ravaging the forms of living and inhabiting the times and spaces of the EIC.

With the Bakhtinian referential, which stresses that we enter into a dialogical chain in the patterns in which we take part – with many, already said, simultaneous and an open field for new words – we point out, in the recognition of processuality in the construction/of Rural Childhood Education, the scope of the struggle for the achievement of social equality in the right to education of young children. In times of imposing cuts in the (if still incipient) social achievements, we conclude by inviting counterwords in order to contribute to the continuation of this agenda in the meeting with new interlocutors, within the horizon of affirmation of social rights, especially the right to education.

NOTES

1. The Constitutional Amendment 59 of 2009 (Brasil, 2009a) determined the compulsory enrollment / attendance in the preschool for children of four and five years. Children who complete six years after the 31st of March must be enrolled in the IE.
2. An Institution with a single room and/or single teacher.
3. An institution with more than one room, usually with more than one teacher.

REFERENCES

Arroyo, M. (2012). Diversidade. In R. S. Caldart (Coord.), *Dicionário da Educação do Campo* (pp. 229–236). Rio de Janeiro, São Paulo: Escola Politécnica Joaquim Venâncio, Expressão Popular.

Bakhtin, M. M. (2011). *Estéticada Criação Verbal. 6ª* ed. São Paulo: Editora WMF Martins Fontes.

Bakhtin, M. M. (2012). *Para uma filosofia do ato responsável*. São Carlos: Pedro & João Editores.

Bakhtin, M. M. (2014). *Marxismo e Filosofia da Linguagem*. 16ª ed. São Paulo: Hucitec.

Barbosa, M. C. S., Gehlen, I., & Fernandes, S. B. A oferta e a demanda de Educação Infantil no Campo: um estudo a partir de dados primários. (2012). In M. C. S. Barbosa, A. P. S. Silva, J. Pasuch, F. L. A. Leal, I. Oliveira e Silva, M. N. M. Freitas, & S. S. Albuquerque (Coord.). *Oferta e demanda de educação infantil no campo* (pp. 71–105). Porto Alegre: Evangraf.

Barbosa, M. C. S., Silva, A. P. S., Pasuch, J., Leal, F. L. A., Oliveira e Silva, I., Freitas, M. N. M., Albuquerque, & S. S. (Coord.). (2012). *Oferta e demanda da educação infantil no campo*. Porto Alegre: Evangraf.

Brasil. (1988). Constituição [da] República Federativa do Brasil. Brasília: Senado Federal.

Brasil. (1990). *Estatuto da Criança e do Adolescente*. Retrieved from de http://www.planalto.gov.br/ccivil_03/leis/l8069.htm.

Brasil. (1996). *Lei de Diretrizes e Bases da Educação Nacional* (LDB). Lei Federal n.º 9.394.

Brasil. (2006a). MEC/SEB. *Parâmetros básicos de infra-estrutura para instituições de educação infantil*. Brasília: MEC, SEB, 2006. Retrieved from http://portal.mec.gov.br/seb/arquivos/pdf/Educinf/miolo_infraestr.pdf.

Brasil. (2006b). MEC/SEB. *Parâmetros Nacionais de Qualidade para a Educação Infantil* — Volume 1. Retrieved from http://portal.mec.gov.br/seb/arquivos/pdf/Educinf/eduinfparqualvol1.pdf.

Brasil. (2009). MEC/SEB. *Indicadores de Qualidade na Educação Infantil*. Brasília: MEC/SEB. Retrieved from http://portal.mec.gov.br/dmdocuments/indic_qualit_educ_infantil.pdf.

Brasil. (2011a). Ministério da Educação. Nota Técnica. *Reuniões Técnicas Regionais do Grupo de Trabalho responsável pela elaboração das Orientações Curriculares para a Educação Infantil do Campo*. Retrieved from http://portal.mec.gov.br/index.php?option=com_docman&view=download&alias=7471-nota-tec-reg-2-pdf&category_slug=janeiro-2011-pdf&Itemid=30192.

Brasil. (2011b). MEC/SEB. *Deixa eu falar*. Brasília: MEC, SEB.

Brasil. (2013). *Monitoramento do uso dos Indicadores da Qualidade na Educação Infantil*. Retrieved from http://portal.mec.gov.br/index.php?option=com_docman&view=download&alias=13119-relatorio-versao-internet-final-pdf-pdf&category_slug=maio-2013-pdf&Itemid=30192.

Brasil. CNE/MEC. (2009a). *Resolução nº 5, de 17 de dezembro de 2009a*. Estabelece Diretrizes Curriculares para a Educação Infantil. Retrieved from http://portal.mec.gov.br/index.php?option=com_docman&task=doc_download&gid=2298&Itemid.

Caldart, R. S. (2000). *Pedagogia do Movimento Sem Terra: escola é mais que escola*. Petrópolis: Vozes.

Caldart, R. S., Paludo, C., & Doll, J. (2006). *Como se formam os sujeitos do campo? idosos, adultos, jovens, crianças e educadores*. Brasília: PRONERA: NEAD.

Cerisara, A. B., Rocha, E. A. C., & Silva Filho, J. J. (2007). Educação infantil: uma trajetória de pesquisa e indicações para a avaliação de contextos educativos. *Revista Zero-a-Seis: Santa Catarina*, *9*(15), 2–24, Jan/Jun.

Conde, S. F., & Farias, K. H. (2011). *Desafios da Educação do campo na atualidade: Educação Infantil e Classes multisseriadas na Serra Catarinense*. Natal: Anped. Retrieved from http://34reuniao.anped.org.br/images/posteres/GT03/GT03-1061%20int.pdf.

Côco, V. (2011). *Educação infantil do campo: aproximações ao cenário do Espírito Santo*. Natal: Anped. Retrieved from http://www.anped.org.br/app/webroot/34reuniao/images/trabalhos/GT03/GT03379%20int.pdf.

Côco, V. (2013). Conquistas, avanços, desafios e disputas na política de educação infantil: Transformações na docência... em nós. In I. S. Rangel, K. R. Nunes, & V. Côco. (Org.). *Educação Infantil: redes de conversações e produções de sentidos com crianças e adultos* (pp. 181–199). Petrópolis: De Petrus.

Côco, V. (2015). Docência na Educação Infantil. De quem estamos falando? Com quem estamos tratando? In M. L. R. Flores & S. S. Albuquerque, (Org.). *Implementação do Proinfância no Rio Grande do Sul: perspectivas políticas e pedagógicas* (pp. 143–160). Dados Eletrônicos. Porto Alegre: EDIPUCRS.

Côco, V., & Salgado, R. G. (2018). Reafirmando o direito a educação infantil. In J. F. Oliveira, A. B. Gouveia, & H. Araújo (Eds.), *Caderno de avaliação das metas do Plano Nacional de Educação: PNE 2014-2024* (pp. 8–9). Brasília: ANPAE. Retrieved from https://www.anpae.org.br/BibliotecaVirtual/4-Publicacoes/CadernoAnlisePNE.pdf.

Fernandes, B. M. (1999). *M. S. T. Movimento dos Trabalhadores rurais sem terra: formação e territorialização em São Paulo*. São Paulo: Hucitec.

Freire, P. (2013). *Extensão ou comunicação?* Rio de Janeiro: Paz e Terra.

Freitas, M. C. (Org.). (2006). *Desigualdade Social e Diversidade Cultural na Infância e na Juventude*. São Paulo: Cortez.

Gonçalves, R. D. F. S. (2013). *O estado da arte da infância e da educação infantil do campo: debates históricos, construções atuais*. (Master's thesis, Feira de Santa Federal University). Retrieved from http://www2.uefs.br/ppge/dissertacao/dissertacao_goncalves_2013.pdf.

Movimento dos Trabalhadores Rurais Sem Terra. (2018, September 17). Cerca de 15 mil pessoas participam da 3ª Feira Estadual da Reforma Agrária no ES. [Web log post]. Retrieved from http://www.mst.org.br/2018/09/17/cerca-de-15-mil-pessoas-participam-da-3a-feira-estadual-da-reforma-agraria-no-es.html.

Nunes, M. F. R., Corsino, P., & Didonet, V. (2011). *Educação Infantil no Brasil: primeira etapa da educação básica*. Brasília: UNESCO, MEC/SEB. Fundação Orça. Retrieved from http://unesdoc.unesco.org/images/0021/002144/214418por.pdf.

Padilha, A. M. L., & Oliveira, I. M. (2013). Quando a diversidade (não) é o mesmo que desigualdade: Educação infantil e trabalho docente. In I. S. Rangel, K. R. Nunes, & V. Côco, (Org.). *Educação Infantil: redes de conversações e produções de sentidos com crianças e adultos* (pp. 125–138). Petrópolis: De Petrus.

Pamphylio, M. M. (2010). *Os dizeres das crianças da Amazônia sobre a infância e escola*. (Master's thesis, Pará State University). Retrieved from http://paginas.uepa.br/mestradoeducacao/index.php?option=com_rokdownloads&view=file&id=258:marisnia-matos-pamphylio.

Pasuch, J., & Santos, T. M. D. (2012). A importância da Educação Infantil na constituição da identidade das crianças como sujeitas do campo. In M. C. S. Barbosa, A. P. S. Silva, J. Pasuch, F. L. A. Leal, I. Oliveira e Silva, M. N. M. Freitas, & S. S. Albuquerque (Coord.). *Oferta e demanda de educação infantil no campo* (pp. 107–151). Porto Alegre: Evangraf.

Reforma agrária em dados. (2006). *Educação do Campo: Direitos de todos os camponeses e camponesas*. [Web Page]. Retrieved from http://www.reformaagrariaemdados.org.br/.

Rocha, M. I. A., & Hage, S. M. (Org.). (2010). *Escola de Direito: reinventando a escola multisseriada*. Belo Horizonte: Autêntica Editora.

Rosemberg, F., & Artes, A. (2012). O rural e o urbano na oferta de educação para crianças de 6 anos. In M. C. S. Barbosa, A. P. S. Silva, J. Pasuch, F. L. A. Leal, I. Oliveira e Silva, M. N. M. Freitas, & S. S. Albuquerque (Coord.). *Oferta e demanda de educação infantil no campo* (pp. 13–69). Porto Alegre: Evangraf.

Scott, J. W. (2005). O Enigma da Igualdade. *Revista Estudos Femininos*, *13*(1), 11–30.

Silva, A. P. S., Felipe, E. S., & Ramos, M. M. (2012). Infância do Campo. In R. S. Caldart, I. B. Pereira, P. Alentejano, & G. Frigotto (Org.), *Dicionário da Educação do Campo* (pp. 417–424). Rio de Janeiro, São Paulo: Escola Politécnica Joaquim Venâncio, Expressão Popular.

Silva, A. P. S., & Pasuch, J. (2010). *Orientações Curriculares para a Educação Infantil do Campo*. Retrieved from http://portal.mec.gov.br/index.php?option=com_docman&view=download&alias=7396-oreint-curric-pdf&category_slug=janeiro-2011-pdf&Itemid=30192.

Silva, I. O., & Luz, I. R. (2012). Espaços, ambientes e contextos: reflexões sobre a Educação Infantil para crianças de 0 a 6 anos residentes em área rural em dois municípios da região sudeste do Brasil. M. C. S. Barbosa, A. P. S. Silva, J. Pasuch, F. L. A. Leal, I. Oliveira e Silva, M. N. M. Freitas, & S. S. Albuquerque (Coord.). *Oferta e demanda de educação infantil no campo* (pp. 181–217). Porto Alegre: Evangraf.

União Nacional dos Conselhos Municipais de Educação do Espírito Santo. (2015). Sistemas Municipais de Educação. [Circular Letter]. Retrieved from https://www.uncme.org.br/.

Vieira, M. A. F. O. (2016). *Educação infantil do campo e formação continuada dos educadores que atuam em assentamentos*. (Master's thesis, Espirito Santo Federal University). Retrieved from http://educacao.ufes.br/pos-graduacao/PPGE/detalhes-da-tese?id=9958.

Vieira, M. A. F. O., & Côco, V. (2016). Da educação rural à educação do campo: percursos históricos da educação infantil a partir das produções acadêmicas e da legislação brasileira. In E. C. Souza & V. L. J. Chaves (Org.). *Documentação, memória e história da Educação no Brasil: diálogos sobre políticas de educação e diversidade* (pp. 83–105). Tubarão, SC: Copiart.

Vieira, M. A. F. O., & Côco, V. (2017). Educação Infantil do Campo e formação de professores. *Cadernos CEDES*, *37*(103), 319–334. Retrieved from http://www.scielo.br/pdf/ccedes/v37n103/1678-7110-ccedes-37-103-319.pdf.

PART II
CHILDREN, YOUTH, SOCIOCULTURAL DIFFERENTIATION AND UNITY

FORMS, IMPACT AND CONSEQUENCES OF VIOLENCE AGAINST CHILDREN IN ROMANIAN CHILD PROTECTION SETTINGS

Maria Roth, Imola Antal, Ágnes Dávid-Kacsó and Éva László

ABSTRACT

Since the reforms started in the Romanian child protection, and in spite of adopting children's rights, and investing in the professionalization of the child protection staff, research has indicated that children continue to suffer violence in care settings.

This chapter contributes to the literature that documents children's rights violations in Romanian residential care, before and after the political shift in 1989, including the period after the accession to the EU, by presenting and discussing interview data of 48 adults who spent parts of their childhoods in child protection settings.

The conceptual framework of this analysis is based on the human rights perspective and the transitional justice. The main body of the article presents the testimonials of adults who grew up in institutional care in Romania, as collected in the framework of the SASCA project, funded by the European Union.[1]

Keywords: Violence; Romanian children protection; residential care; care leavers; institutional abuse; transitional justice

Human Rights for Children and Youth: Sociocultural Differentiation, Resistance and Unity
Sociological Studies of Children and Youth, Volume 24, 99–131

ISSN: 1537-4661/doi:10.1108/S1537-466120190000024006

Three decades after the universal recognition of Children Rights as foundation of child protection, it is justified to assume that Child Protection systems over the world have undergone thorough analysis for their previous failures and have rebuilt their institutions based on human rights principles. Such revaluation should be a basis for contemporary systems to assure that the millions of children and youth fostered in families or different forms of residential care spend their childhood in a nurturing environment, for the full realization of their potential. Notwithstanding such assumption, data of the Global Violence Reports in 2006 and 2015 reflect that children placed in institutional care, including residential care, family foster care, correctional facilities and settings for children with disabilities continue to be at high risk for violence (Office of the SRSG on Violence against Children, 2015; Pinheiro, 2006). Despite the progress which has been made all over the world due to the global commitment of governmental bodies and civic society to the Children's Rights Convention (CRC),[2] analysis has often pointed to the multiple victimization faced by children 'looked after' in care institutions. The UN's Secretary General Report on Violence (Pinheiro, 2006) has brought to public attention that child protection and justice systems authorities worldwide are responsible for supervising and controlling the lives of millions of children in their care, and often fail to safeguard them from the risk of violence from staff and peers, and also to develop effective mechanisms for complaints. In the last two decades, researchers have often found residential facilities to be poorly financed, endangering the lives and development of many children (Rus, Parris, Stativa, & Popa, 2017). Children in large institutions and those with disabilities are especially at risk, as they may lack the satisfaction of their basic needs, access to education, medication, recreation, or rehabilitation, which can cause or aggravate cognitive delays and psychological disorders (Larsson, 2016). In such institutions children's voices are not heard, and leadership withdraws from monitoring violence and quality of life for children in institutions, allowing the development of a culture of violence committed with impunity either by the staff or by the children themselves (UN, 2009). The gap between child protection laws that ban violent punishment and prevent all forms of violence and the enforcement of the legislation remains a key issue for most national governments (Office of the SRSG on Violence against Children, 2015). This covers the perpetual use of physical punishment as a child rearing method not only in families, but also in care institutions, in spite of the legal bans, resulting in poly-victimization of children. Although legal systems include opportunities to remedy and compensate victims of violence, access to these is limited to a few countries with better economic status.

Compared to other categories of maltreatment against children, research covering institutional abuse is scarcer, although it was already denounced back in the 1970s (D. Gil, 1975) and a solid mass of data has been accumulated. Data on violence in residential settings has been collected both in the historical past and present in all regions of the world (Rus et al., 2017). Historical institutional abuse affecting large numbers of children, from low social-economic backgrounds and often minority origin, was revealed in the United States (Finn & Coleman, 1985; Nunno, 1997), the United Kingdom (Gallagher, 2000),

Australia (Mathews, 2004), Canada (Barter, Renold, Berridge, & Cawson, 2004), Ireland (Fitzpatrick et al., 2010), Norway (Pettersen, 2010); Sweden (Sköld, 2013; Sköld, Sandin, & Schiratzki, 2018), Denmark (Sköld, 2013), New Zealand (Winter, 2018), Brazil (Salomão, Wegner, & Canabarro, 2014; Silva, Lunardi, Lunardi, Algeri, & Souza, 2016), China (Kim et al., 2000) as well as in the former communist countries of Central and Eastern Europe and the former Soviet Union (Carter, 2005; Tobis, 2000).

OBJECTIVE

The objective of this chapter is to analyze institutional child abuse in Romania from the perspective of adults who have spent their childhoods in residential child protection homes, and to discuss the willingness of Romania to join the transitional justice movements and respond to the victims' needs.

The conceptual framework of this chapter is based on the Human rights perspective, mainly on the contradictions between the declared commitment to the wellbeing of all children, and the way society handles its responsibilities, by admitting to and redressing the victims' childhood sufferings. The main body of the article consists of the analysis of testimonials of adults who grew up in institutional care in Romania, as captured in the recent SASCA project,[3] which is looking at the ways victims of institutional abuse and professionals in residential care view the issue of justice for those who experienced adversity and suffering in child protection settings.

THE CONCEPT OF INSTITUTIONAL ABUSE

Soon after the concepts of child abuse and neglect in the family were defined by Kempe and his collaborators (H. Kempe et al., 1962), the number of children taken into care increased. In the 1970s the quality of care became a concern, and David Gil (1975) expended the level of analysis from family level to institutional and societal level. The specificities of institutional abuse were defined by Eliana Gil (1982) according to whom institutional abuse has three forms: the first is committed by certain members of the care staff or associated persons against institutionalized children, similar to the physical, sexual or psychological maltreatment suffered in a family; the second is called program abuse, when specific settings operated below child welfare standards, affecting the children they cared for by administering a regime or an intervention method or treatment or other behaviour modification technique which may be acceptable for some staff members, but not acceptable according to general children's rights principles; the third form is system abuse where maltreatment is not committed by a single person or an isolated operational program, but because the child protection system is stretched beyond its limits and it results in the lack of sufficient child care units to respond to the children's needs, followed by misdiagnosis, misplacement, unnecessary removal from family or prolonged treatment due to inadequate assessment, monitoring or supervision (Barter, 1997; Popwers & Nunno, 1990). The concept of institutional abuse refers to the responsibilities of child welfare institutions, public administration services, courts of law and legislative bodies for the respect of children's fundamental rights (Pinheiro, 2006). It is the expression of how systematically they take into consideration children's interests when they design policies, run programs and activities, define behavioural management, train and support staff, assess and monitor children. The UN report also revealed that in such institutional systems staff lacked behavioural management methods, was generally poorly educated, and withdrew leadership from monitoring foster care, which contributed to a culture of impunity and tolerance for violence committed either by the staff or by the children themselves.

Centred on the concept of institutional abuse, this article looks at interpersonal, program and societal violence, as reflected in the narrations of adults, who spent their childhood, or part of their childhood in the child protection system. The analysis is based on the conceptualization of the General comment No. 13 (2011), which includes institutional and system violations of child rights as direct or indirect harm caused to children:

> Authorities at all levels of the State responsible for the protection of children from all forms of violence may directly and indirectly cause harm by lacking effective means of implementation of obligations under the Convention. Such omissions include the failure to adopt or revise legislation and other provisions, inadequate implementation of laws and other regulations and insufficient provision of material, technical and human resources and capacities to identify, prevent and react to violence against children. It is also an omission when measures and programmes are not equipped with sufficient means to assess, monitor and evaluate progress or shortcomings of the activities to end violence against children. Also, in the commission of certain acts, professionals may abuse children's right to freedom from violence, for example, when they execute their responsibilities in a way that disregards the best interests, the views and the developmental objectives of the child. (art. CRC/C/GC/13, IV, A, 1/32)

This interest to respect children's rights in alternatives to family care has been emphasized in the UN Guidelines for the Alternative Care of Children and prompted greater attention to this issue. (Brodie & Pearce, 2017).

TRANSITIONAL JUSTICE

The willingness to change past practices to handle such issues and bring justice to victims of violence in residential facilities run by churches or public institutions in past regimes in different countries has been described as transitional justice (Moffett, 2017). In cases in which states admitted to bearing the responsibility for atrocities against vulnerable groups of people committed previously, redress schemes were developed addressed to the survivors of those forms of violence. In a transition period, this has the potential of a political project of solidarity with and reparation for a group who had suffered human rights abuse. In case of children being robbed of their childhood while being victims of undifferentiated care, emotional neglect, physical and/or sexual abuse, or other torturous treatments during their time in foster care, reparations in transitional justice processes respond to the need of victims to be treated as full citizens with rights whose lives matter and whose voices are finally heard. Reparation schemes in such case are meant to give a clear cut signal of the unacceptability of all forms of violence against children in any context and the need to build a child rights based attitude 'by remedying the violations of the past and preventing future victimization' (de Greiff, 2006, p. 454). Transition justice schemes are being practiced in more and more affluent countries in an attempt to face and deal with historical abuse of children in public or religious settings. Australia, Austria, Belgium, Canada, Germany, Iceland, Ireland, New Zealand, The Netherlands, Norway, the States of Jersey, Sweden, Scotland, Switzerland and the United States have such schemes, while other countries have undertaken inquiries but did not establish redress schemes for those victimized in their childhood, like the Aland Islands, Denmark, England, Finland and the Northern Islands (Daly, 2017).

Confronted with scarcity of resources, necessary reforms in the child protection systems are much slower to be adopted by developing countries. In ex-communist countries institutional child care has been denounced as impersonal, with poor standards of care, inadequately resourced (both for human and financial resources), uncaring, neglectful, abusive and oppressive for minorities and families with social and economic disadvantages (Carter, 2005; Csáky, 2009; Roth, 1999). Due to the recent economic crisis, and the ongoing political conflicts, wars and migration, there are several regions in the world where the numbers of children in public and private care institutions have been maintained or even increased; community services have been non-existent or scarce or drained of resources, and consequently, residential care got to be seen 'as the only way to access education and other services' (Better Care Network & UNICEF, USAID & PEPFAR, 2015, p. 7). Discrimination and prejudices around children born out of wedlock, with disabilities, girls, Roma and other ethnic groups or races have an impact on parenting, foster parenting and adoption in several ex-communist countries in Eastern and Central Europe, China and many other regions. These cultural attitudes contribute – with particular regularity – to the maintenance of parental abandonment and to the low rate of foster parenting and adoption in many countries affected by poverty, wars, natural disasters and 'supply' plenty of children for the maintenance or the expansion of residential child care. Such tendencies continue in the former communist countries of Eastern and Central Europe, with different characteristics, depending on specific social-economic, political and cultural contexts.

OVERVIEW OF RESEARCH ON INSTITUTIONAL VIOLENCE IN ROMANIA

The Romanian child protection system inherited from the former communist regime was based on a large network of residential care institutions, organized by age, gender and disability: medicalized institutions called 'cradles' for children aged 0–3 ; orphanages for children aged 4–6 and 7–18 as well as hospital-homes for children with disabilities, evaluated as uncurable. Conditions in many of these institutions were extremely poor, and the more severe the disability, the lower the quality of the living conditions, endangering children's health, survival, intellectual and emotional development, and their capacity for attachment in social relations. Conditions in these homes were severe: lack of adequate nutrition and medical care, inadequate clothing, unheated, isolated and defective dwellings. The organizational culture of these institutions was dominated by neglect of children's physical and emotional needs and all forms of abuse committed by peers and staff, accompanied by lack of monitoring and impunity for any forms of violence against children (Dumitrana, 1998; Greenwell, 2001; Macavei, 1989; Roth, 1999).

After the fall of Ceausescu's communist regime, in 1990, the horrors of more than 100,000 children living in Romania's child welfare institutions were revealed to the world, showing images of children of different ages crowded in large institutions, all dressed alike, without adequate stimulation, education and supervision, often malnourished, poorly dressed, and suffering from chronic diseases, including AIDS, due to institutional contamination:

> Romania's abandoned children remain unforgettable, indelibly stamped on the memory. Shaven-headed, semi-naked and malnourished, the cameras showed children in their hundreds dressed in rags trapped in barred, airless rooms, many tied to beds or rocking back and forth out of mind-numbing boredom. Of the injustices generated by the Ceauşescu regime this was to prove the most graphic, the most shocking. Beamed into homes across the world, the footage prompted global outrage, and medical provisions and aid poured into a country that had kept its abandoned children under lock and key for decades. (UNICEF, 2009, p. 4)

Changes began by opening adoptions, allowing international aid agencies to bring material aid, but also consultation and professional service models to Romania. In the first decade after the political shift, the Romanian civil sector and the training of social science and support professionals was reborn from its ashes where the dictatorial regime of Ceausescu had buried it. Universities embarked on developing training programs for social workers, sociologists, psychologists, special educators and public administrators, encouraging the development of social, medical and psychological public and private services. In spite of all these efforts, reforms were enacted slowly and the organizational culture in child protection survived long after the political shift. It took 14 years for the legislators to ban the placement of infants and toddlers under the age of two in children's homes, and to create the legal bases and the standards for professional foster care (Greenwell, 2001; Roth, 1999). In cooperation with international civil and political forums, the Romanian Government has embarked on the politics of deinstitutionalization, meaning to decrease the number of children already living in institutions by reintegrating them in their own biological family, with relatives or foster families or by adoption, albeit mostly international adoptions. In 1997 it issued legislation that defined child abuse and neglect and created the grounds for professional family foster care. But only the Child Law 272[4] dated 2004, has been the first child rights document designed to transpose the UN Convention into a comprehensive Romanian law accompanied by guidelines and application standards. Among others, it legislated the prohibition of all forms of physical punishment aiming to prevent child abandonment and violence against children, it imposed compulsory reporting by professionals and monitoring of all forms of violence against children, it encouraged the development of public services for children and families in communities, and it prioritized family foster care, or small family type centres over large institutions (Cojocaru, 2007; Neagu, 2017; Roth, 2005). In order to avoid the effects of hospitalization of infants and toddlers in medical type institutions, law 272 and the standards for child care that followed it limited the placement of children in residential child care institutions for those under the age of two, extending it later in 2013, to the age of three. It was followed by the Civil Procedures Code (134/2010) (referred to as CRC hereon) and the Penal Code (135/2010), also reinforcing children's rights to be protected against violence, which instated the rights of children to file reports and get professional help, as well as compensation for suffering violence (Călian, 2018). In spite of the declared aims of the Romanian child protection strategies[5] to end institutionalization of children and shift towards community and family foster care, the large public institutions of child protection have been maintained in Romania, as a response to the high rate of child abandonment by families (Stănculescu, Grigoraş, Teşliuc, & Pop, 2016).

In 2018, Romania still registered 17,718 children in residential care, with 14,033 of them being in public residential placement centres and 3,685 in private settings, as shown on the official site of the Romanian Agency for Protection of Children's Rights and Adoption[6] for June 2018.[7] Although the topic of deinstitutionalization has been permanently maintained on the agenda of all the governments, Romania has not yet mobilized enough resources to counteract the generalized high poverty rate and the lack of social housing affecting a large percentage of the population especially its most deprived and marginalized community, the Roma (Antal & Tonk, 2017; Neagu, 2017; Stănculescu et al., 2016).

Since the reforms started, research data have been collected to document the changes in the children's quality of life. In spite of adopting a discourse centred on children's rights, and investing in the professionalization of the child protection staff, the data collected after the legalization of CRC over the last two decades indicated the perpetuation of hardships in living conditions and violence suffered by children and young people in care (Rus et al., 2013; Rus et al., 2016; Stativa, Anghelescu, Palicari, Stanescu, & Nanu, 2002), demonstrating the weaknesses of the system, that could not stop psychological, physical and even sexual abuse by staff and\or peers. Such violence was documented both before and after the period of accession of Romania to the EU. Researchers collecting children's views in different regions of the country documented physical, emotional and sexual abuse committed by staff and peers, as well as all forms of neglect (Brătianu & Roşca, 2005; Câmpean, Constantin, & Mihalache, 2010; Gavrilovici & Groza, 2007; Neagu, 2017; Onica-Chipea, Stanciu, & Chipea, 2008; Porumb, 2010). According to this body of studies, children in residential care were left without individualized treatment; staff was not properly trained for dealing with abused, neglected or/and abandoned children; young people in care did not benefit from the proper treatment they needed, and were not sufficiently prepared for either an eventual family reunification or for independent social life, employment and family formation, nor for the transition to independent housing.

The report of the Center for Legal Resources (2014) has reiterated that children and young people with disabilities were treated in worse conditions than those with more capabilities; they were kept outside the mainstream system of education and social life: education in special schools, where children do not learn basic skills that would help them live an independent life. Children with disabilities are cared for by mostly untrained staff, who do not seem to know these children's needs for treatment and recovery. Even hygiene conditions are affected by insufficient resources, treatment is not sufficiently individualized and revised, in spite of the existing regulations, and in such institutions the mortality rate has been maintained high.

METHODOLOGY OF DATA COLLECTION

The goal of this chapter is to analyze the state of art of the Romanian residential care system as described by 45 interviews and a focus group, with a total of 48 young adults who have spent part of their childhood in a residential care setting.

The interviews were carried out with the following objectives:

- To describe the perspectives of the interviewed adults on the living conditions in the residential settings and to identify the aspects related to children's rights in relation with the reforms taking place in the country.
- To address the problem of violence against children in institutional settings from the perspective of adult survivors and understand the long-term effects of such events.
- To understand the expectations of the survivors of violence in institutional settings for compensation for their suffering.
- To build on the testimonials of the adults experiencing violence in residential settings and to suggest violence prevention strategies for the protection of children still living today in residential care.

Sampling was developed using the snowball technique, mainly through recruiting students enrolled in Social Work studies, contacting associations and informal groups of out-of-care young adults (The Council of Institutionalized Young People and „Gyeri" Club), public and private services for vulnerable adults, and through social media (through personal and Facebook page (SASCA.ro), radio and newspaper announcements, as well as distribution of project flyers. We managed to recruit 48 persons aged 19 to 35, within which the age group 20 to 30 being best represented, with only 4.4% of respondents (2 persons) under the age of 21, 58% (26 persons) between 21 and 33, 32% (15 persons) between 31 and 40, and 4.4% (2 persons) between 41 and 50. Regarding their professional status, 23 persons (51.1%) had full-time jobs at the moment of the interview, five persons (11.1%) had part-time jobs, two persons were students (4.4%) and four were on maternity leave (4.4%). The rest of the persons weren't in formal employment, seven of them were unemployed (15.6%), four were on disability allowance or on ill health retirement and three were working occasionally. A large proportion (48.9%) had higher education diploma, among whom six (15.4%) graduated a masters or doctoral program, 11 persons (24.4%) had an upper-secondary education level, eight persons (17.8%) graduated a vocational form of education, three (6.7%) had middle school education and two (4.4%) graduated primary school. Among the interviewees, 10 (22.2%) were married and had children of their own.

For ethical considerations, invitations for collecting narratives were accompanied by letters addressed to potential respondents with information regarding the scope of the project, to fact of voluntary participation, the anonymity of the interview transcriptions in all reports and scientific publications, and the possibility to end and drop out of the interview at any moment, without any consequences. Respondents were invited to sign consent forms for the use of fragments from the registered materials. A number of the respondents expressed their wish to openly state their names in the project reports, but the ethical committee of the project had decided to anonymize all names, coding their initials, in order to prevent their recognition. The interviewers did not promise financial compensation, as this was not covered by the project but made it possible for participants to participate in sessions of counselling and social support. A few of the respondents have used this opportunity, taking part in psychotherapy, legal counselling and benefitted from social support and social services in applying for shelter, social benefits or health care.

PERSONAL HISTORIES

The life-stories revealed that the interviewees have been through several types of care settings before leaving care: only six persons (14.3%) grew up in one, 13 persons (31%) in two, 12 (28.6%) in three, nine persons (21.4%) in four, one person (2.4%) lived in five and one (2.4%) in six different settings. Sometimes the changes were positive, like moving from a large institution to foster care, or moving from a family type residential home to a transition home or from abusive foster parents to a 'good enough' foster family, there were many negative changes as well: from caring foster parents to residential home, from a family type institution to abusive foster parents. In a few cases, even with severe abusive experiences, there were no changes. Children were kept in the same families or the same residential homes.

Although all 48 interviewed persons grew up in at least one form of residential care (large institution or family type institution), many of them had experiences in foster care and transition homes as well. Among the 48 persons, 36 (80%) had experience in growing up in large institutions, 28 (62.2%) in family type residential homes, 29 persons (64.4%) in foster care and 14 persons (31.1%) in transitional homes for young people. Regarding the age of institutionalization, 20 persons (44.44%) were institutionalized before they were two years old, 15 (33.3%) after their birth, 18 persons (40%) at age 3–7, the rest of seven persons were older than eight years old at the time of their institutionalization. The maximum age of institutionalization in our sample was 16 years, the average age was 3.93. They spent on average 17.6 years in the child protection institutions, a minimum of seven and maximum of 30 years. The period of institutionalization is estimated according to the lifecourse drawn by the respondent. It is indicated by the acronym p.i. In cases when the period of experiencing violence could be approximated more exactly, this is indicated by the acronym p.e.v.

RESULTS

For several respondents the institutional atmosphere was frightening, stressful, disorganized and wild. Many things were frightening for the small children, when they entered the institutions: the crowded places, the noises, the fights, the beatings, the shouting and even serious accidents.

This was illustrated, for example, by RC (24, male), who compared the large residential home where he spent his childhood to the jungle:

> The atmosphere? Like in the jungle; it was the jungle. [...] Many abuses were hidden there. Can you imagine the residential home having four floors, with long corridors, and full of children?". "I even saw a child falling down from an upper floor. (RC, 24, male, p.i 1995–2010)

The daily experiences in residential homes were frightening, children felt exposed, scared, insecure.

> For me it was very frightening, and it made me so nervous. I saw myself so small and they were beating so hard. From this I accumulated so much need of revenge. (MC, 25, female, p.i. 1995–2010)

Fear was felt both in public and private homes. In spite of the sponsors who regularly visited the home, the leaders of the home of AL (22, male) managed to keep them under control by inspiring fear.

> One heard very frightening, even dramatic things as a child: you were threatened to be pinned by the ears, put in a hole and locked inside. Of course we were frightened. (AL, 22, male, p.i 2000–2014)

SEXUAL ABUSE

Sexual abuse by older boys was a well-known phenomenon, targeting mostly boys; only 5 respondents (4 men and one woman) of the 48 interviewed people recounted personal experiences of sexual abuse, where the aggressors were professionals/caretakers from the residential home (an educator from a family type foster-home, a volunteer-journalist, a couple of educators in a large institutions and a doctor). The abusers were men in all of these situations. In one of the cases, the abuse had lasted for one year, when the 17-year-old girl disclosed the abuse to the school psychologist. In another case, the perpetrator had access to the victim many times, as well as to other children in that setting. When this victim met the second perpetrator, he was already aware of his opportunities and stopped the abuse, but the interviewee knew about other boys who may have been victims. For example, IO (*29, male, period of abuse 1998–2002*) had been abused by two educators from the large institution he grew up in, who gave money and other advantages to the boys whom they abused. Other testimonials explained the devastating effects of sexual abuse on care leavers' lives.

> But I also experienced sexual abuse, there were quite hard situations there. It started when I was in the 11th grade, at the beginning [...] It lasted for one year. 'Cuze I couldn't bear it anymore, I broke down. (E, 29, female, p.e.v. 2006–2007)

> And in fact he liked not only my speech, but maybe me too, when I was little. And of course he asked permission to take me from Odorheiu Secuiesc, to various places, but I was always sleeping next to him, and I woke up many times that he was caressing me, or I fell asleep or woke up without pyjama bottoms, and all these events left harsh, deep marks on my life, I didn't dare to tell about it. [...] I was still in the 10th grade. (AN, 36, male, p.e.v. 1997–1998)

> Yes, also sexual abuses occurred, a lot of them. I suffered abuse uncountable times. These sexual abuses stopped when I turned around 15. By other older youngsters and educators and [...] The thing is that it didn't occur just once. They woke up one of us, I was waken up too, first you had to clean the bathroom, then you were called in the room where he stayed, in the educator's room or the service room, it was called the service room. And there you had to do things like [...] do him oral stuff, masturbate him and let him [...] well, let him do it to you. You couldn't resist, you couldn't say anything; in fact he tried to buy me, he eventually gave me money [...] (So there was one specific person who requested this from you?) Not only one, no. There was one also among the younger (educators)s and the older; [...] at a certain point there were some who did this for cigarettes, other kids for I don't know [...] for money. (RC, 24, male, p.e.v. 2000–2005)

The accounts of sexual abuse also described situations when the interviewed person talked about the experiences of his or her colleagues:

> Or alike, the girls, those in professional school were sexually assaulted by male educators. My cousin told me the same, that they wanted to do this to her too, and to her classmates as well, and it also happened that they raped girls. (MA, 31, female, p.e.v. 2003–2005)

> There was an educator who abused a child, who was well developed, at around 3 in the morning. And, unfortunately, this woman is still working in the system, who abused my colleague, who's 30 years old now. (RC, 24, male, p.e.v. 2003–2010)

Sexual abuse by peers, committed by older children, especially boys was a well-known phenomenon to many of the interviewed persons coming from various large institutions. Although the interviewees related events in which the victims were both girls and boys, many of them told us that sexual violence against younger boys was a routine in the institution they grew up in. In most of the institutions there were rules in place for stopping the access of older boys to younger girls, but the younger boys were within sight and reach of the older ones most of the time, and thus they were extremely vulnerable to victimization. Among the most frequently mentioned forms of abuse they described was oral penetration, forcing the young boy to fellate the abuser. But touching of the genitals of the young boy, making the younger child touch and manually manipulate the older boy's penis and forcing sexual interactions between two younger children (two boys or a boy and a girl) were also detailed.

> It was well known that the older were sexually abusing smaller children. Watch his penis, and if not, you got beaten, or you were surrounded by several boys, they took out your penis and kept pawing it, things like that [...] It also happened that they took out their penis, now touch it, hold it, if not, they beat you. You had to do it even if you didn't want to. (GE, 27, male, p.e.v. 2000–2007)

> Me too, I went through this: when I went to a camp, an older boy in institutional care raped me, forced me to have sexual intercourse with him. (VI, 33, male, p.e.v. 1995–1997)

> I had to suck the sex organ of an older boy to be able to stop something. It wasn't the most pleasant thing to do. [...] I was 8 or 9. (BA, 23, male, p.e.v. 2003–2004)

> I remember also that, oh it was very bad, the older boys abused older girls, and once I... I was sent to sleep in a place where an older girl was laying, I didn't understand why I had to sleep next to her anyway, because I was little. And this SZ came in, you see, he was beating this girl, because she didn't let him to [...] So he kept being violent, I remember him getting on top of her, and I was so scared. I covered my head, I kept praying, Jesus, my Lord, please watch over me, but I couldn't sleep. I didn't get hurt, but that fear you experience, when the other is being abused next to you. It was hard. (MA, 31, female, p.e.v. 1998–2000)

In a few instances the abuse was known to the personnel but was not followed by any intervention due to a misconception of 'confidentiality' of the institution and colleagues. A report from a specialist outside the institution was needed for something to happen. In sexual abuse situations, the reasons for children not requesting help sometimes included loyalty towards the perpetrator, other times fear of the perpetrator or fear of the consequences and shame.

> And it [the relationship] didn't result in any trouble, it didn't become known. If it came out – but it happened very rarely, one had to be very brave for that – then the educator was fired for real, in that case, of course. But the educator could get away only with that, with being fired. (MA, 33, female, period unclear)

> I didn't dare to tell about it, because he threatened me. So they didn't know in the institution, but I could do nothing. I feared the consequences and what the institution would say. I also wanted to go to university [...] There was an educator whom I told everything, but I asked them not to do anything, so they couldn't take measures, but I always talked about it with that educator and cried on their shoulders. (E, 29, female, p.e.v. 2005–2007)

Other times, girls asked for help, but only after long periods of victimization

> I kept on bearing it until I got in the 12th grade, then I told the school psychologist, and they took measures. They made my write it down and submitted my letter. (E, 29, female, p.e.v. 2005–2008)

PHYSICAL ABUSE AND OTHER METHODS OF PUNISHMENT

Children got beaten and hit in various ways by the staff as well as by other children, in public institutions and private ones alike, and in large institutions as well as in smaller, family type homes. Some of them suffered extremely brutal forms of physical violence. Witnessing the suffering, in some cases the death, of their mates and friends was also a traumatic experience for many. In large institutions, the different forms of physical violence were applied throughout the daily life of children: when they woke up, when they were late for breakfast, when studying, doing their homework, working, when they were sick and wouldn't eat, when they went to bed, when they didn't sleep, when they were disobedient or sometimes simply for the fun of adults, or older children.

Physical violence sometimes continued in the family type children's homes as well, or in the foster family, since the 'professional' foster care personnel was the former staff member from the children's homes, thus the same people continued to work with the children, even if much fewer children were living in a home. We have few accounts of physical violence that occurred after 2008, but the majority of the interviewed people were already teenagers or adults at this time. After the large institutions were closed, the rate and intensity of violent acts by older children against younger ones were reduced. Hitting and beating were usually used as disciplining methods but sometimes as entertainment as well.

> My colleagues were beaten so badly, worse than animals. And they hit in the head [...] They were beaten with the hose. The nephew of the director was the person appointed to beat the children. (AL, 22, male, p.e.v. 2005–2011)

> I remember that the male educator, when we didn't know the math homework, called us to write it on the blackboard [...] He would step behind you, and you see, he would push your head against the blackboard. It even happened that he kicked a girl so hard, a classmate of mine because of math that we thought she would die, I swear she couldn't breathe, and he kept kicking her. And we didn't dare to tell him to stop. 'Cuz if we had, he would have kicked us as well. Oh, one could easily just die in front of our eyes, and we would do nothing, because we didn't dare. It was very rough. (MA, 31, female, p.e.v. 1997–2002)

> In fact I had two very good friends I couldn't save. I recall it well, in bedroom number 8, one of my friends died after getting beaten by his colleagues. There was a guy, H, who made his colleagues, older boys, beat my friend, and in 5 seconds he passed away. The other one, the same thing, also because of the beating, I was terrified, not only me, all 17 of us from there, and we were shaking and staring at him, we knew he was dead, for his face was yellow. I tried to mutter that he was deceased, but he scolded me: 'Did you say something? You, in the corner! I didn't say anything then, 'cuz I knew if I was to say something, I could be the next. (AD, 32, male, p.i 1990–2005)

Educators used a large variety of forms of physical violence in order to discipline children, some of them milder, other extremely severe. Several respondents mentioned how terrified they were when locked up in isolation rooms. Two of the four focus group participants reported being locked up for variable number of days, and even weeks in the 'white isolator', together with tens of other naughty children. This was a small room, very crowded, full of bunk beds, with very little space for moving for the children, with no windows, and a locked door. They had a TV which was playing all the time on the same channel. Food was portioned, but never enough. They were medicated, and the personnel was checking on them sometimes 'when they heard too much noise', but otherwise the children were 'entertaining themselves' i.e., fighting among each other. 'We were injected, to calm us down'; 'The isolator was like a boxing-ring' (RC, 24, male, p.e.v. 2003–2005). The boxing ring is a metaphor meaning that the strongest remains on his feet, the rest are knocked down, and that they had to stand up for themselves if they wanted to survive.

According to the respondents, among the experiences that marked them the most, were the hitting and beatings, which were usually used as disciplining methods, but sometimes as entertainment for some staff as well. The contexts in which hitting and beating were used could be related to any aspect of the children's lives: getting up, being late for breakfast, studying, doing homework, going to bed, disobeying the adults, etc.

> At breakfast, precisely at 8, if you weren't punctual, they came and pulled your earlobe, they would call it the pulling of the ear-hair. This was the system like, you had to be punctual. (AL, 26, female, p.e.v. 2001–2005)

> I remember that I had another teacher, she lives just across the street from the care home. Well she was busy with the alphabet, so don't worry, I know it by heart now. Oh, she beat me so hard because we couldn't learn the alphabet. (DM, 31, female, p.e.v. 1993–1999)

The evening routines were another occasion when many children were hurt, slapped and beaten. Bathing in the large institutions was usually not a good experience when they were washed quite roughly and many children were disciplined by putting soap in their eyes. Children were often beaten for not sleeping or beaten before going to bed.

> Going to bed was like this: first going to the toilet, and before going to bed, we stood in line again, and I remember one more educator, who had this habit that she had a plank, I think, or it seems to me it was a plank from a bed, so we lined up, and she gave two paddles to each of us, so we went to bed with that so that we would fall asleep crying. This was everyday practice. After a while, whoever became a favourite child, so I remember holding out my arms, and she didn't hit my hand, so those who became favourites or she liked, those didn't get paddles, but at the beginning everybody got the same. (PI, 30, female, p.e.v. 1994–1999).

> And it also happened that – out of fun – whoever wasn't sleeping, they called them out to the corridor, now you squat, walk like a dwarf, I don't know how meters long, and the night guard came in and watched. And if you didn't do it properly, they would kick you, in the ass, or beat you right there. And if you cried, [...] 'Are you crying, miss?' if you cried, they hit you harder, and on and on [...] It was very tough. (D., 31, female, p.e.v. 1993–1999)

Being sick, having different kind of problems: vomiting, enuresis, speech problems were all reasons to get physically abused behaviour by the staff.

> The night shift came, and if someone wetted the bed, the night guard didn't mind we were all sleeping, switched on the light, took the kid out of bed and beat him hard for wetting the bed. (IR, 33, female, p.e.v. 1989–1995)

> Or there was a woman, I couldn't pronounce her name, it had an 'r' in it, and I said I don't know what instead. So she didn't beat me, just kept frightening me with a stick, 'Say it again!', she hit the table, and repeat it again, and I fucked it up. Now again! (M, 31, female, p.e.v., 1991–1995)

> I was vomiting and she beat me hard for vomiting. (I, 33, female, p.e.v. 1989–1995)

Beatings were administered by hand or with different tools: hose, sticks, stripes, plank, etc.

> I remember it even now, he had a plastic stick, with stripes, and with that. It was so painful, we got such hard blows on our bottoms and backs you wouldn't believe. Or we would get taws, those with a rod. (IR, 33, female, p.e.v. 1989–1995)

Other forms of physical abuse were: kneeling on pebbles, kneeling in the snow, being denied food, forcing the spoon into the mouth of children, cutting their hair, washing the kid's eyes with a sponge.

> They gave us some syrup, which we didn't like, because it was bitter, but they forced us to drink it. They grabbed us and forced the spoon into our mouths. (IR, 33, female, p.e.v., 1989–1995)

> It also happened that we had to kneel on pebbles, because we didn't listen to the educators, to the nannies or teachers, so we got beaten hard by the nanny. It even happened that because of one kid we all got beaten. (I, 33, female, p.e.v. 1991–1995)

> He made us smell the toilet as a punishment, or didn't give us anything to eat. He did quite odd things. (EA, 27, female, p.e.v. 1995–2007)

Not everybody was equally punished; Roma children with dark skin, children the staff didn't like were punished more often than the others:

> There were children they didn't like, or there were naughty children, they sometimes brushed those kids' eyes with a soapy sponge. (RO, 34, female, p.i. 1988–1994)

> I tell you that they didn't hurt those with white skin, I was one of these, but whoever had brown skin, got trashed. (IR, 33, female, p.e.v. 1989–1995)

Relationships between children and children or relatives of educators were not allowed:

> Or I recall that this B had a, I'm not quite sure, it wasn't his daughter, but his sibling's daughter or what, she was of the same age as we, and one boy [...] well some sort of childish love, we were small, we were learning the alphabet, so this boy liked that girl, and he kissed her lips. Wow, how hard he beat him. He beat him so hard, we couldn't understand at that age why. Later he told us that the boy kissed her on her lips. Anyway, to beat him so hard just for that? (IR, 33, female, p.e.v. 1991–1992)

Respondents remember children being turned against each other:

> He made 2 children hit each other. (E, 29, female, p.e.v. 1995–2000)

> Once he (the educator) convinced my little brother to hit the other child and he got money for that. He rewarded him for beating the other kid. (EA, 27, female, p.e.v. 1999–2001)

Terrifying physical abuse was also committed by older children who were doing it either for their own entertainment or interest, lack of monitoring by the staff, or sometimes encouraged by 'educational' personnel to discipline and abuse younger children. These could take very harsh forms as well, even resulting in the death of children.

> Yes, there was another child close to me. That was in 2000, or 2001. He was burnt alive, they actually set his bed on fire, because the mattresses are made of foam and the child didn't wake up. Only we smelled it when we saw the smoke coming out from that room and they took off the bars, but by that time the boy turned to ashes. (Who burnt him alive?) His roommates. (AN, 32, male, p.e.v. 2001–2002).

> They told me: get on the chair and bend your head down, don't look at them. And you wetted your pants because of fear, because you knew it would be your turn too to get tortured thoroughly: they made you run from one place to the other, and they would put their leg in front

> of you to make you trip, you weren't allowed to jump to avoid falling, because they beat you so hard, as you can't imagine. (VI, 37, male, p.i. 1988–2002).

> I could see them taking him and pulling him from the leg, they put him on the bed and put those very thick blankets over him, those brought by the English, and five persons put him on the ground, an angel of 4 years. When we were praying one night, that night they killed him. (Older boys [killed] a little child) (AD, 32, male, p.e.v. 1991–1994)

Most peer abuse incidents were committed by men against men. According to Popwers and Nunno (1990), most research on bullying shows that boys are far more likely to be both the perpetrator and the victim of physical assaults. But in residential homes peer abuse was not only specific to males, but also to female children in residential homes:

> But there were moments when older girls enjoyed watching us, children fighting: they put us in a circle and chose: you, kiddo, with that one, now fight. And if you said you didn't want to fight, you got beaten by all the kids. And rather than being beaten by all, you preferred to get a trash from one. That was the moment of survival. But most of the time it was me who got beat up. (AM, 36, female, p.e.v. 1989–1995)

The children who had the opportunity to be placed from the institutions in family foster care could not always benefit from a better treatment, depending on the good will of the foster parent. Monitoring by the child protection agency was not effective. Our respondents recall being subject to physically abusive behaviours: hitting, keeping the children outside the house, switching off the heating in their rooms, gripping their neck and forcing them to kneel for long periods of time.

> If we left school at two and didn't arrive home let's say at two and a quarter, she would keep us in front of the house for two hours, no matter if it was winter or summer, if we moved away, she shouted to us to stay there, in wintertime she was leaving the door of the balcony open to let the room become cold, she was switching off the heating. (ASz, 24, female, p.e.v. 2005–2009)

> If I did something she disliked, she would make me kneel for an entire night in the hall, so there are things which can't be surpassed, once she gripped my neck because she was angry, I think that was the last nastier thing she did, then my sister went to the centre and told them it was over, we had to stop. You have to move us from here, because it's not good, 'cuz she kept on saying that when they were visiting us, we needed to say we were fine, because if we didn't, she was very harsh. She wasn't held responsible, because everybody thought it was ok. There were visits from the social workers once in month or once a while. She knew when it was going to happen, and tell them it was fine, bla-bla, but it wasn't. Perhaps we were quite little, and we were afraid of her, we kept on saying everything was just fine, we were very happy, [...] but it was terrible, we weren't happy at all. It wasn't a good period for us. (ASz, 24, female, p.e.v. 1998–2006)

It is no surprise that disclosure of abuse was difficult in all these institutions because of the impact of organizational culture and the role of formal lines of accountability (Biggs, Stevens, Tinker, Dixon., & Lee, 2009). Children really didn't dare to disclose the violence as they felt threatened, ashamed or didn't know whom to disclose it to, or if it happened children were rarely listened to or their situation worsened after they filed a complaint.

> There were educators, who paid attention not to leave any trace, if they beat us, and this was like that, he knew that he shouldn't leave any trace if he beat us. (PI, 30, female p.i. 1990–2005)

One of the participants related that himself and others tried to complain about beatings, but the directors, police, medical personnel, teachers or representatives of the Child Protection Directorates did not listen to them, did not react to what they disclosed, which exposed children who complained to even more abuse. This contributed to the feeling of helplessness, and being left alone.

> They do not beat you so that it can be seen. And if you complain, they do not believe you. There is a lot of incompetence shown by the professionals, but also the DGASPC. If I would do an inspection, I would ask educators, personnel, but also the children. (LU, 23, male, p.e.v. 2001–2007)

EMOTIONAL ABUSE

According to several respondents, emotional abuse was the hardest to bear, due to its repetitive character: 'Words were the most painful, they didn't help us heal.' (GF, 28, male, p.i 1992–2007). In most of the large institutions, but, unfortunately, in many smaller children's homes as well, positive relationships between staff and children were rather the exception than the rule. The majority of young people didn't recall expressions of positive feelings towards them. They did not feel loved or appreciated by the staff. Accordingly, kids didn't feel attached to staff as a reaction to the lack of concern, anger, contempt and disgust they sensed from staff members.

> They talked to us as if we were dull and handicapped. This word 'handicapped' killed me. I felt it constantly bumping in my head. (MC, 25, female, p.i 1995–2010)

Most of the interviewed persons had experienced regular humiliation and ridicule in the institutions.

> I don't know how many times I was told that I was a stinky gyppo.[8] Yes, all of the educators kept on saying things like this, repeating it from day to day! (PI, 30, female, p.i. 1990–2005)

> They called us gyppos, they called us fags, and they called us stinky. (VI, 37, male, p.i. 1988–2002)

Emotional abuse is construed by some youngsters as a tool for controlling children in care, and it was paired with different forms of punishments, in case they did not submit. 'They told us all the time that we are handicapped and are not able to do anything right. I tried to respond' (RC, 24, male, 1995–2010). One quarter of the respondents related that regarding their educational goal they were often discouraged by staff, being confronted with systematic name calling, like 'you're stupid', 'you're good for nothing' and 'you'll end up on the streets, or in jail'. The verbal insults discourage youngsters from choosing a certain career, either by telling them that he or she was not good enough for that, kind of work, or by prohibiting them to pursue a high-school or university education, or by outright denying any form of support in pursuing studies. A few of these accounts unfortunately refer to quite recent experiences in small, familial type centres.

> And then this dream was born in me to become a nurse or a doctor, and no, they didn't support this idea. They said to me: 'Cool down, you'll be nothing. Two years of vocational school would be enough for you, then you're on your own. (AT, 36, female, p.e.v. 1999)

> Once I went to the director and told him I wanted to continue my studies at the Faculty of Sociology and Social Work in Cluj-Napoca, and I was expecting him to encourage me, but he told me: 'Do you think you are worthy to go to university? Look at so-and-so, you're not at their level.' And I said: 'I was expecting you to encourage me somehow, but I'll keep up with my goal to go to the university, the Canadians would help me pay for my studies, I'll continue to go, and if it will not be good for me, I'll give up. But I want to see what would happen for one year.' They said: 'Go then, but you're not fit for a university anyway.' (AN, 26, female, p.e.v. 2004–2009)

> They didn't help or support me with anything; on the contrary, the housemother permanently kept on putting mental pressure on me. When the first holidays started during university, and the campus closed, I had to go home; well I didn't have any other place to go to. When I arrived at the institution, she asked me what I was doing there, I didn't have any rights to be there because I had enrolled to university, which wasn't right at all, and she had no reason to say this. (PI, 30, female, p.e.v. 2006)

> I told you they cut off the girls' hair, and everybody was equal, all the boys and girls. One couldn't tell if you were a boy or a girl, because of the short hair. (A, 26, female, 1994–2000)

> They very often talked disparagingly to the children, like: 'You little snotty, go to bed, who do you think you are to jaw. (E, 29, female, p.i. 1991–2005)

> Who was beautiful, was treated like a princess, who was ugly, could go to hell, to say it frankly. (EL, 31, female, p.i. 1990–2004)

In family type homes, basically in many homes, the same behaviour continued because the staff didn't change and the same people continued to work with smaller groups of children.

The interviewees recalled many other expressions of emotional abuse when they felt blamed, threatened, frightened, manipulated against each other, blackmailed, or discriminated mostly by ethnicity (for being Roma), but also by gender and looks etc. These clearly show that psychological violence was part of the organizational culture for institutional care.

EXPLOITATION BY EDUCATORS AND OLDER RESIDENTS

In many institutions the staff delegated many of their responsibilities to older children, and by failing to supervise the activities, the institution functioned under the law of the jungle. In certain institutions there was a supervisor for each room, an older child, who was responsible for younger children, and who had full rights to discipline and exploit younger children, no matter how.

In certain institutions, some of the chores were supervised by older children, while the staff didn't participate in the process, or consented to the cruelty of the older children towards the younger ones. There were institutions where the unpleasant duties (for example, washing the toddlers and changing their diaper) were the task of children, even if they were too young to be able to perform these tasks:

> Or the weeding [...] in the large courtyard. We had this big garden [...] we had a lot of vegetables growing etc. I remember we were lined up, and you had to collect the leaves with your bare hand. If we left one there, a leave or perhaps a piece of wood, or if you dropped behind, you were finished. They beat you hard, and the educator didn't say a word, although he should have supervised all this, but he rather went to the teachers' room to have a coffee. (MA, 33, female, p.e.v. 1991–1997)

> In general there were a lot of children who wetted or made a mess in the bed during the night, and when we grew older, we, the older children had to change them, wash them, replace the linen, so that's how the morning usually began. (PI, 30, female, p.e.v. 1999–2005)

> In the night, they introduced these chores in the night, they came to your room or called you to give you a job in the night, go clean the bathroom, go [...] they didn't do anything, don't imagine they would have to do the cleaning or anything else. We were doing everything. (RC, 24, male, p.e.v. 1995–2010)

Children were also requested to perform personal services for the staff members, which made them feel uncomfortable starting from massages, manicures, washing their car or the staff's own clothes:

> They treated us unscrupulously, made us do things, massage or doing the nails of the educator. To give a massage to the educator. To deliver various services. Or cleaning the car with which they came to work or whatever they wanted. filing the nails [...] to women, who wanted this. You think it isn't happening now? It is. (RC, 24, male, p.i. 1995–2010)

> It happened that we came home from school and we were tired, and me and my roommate, we had to take the educator's own clothes to her home, at half past eleven in the night, because she had her clothes washed in the children's home. And we had to take them home for her. We were very much afraid, because she lived in the other part of town, where it was quite dangerous. And we had to do this every second night, while she invited her friends to our house and drank there. (AL, 26 female, p.e.v. 2004–2009)

In children's homes, personal objects like toys, clothes, hygienic products, sweets were especially desired and valued, especially those received from abroad as aid:

> When we were getting packages from foreign people or neo-protestants who were bringing bananas and chocolate, they (the staff) would take it away and put it in our wardrobe saying that we should keep some for the next day too, but we didn't find those things anymore, we didn't see them ever: chocolate, clothes the Danish people had given us, we didn't have them anymore. I don't know what they did with the stuff. (CC, 25, male, p.e.v. 2004–2009)

> We were receiving washing powder, shampoos like Dove, Palmolive. He (the director) would seize them and give us shampoos made from nettle, which was worse. Sports-clothes, socks, shoes, blankets, duvets, he would take all these to his storeroom. He would give us a pillow, duvet and bed-sheets once a year. (CA, 22, female, p.i. 2004–2013)

Several respondents told us that the educators, as well as the cooks took away some of the children's food for their own benefit decreasing the portions given to the children. In some of the institutions, children's dessert was regularly taken away by the staff:

> The food was very little. It was far from being enough, and we couldn't get full with what they've been giving. We kept saying we wanted more, but if they wanted, they gave us, if not, then not. It also happened that when the food was poorer, they said they have more, and when it was better, they said it was over. 'Cause they also used to steal there, in the centre. And they were stealing. Also the people working in the kitchen. (VI, 37, male, p.i. 1990–2006)

> Oh, [the dessert] was taken from us each day. Each day they would take away what was better. The educators. They would come to our table, and put things in their bags. 'If someone asked, they told us: you had eaten your dessert.' (CR, 35, female, p.i. 1985–2000)

> At a certain point I had a phase when I hated children, because there was an educator, who took something sweet from the portion of a child, and gave it to her own child. I was very upset at that moment, I didn't know how to express myself, but I kept thinking: 'Why is she taking it away from my mate who can't afford to buy it, and give it to her child, who can afford to buy?' And I said: 'These children are too spoiled, I don't like their children!' (AM, 36, female, p.i. 1988–1997)

In family foster care, the most common form of exploitation was to involve children in hard work, which solicited their free time entirely, or to take away their rewards.

> At first it was very odd, because just as I got there, at seven in the morning the next day they woke me up to go to the field, to work; from the beginning, I had to work. They said it was good to get used to how rural life was, because I had grown up and lived in a town. Well, it was very hard and terrible for me, because we were also travelling a lot, I was tired, and we got to the foster parents at 9 in the evening, and at 7 in the morning they already called me to go to work. It was a terrible feeling for me [...] I never had any time for myself, some free time to go playing, to feel how it was to be a child, because I had to go to the field all the time. I was biking 20 km to get to the field after school. I never had a free day, I said at least let Sunday be a day when I could feel I was free for a while. (AL, 26, female, p.e.v. 2000–2005)

> I was living in a huge house, a three-storey villa [...], and my sister and I had to clean the entire house. (AS, 24, female, p.e.v. 2002–2007)

> Yes, I was sent to work, they were building two houses in the courtyard where I lived, and they made me to carry buckets full of sand, cement, finally, they put me work at the construction of a house. I was working in construction." "The money I got at school or even the money I got at the corner of the street when somebody had died had to be given to them, no matter what. (LU, 23, male, p.e.v. 2007–2011)

> When we left from her, she didn't give me all my clothes, later on I couldn't get them back all, she had put them in sacks in the attic, the better ones. (AN, 19, female, p.e.v. 2005–2016)

DEPRIVED OF FOOD, PERSONAL GOODS AND GIFTS

Older children and staff were taking away the goods from younger children both in large institutions and in residential children's home, and were imposing on the younger ones to deliver all kinds of services to them. The room supervisor, where there were such children assigned, had full powers over young children day and night: he/she made them wash clothes, make the beds, clean, bring water, make sandwiches at any moment of the day, took away their food received from home, their dinner, their toys, and everything the little guys had; anything could be seized by the room supervisor, if he so desired.

> [Did you have toys, did you play with them?] At Christmas, yes; we were examining them for a while, and there were the group supervisors in the bedroom, they took hold of them, and that was it about our toys. (SE, 30, female, 1992–2000)

> One or two of the girls already came of age, were having their period, and they got their pads, but she took them away from us, and we had to use cotton wool. She didn't care if we were having our periods or got stained because of the cotton wool. (IR, 33, female, p.e.v. 1997–2002)

> When my parents came to see me and brought me something, I usually tried to eat everything my mother brought me, but I didn't always manage to. So she always brought me home-made chocolate, hotchpotch, all sorts of tasty stuff, but no way I could eat them all at once, and when the night came, I had to deliver it to the room supervisor. (PI, 30, female, p.e.v. 1992–2000)

> Guests from France brought us many presents, they brought us everything. But we couldn't enjoy these, because when we were little, in the children's homes, we had grown-ups who took these away, they beat us, sent us to steal, to collect butts in the village, they made us fight against each other. (VI, 37, male, p.i. 1990–2000)

> [...] we got a lot of beatings, and our desserts were taken away the. We got already used to it, so we were putting the dessert in our pockets, and I remember there was a door where 4 boys older than us waited, and they would stop you at the exit, if you gave them the biscuits, ok, if not, they took you behind, and there was their world. (AD, 32, male, p.e.v. 1990–1995)

CONSEQUENCES OF INSTITUTIONAL CARE

The accounts of young people who had lived in the residential child protection system unanimously show that their childhood was marked by traumatic events. Their stories reveal that living through experiences of violence and being witness to what their colleagues have suffered had and continues to have consequences on their personality, both at the physical and emotional-cognitive level, on their interpersonal relationships, performance at school and at work and on their self-esteem.

Mental health issues like helplessness, lack of hope, suicidal thoughts and attempts, anger, lack of initiative and motivation were frequently mentioned by the interviewees and their effects were strongly felt, as they often felt alone, without emotional support, or professional therapeutic support.

> I get upset and cry and swing.(IR, 34, female, 1989–1995)

> You could see many cutting their bodies, hands, breaking windows, doors, and fighting, it was like at the lunatics. (CA, 22, female, p.i. 2004–2010)

> For many years I had a phobia of men, if there's such thing. [...] I was afraid of men. I was so afraid of them, if a man touched me, I replied with aggression. Even a simple shaking of hands disgusted me. (AR, 22, male, period unclear, after 1998)

> I fell into a heavy depression with three suicide attempts. I wasn't chatting even with my colleagues, I went wild. (PC, 26, female, p.i., 1995–2012.)

> When I was in a children's home, until I got into the seventh grade, I didn't have any future dreams, I didn't see any meaning of life. [...] when I was in the first year of high school, I wanted to jump out of the window. And then, when I was in the second grade, again, yes, I wanted to jump out of the classroom. (AM, 36, male, p.i 1982–1998)

Negative emotionality was associated with drug abuse, gambling, delinquent behaviour, prostitution, begging.

> Then they go bad, they lose control and don't care. And they become either prostitutes, or thieves or [...] So you just don't care anymore. (AN, 19, female p.i. 2005–2016)

> Then I finished first year, I started the second, and at a certain moment somehow it occurred to me that now nobody is telling me what to do, if I don't want to, then I'm not learning, if I want to, I can spend my money on slot machines, drinks, drugs, I tasted freedom. So in those times I tried out everything: I was drinking, using drugs, womanizing, playing on slot-machines [...] They expelled me from the university, because I didn't have enough credits. (GDF, 28, male, 1995–2010)

Regarding the persistent recalling of traumatic experiences, the respondents referred to nightmares, intrusive memories, obsessive struggles connected to the past. As coping strategies, some try to avoid memories, others isolate themselves in order to avoid letting others see their weaknesses.

> I don't feel the need to remember.(CR, 35, female, p.i. 1985–2000)

> When it affected me (the suffered violence), I withdrew from playing or the activities etc. Many times I'd rather isolate myself not to get hurt. (AR, 22, male, period unclear)

For others negative thoughts, feelings of hopelessness, anxiety, anger, irritability, revengefulness are associated with a reduced ability to control these emotional conditions.

> I burst out at one of them and I gave a blow, not because I wanted to, but out of despair. (AN, 19, female p.i. 2005–2016)

> I had these two feelings: to get revenge on those who had hurt me and to die. (VA, 33, male, p.i. 1989–2002)

Repeated exposure to traumas as a child, left without emotional support, resulted in many cases in a traumatic development of the personality (van der Kolk, 2014), in a reduced ability of self-control, with difficulties to establish and maintain positive, long-lasting relationships. Trusting people, asking for and accepting help, investing in friendships and intimate relationships are difficult tasks, and many repeat failing at them. This affects the functioning as a child, adolescent or adult in many fields of life: family, professional, social and economic. The respondents were aware of many of their problems, and they could see the causation relationships between institutionalization and their personality traits. For example, VL (22, male) was aware of his own delays in physical and psychomotor development when he started school, VI (22, male) linked his stomach pains with malnutrition in childhood, MB (50, female) linked her traumas with her psychosomatic illnesses, AR (22, male) saw the links with low academic functioning and parenthood. VI (37, male) and AM (36, male) discuss the consequences of trauma on intimate relationships:

> When my foster mom came to take me I was 6 years old but I looked like a 2 year-old. I couldn't even speak properly. (VL, 22, male, p.e.v 2001)

> I had problems with my stomach. I cannot eat excessively even now. I keep having the impression that I have limits. Maybe it was left a little in my memory that there isn't enough food. That's my way of thinking. (IP, 28, male, p.e.v. 1993–1997)

> I got ill of stress, 'cuz e too many things accumulated, you know? Many problems in my family, many things happened in my life, and I developed many diseases. (BM, 50, female, p.i. 1969–1988)

> I am the only one that studies at a university. I have colleagues who use drugs, are on the streets. 2 of the girls are prostitutes. (AR, 22, male p.i. 1997–2013)

> Only a very few managed to integrate into a family or create a family. Those are only one or two. The rest are lost and sad cases. (V., 37, male, p.i. 1979–1997)

> Well I'm still [...] a single, but I think that partly some sort of grief persisted, that I was sexually assaulted and [...] So I think this image of a family [...] oh, of course that in addition we weren't provided a true family image to be able to establish a family, so I'm seeing several youngsters from children's homes, of my age or even older ones, there are only a very few who could establish a family. [...] I think that so many of us are lagging behind from the point of view of not receiving a family image, a big picture of what a family looks like, or encouragement related to this; or for example many girls got married rather to older guys to substitute their father. My sister too, who married an older man. (AM, 36, p.i male p.i. 1980–1998)

> I have a colleague who became a mother and behaves with her child in the some ways as they behaved with her. She is yelling and shouting and beating him. (AR, 22, male p.i. 2004–2012)

As shown in previous research with care leavers (Bejenaru & Tucker, 2014; Neagu, 2017; Porumb, 2010), our interviewees demonstrated awareness of incurable marks due previous traumas while in child protection. In spite of the predominantly negatively charged narratives focused on the experiences of violence of the respondents, we also collected expressions reflecting the efforts of respondents to cope with the challenges of education, social relations, identity formation and grounding a vocational career to demonstrate their capabilities to 'fit-in' and become success cases (as described also by Porumb, 2010). These data will be presented on another occasion.

NEEDS OF PEOPLE OUT OF CARE AND THE COMPENSATIONS FOR VICTIMS OF ABUSE

When asked about their needs, most of the respondents referred to the necessity of material and instrumental compensations, which would assist young people in handling difficulties upon leaving the institution, who are left without resources when starting an autonomous life.

> First, a little bit more of state support. [...] Yes, We need state support, because we were provided for in all respects for years, then, after finishing school, I have been told that I have two weeks to leave. That's it, two weeks, no state support [...], no apartment where I could stay. [...] They should provide at least an apartment for a while, until you can provide for yourself.

> Let them live in hostels or something. I know that in Germany they have this, that if you're from children's home and you work, they give you housing. And if you work for 30 years, that house would be yours. You don't need to pay rent, only the electricity and things like that. (AR, 22, male p.i. 2004–2012)

> Emotional support is very important as is material support. But before you get out [from care], and also after you get out, it should be the evaluation, but on a friendly basis, at a professional level, with someone like me, a social worker. What are your thoughts? Where are you staying? What are your goals? What do you need? Can we help you? Of course there should be [evaluation], at least for three or four years, and later on they should help too. Because in some way you're also responsible, meaning the child protection, the educator and the social worker, the psychologist that the child grew up like that. And it's not that person's fault that they can't stand on their two feet, but only on one, or not even on one. (DM, 31, female, p.i. 1988–2003)

> These, who come out of the orphanages, should be given a job and a place where to stay. It's not ok that they let them out and let them get on by themselves. [...] That's what I'm telling you, these kids, after they are done with the school, should get a place where to work and not to stay alone and go and do foolish things, 'cuze that's what happens to them, they should get a place to stay. (LU, 41, female 1978–1994)

> Certainly, yes. Well, from the point of view of [...] if they could pay attention to the youngsters who are out, where they are, and to help them find their place, in life, at work, if they have difficulties in this respect, or to find an apartment. Yes, for example in this field. (AM, 36, male, p.i. 1981–1988)

Regarding the means to provide compensation for traumatic experiences suffered in residential institutions, most of the interviewees were surprised by the question, as this has not yet been discussed in society, and this is a culturally new question. We have collected three categories of answers. Some of the interviewees think that they don't need compensation. These respondents argue that they have already succeeded in processing past traumas, respectively they can't imagine any compensation which could neutralize the negative experiences they had suffered.

> I don't think it exists now, I don't even think about it, in the sense that I left it behind, in the past, I'm quite relaxed, I wouldn't say I'm careless, but I don't take these seriously, so they passed and it's over, that's it. (AS, 24, female, 1997–2006)

> Me personally I am not asking for any compensation for myself, because I made the best thing out of the worst. (SzM, 28, male, 1993–2000)

> In my opinion it can't be repaired anymore. Nobody and nothing [could be a compensation for the young people who are already grown up, and had suffered so many things in care homes]. (KR, 36, female, 1990–1999)

We also placed in this category those who do not think that compensation could be a practical possibility for people who spent their childhoods in institutions.

> Well, who grew up in this system or grew up like this, whom could they ask for compensation, who can account for that? I think it would be useless. (IS, 31, male p.i. 1988–2004)

For those who admit to the necessity of compensations, they either refer to certain legal rights to satisfy mental and material needs of people who were in institutional care when they were children, or underline the importance of being offered moral compensation for the abuses they suffered. Providing psychological counseling for those who didn't manage to overcome their childhood traumas is a form of compensation frequently mentioned by the respondents:

> Well, for example they should be taken to psychologist, to recover mentally, to relieve them from all that poison. (SE, 30, female p.i. 1989–2005)

> Emotionally yes, by all means [they would need compensation]. (GZ, 27, male, p.i. 1991–2007)

As a practical solution, one respondent thought about establishing an organization, which would help individuals:

> [...] and also an organization could be founded, which would follow the development of a group or of an entire institution. (DF, 28, male p.i. 1991–2007)

The importance of granting moral compensation for the abuses suffered is mentioned in many interviews. Some of the respondents mentioned an official public apology by the state or the institutions where they suffered abuse, as a form of moral compensation:

> Yes. [for the compensation.] First of all, psychological. To relieve ourselves emotionally (MI, 20, female, p.i. 2000–2015)

> [...] and the first thing, which is very important, that they ask to be forgiven. The apology [...] they should ask to be forgiven for each of them separately. (DM, 31, female, p.i. 1989–2005)

There are survivors from residential child care institutions who would address the media in order to make public the abuses suffered in the institutions, which is seen as a first step in the impeachment of the abusive staff:

> A lot of them, there are certain youngsters, who keep thinking about making a film about this, so to reveal at least for the media how these institutions were, how those people were, or there are people who still work in the system, and committed those things, they should be exposed, so that they would never ever be allowed to work with children again. (RO, 34, female p.i. 1985–2001)

> In the newspaper too, with a big smiley, yeah [I would make them publish the events]. (PI, 30, female p.i. 1991–2006)

For some respondents the impeachment of abusive staff members would mean the moral compensation for the experiences they suffered, but without financial compensation for the victims. The mentioned methods of making staff liable are to fire those who committed violence against children and financial liability.

> They should be kicked out. [...] But replace the entire system. Well, in this system, these educators work. (PI, 30, female p.i. 1991–2006)

> And let them pay a lot of money, I mean to the state, because the child wouldn't know what to do with that money, for being too small. I don't know, but to impose on them such a punishment [...] (PI, 30, female p.i. 1991–2006)

> I think that the family where I stayed should be punished in the following manner: material compensation, but all their goods should be seized, and they should work for the community (LU, 23, male, p.i. 2001–2012)

Others have more information about possible legal actions against those who caused their sufferings, and wish the impunity to end:

> I would [sue the system] if I was there with the mind I have now, I would be the first. (PI, 30, female p.i. 1991–2006)

> To prison with the management of the child protection system. (LSz, 31, male p.i. 1990–2005)

> I think they would have the right to sue the educators who hurt them, let them get what they deserve. (AL, 26, female, p.i. 1997–2009)

The survivors' feelings of justice are related to the needs of the many young people who are released each year from residential homes, without enough provisions for their security and social inclusion:

> I want that the state helps young people to be better integrated in the society. (L, 23, male p.i 2001–2013)

A bachelor student proves he can link needs and rights, when he explains:

> I think that at least afterwards you should be getting support. You have suffered a lot, so the state should help start your life: give such people a piece of land, so you can build a house with two rooms and have a family, money to build a home, counselling and some social services. There are so many (of us) who cannot deal with the start of adult life. (AR, 22, male, p.i. 2000–2011).

DISCUSSION

Unfortunately, growing up in the child protection system was not a smooth childhood experience for most of the interviewed persons, and encounters with violence were often recalled. Many adults who spent their childhoods or part of it in child protection institutions have been marked by coercive, unpleasant routines and experiences of physical, sexual and emotional violence committed by staff or other adults, as well as older children, and by a general lack of interest in protecting their rights and providing for their developmental needs. In fact most of the interviewee had experienced multiple forms of violence which were defined by Finkelhor, Ormrod, Turner, and Hamby (2005) as polyvictimization, which increases the risk of clinical range symptoms and has a poor prognosis in terms of psychological adjustment (Rassenhofer, Spröber-Kolb, Plener, Kölch, & Fegert, 2017).

Beyond the testimonials of the men and women who recounted their childhood memories, we could grasp the general atmosphere of the whole institutions, as described by Goffman (1961), which left profoundly affected on children's personalities. Daily routines like sleeping, eating, playing, studying were marked by fear of discretionary punishments, which left the children at the mercy of an unprepared, sometimes wicked and corrupt but mostly uncontrolled staff who sometimes exploited children, or took away part of their food. Such ruthless behaviour management methods and the existence of a system of privileges, of obedience and the climate of fear have impeded on the process of identity development, leading to distrust in the self (low self-esteem, low self-efficiency) and in fellow human beings. Children, who asked for help against violence while in care had generally been ignored by care staff and by the leadership of the institutions. As described by the literature on institutional abuse (for example Biggs et al., 2009; Sköld, 2013), staff in Romanian child protection care has been generally reluctant to report based on children's accounts only, therefore the severity of abuse has been extreme in the situations where action was taken. Within this context, the conspiracy of silence (Barter, 1997) is central for avoiding complaints within the settings and reporting outside it. The trauma of violence was amplified by the feeling of being left alone, without appropriate help, a phenomenon also observed in other research (Sperry & Widom, 2013). In addition, research has shown that when children victims of violence were not listened to or believed if they tried to get help, the long-lasting psychosocial consequences of the violence increased. (Spröber-Kolb et al., 2017).

Victims' narratives of the violence they suffered or witnessed during their stay in Romanian child protection settings have shown that the staff employed by the child welfare system was incapable of rapid reactions to contain violent behaviour of adults and peers. One proof of such lack of responsiveness is keeping some of the most abusive employees on their jobs (including coordinators and directors). Silence around the ongoing violence before and after the fall of the communist regime encouraged those who committed it. Both the personnel and the members of leadership have often condoned the violence, instead of preventing, stopping, or professionally responding to it. Such characteristics qualify for the definition of institutional abuse, as described in the introduction (Gil, 1975; Gil, 1982; Goffman, 1961; Pinheiro, 2006). This confirms once more the use of the term institutional violence for the phenomenon described by our research with the characteristics mentioned by the General Comment No. 13, which describes direct harm as allowing situations when children's rights and developmental interest are disregarded, and also indirect harm, by lacking effective means to implement legislation and by not providing sufficient resources, including human resources, as well as lacking the capacities to identify, prevent and react to violence against children (CRC/C/GC/13, IV, A, 1/32, 2011). This kind of institutional behaviour justified the numerous law suits in countries like Canada, Australia, Norway and Ireland, where victims have organized and asked for justice. Contemporary governments in more than 15 countries have apologized for historical violence in public or faith-based child care institutions, and financial schemes have been put in place for victims of violence in child protection settings in the last decades (Daly, 2017; Sköld, 2013). Ignoring the suffering of children during the communist regime, no historical abuse judicial trials followed the discovery of the horrors against children in centres for the disabled children and in the large residential homes in Romania, Bulgaria, Russia, Ukraine, Belarus (Carter, 2005; Daly, 2017; Stativa et al., 2017), no ex-communist country in the European Union or on the territory of the ex-Soviet Union has followed this trend (Daly, 2017). Even if on the political level

Romania embarked on a trajectory of steady political reforms and deinstitutionalization (Government of Romania, 2001, 2006, 2008, 2014), the lack of official recognition of the abuse suffered within the walls of child protection settings for healthy or 'unrecoverable' children contributed to the perpetuation of the culture of impunity for the violent behaviour by staff and peers against the less powerful residents: younger children, ethnic, racial and sexual minorities, girls, and children with disabilities.

LIMITS OF RESEARCH

The sample of the research is far from being a nationally representative sample, and it does not allow for generalizations. In spite of this limitation, it offers detailed information about institutional violence, which the authors cannot ignore, or keep undisclosed. Although the authors were aware of previous data on violence against children (Brătianu & Roşca, 2005; CRJ & UNICEF, 2006; Dumitrana, 1998; Gavrilovici & Groza, 2007; Macavei, 1989; Onica-Chipea et al., 2008; Porumb (Ciobriş), 2010; Rus et al, 2013; Rus et al., 2016; Stativa et al., 2002), they expected fewer testimonies of violence, or at least less severe ones. As we started our snowball sample by inviting our out-of-care graduates to the interviews, we got a high percentage of respondents in the sample taken in care after the end of Ceausescu's regime (58%), and an overrepresentation of employed people (51.1%), and of graduates or students of a university program (53.3%). Being aware of the effect of institutionalization on educational attainment (as discussed, for example, by Attar-Schwartz, 2014), we think that a larger sample of out of care people, with lower level of education and employment would probably have more accounts of violence. The picture derived from the testimonies of survivors of violence in Romanian child care settings is extremely sad because it shows that violence in Romanian institutional settings has continued long after the legal reforms, showing that laws, strategies and principles are not enough to counteract the institutional culture of violence.

CONCLUSIONS

In the communist regime, Romania had an extensive residential centre system which over the years housed hundreds of thousands of children who grew up in an organizational climate which treated them badly. The culture of institutional violence in the residential centres for children has been maintained long after the political shift, even after the accession to the EU: children were often victims of physical, sexual and emotional abuse, their health, education, capacity of attachment and identity formation was endangered. Unfortunately, abusive adults continue to work with children, being incapable of non-violent behaviour management. According to the interviewed persons, a caring, loving professional (even in foster care) is more of an exception than a rule.

In spite of being aware of the pervasive effects of violence on their personality, the majority of the respondents has not yet envisaged compensation schemes, as collective rights. They limit their wishes to the official recognition and apology for the suffered violence, and some wish for the punishment of abusers. There are some respondents who would like to participate in legal action against abusive staff. Providing material compensation and access to different support services for people who lived in residential child care institutions is not perceived as a right for support towards adulthood, but more as a form of compensation for the experiences suffered within the child protection system, and also as a public recognition of the failure of the child protection system to release young adults more capable of adapting to the outside world on their own.

Besides the planned strategies of deinstitutionalization and professionalization of child care, a mature Romanian child protection system should be able to face its own past failures by developing a safety net for its children and by introducing reparatory measures for its past victims, as well as building effective and accountable safety nets of its most vulnerable children, separated from their biological parents. This needs the reinforcement of communication between law- and policy-makers, researchers and professionals working directly with children in care and youth about to leave the system.

NOTES

1. The project 'Support to Adult Survivors of Child Abuse in institutional settings -SASCA' was funded by the European union through [JUST/2015/SPOB/AG/VICT Access to justice strand/4000009292. More data about the project results can be found on www.sasca.eu
2. All the countries around the globe signed the UN Convention of Children's Rights except the United States.
3. More data about the project results can be found on www.sasca.eu
4. Law 272/2004, has been updated several times (http://www.euroavocatura.ro/print2.php?print2=lege&idItem=1223). After critical reports on the state of art of the child protection system the last proposal (December 2018) submitted to public debate recommended that no child under the age of 7, should be placed in residential care, except those with disabilities and drastically limited the number of places in residential care.
5. The Romanian Governments have elaborated three strategies for reforming child protection (2001–2004, 2008–2013, and 2004–2020) and a strategy for social inclusion of young people out of care.
6. Data are collected periodically and published on the site of the Romanian National Agency for Children's Rights and Adoption (ANPDCA, http://www.copii.ro/statistici-2018/), Accessed on January 15, 2019.
7. The Romanian Agency for Protection of Children's Rights and Adoption (Agenţia Naţională pentru Protecţia Drepturilor Copiilor şi Adopţie). Retrieved from http://www.copii.ro/statistici-2017/
8. Gyppo is an offensive word designating people of Roma origin.

ACKNOWLEDGMENT

The data for this chapter are based on the project 'Support to adult survivors of child abuse and neglect' (SASCA, www.sasca.eu). The project was funded by the European Commission, and coordinated by Artemisia Association. The project is based on a partnership in four countries: Italy, Greece, Ireland and Romania. The project is in line with its specific objectives to facilitate the effective access to justice for all victims of violence, including promotion and support, and compensation for the victims. Retrieved from https://www.researchgate.net/publication/291176929_Institutional_abuse_A_review_of_the_literature

REFERENCES

Antal, I., & Tonk, G. (2017). Raspunsul sistemului de protective a copilului la abuzul si neglijarea copiilor in comunitatile marginalizate (The response of the Romanian Child Protection to child abuse and neglect in marginalized communities). In G. Tonk, J. Adorjani, & O. B. Lacatus (Eds.), *Servicii sociale publice pentru comunitatile marginalizate clujene (Public Social services for marginalized communities in Cluj)* (pp. 124–189). Cluj: IDEA.

Attar-Schwartz, S. (2014). Experiences of sexual victimization by peers among adolescents in residential care settings. *Social Service Review*, *88*(4), 594–629. doi:10.1016/j.childyouth.2012.11.005

Barter, C. (1997). Who's to blame: Conceptualising institutional abuse by children. *Early Child Development and Care*, *133*(1), 101–114, doi:10.1080/0300443971330108 Retrieved from http://housesofempathy.eu/en/wp-content/uploads/2016/05/Who-s-to-Blame-Conceptualising-Institutional-Abuse-by-Children.pdf

Barter, C. A., Renold, D., Berridge, D., & Cawson, P. (2004). *Peer violence in children's residential care*. Vancouver: Palgrave Macmillan.

Bejenaru, A., & Tucker, A. (2014). Voices of youth from romanian residential care homes about rights and participation. In *Child & family welfare* (pp. 95–113). Cambridge: Cambridge Scholars Publishing.

Better Care Network, UNICEF, USAID & PEPFAR. (2015). Making decisions for the better care of children. Vol. Oct., 5. Country Case Studies. © Better Care Network and UNICEF, Retrieved from https://www.unicef.org/protection/files/UNICEF_Gatekeeping_V11_WEB_(003).pdf. Accessed on February 15, 2019.

Biggs, S., Stevens, M., Tinker, A., Dixon, J., & Lee, L. (2009). *Institutional Mistreatment and Dignity: toward a conceptual understanding*, A paper for the Department of Health and Comic Relief. Retrieved from https://www.kcl.ac.uk/sspp/policy-institute/scwru/pubs/2009/biggsetal2009institutional.pdf

Brătianu, I., & Roşca, C. (2005). *Copilul instituţionalizat între protecţie şi abuz*. [The institutionalized child between protection and abuse]. Iaşi: Lumen.

Brodie, I., & Pearce, J. (2017). Violence and alternative care: A rapid review of the evidence. *Psychology, Health & Medicine*, *22*(supl), 254–265, doi:10.1080/13548506.2017.1281980 Brodie, Pearce, Jenny.

Călian, D. (2018). *Institutional Child Abuse: Legal Framework in Romania*, Babeş-Bolyai University, 2018. Retrieved from http://www.sasca.eu/wp-content/uploads/2018/01/National_Raport_LEGAL_Sasca_DoraCalian_ENG.pdf. Accessed on March 9, 2018.

Câmpean, C., Constantin, P., & Mihalache, E. (2010). *Resources and needs in the social integration of children and youth from child protection residential services*. Iaşi: Fondul Român de Dezvoltare Socială (Romanian Developmental Social Funds). Research Report project ACTIN, http://www.crips.ro/doc/rfactin.pdf. Accessed on March 18, 2018.

Carter, R. (2005). *Family matters: A study of institutional childcare in Central and Eastern Europe and the Former Soviet Union*. London: Everychild.

Centre for Legal Resources. (2014). Mobile Legal Clinic. Retrieved from http://www.crj.ro/wp-content/uploads/2018/04/CRJ-raport-clinica-juridica-mobila-engleza.pdf. Accessed on February 12, 2019.

Cojocaru, D. (2007). Evoluţia sistemului de protecţie a copilului din România. *Revista de Cercetare şi Intervenţie Socială*, (18), 31–46.

CRJ, & UNICEF. (2006). *Monitorizarea drepturilor copiilor si tinerilor cu dizabilitati din institutiile publice* [Monitoring the Rights of Children and Youth in Public Institutions], Bucuresti: MarLink. Retrieved from http://www.unicef.ro/wp-content/uploads/monitorizarea-drepturilor-copiilor-si-tinerilor-cu-dizabilitati.pdf. Accessed on July 19, 2019.

Csáky, C. (2009). *Keeping children out of harmful institutions: Why we should be investing in family based care*. London: Save the Childrens Fund.

Daly, C. (2017). Redress for historical institutional abuse of children. In A. Deckert & R. Sarre (Eds.), *Australian and New Zealand Handbook of criminology, crime, and justice* (pp. 449–466). London: Palgrave Macmillan.

Dumitrana, M. (1998). *Copilul institutionalizat (The instituionalized child)*. Bucharest: Editura Didactică şi Pedagogică.

Finkelhor, D., Ormrod, R. K., Turner, H. A., & Hamby, S. L. (2005). Measuring poly-victimization using the Juvenile Victimization Questionnaire. *Child Abuse Negl*, 2005 Nov; *29*(11), 1297–1312.

Finn, T. R., & Coleman, M. D. (1985). The institutional and educational abuse of children in state care. *Suffolk University Law Review*, *19*(2), 227. US, Rhode Island (provides state care for thousands of children).

Fitzpatrick, M., Carr, A., Dooley, B., Flanagan-Howard, R., Flanagan, E., Tierney, K., ... Egan, J. (2010). Profiles of adult survivors of severe sexual, physical and emotional institutional abuse in Ireland. *Child Abuse Rev*, *19*, 387–404. doi:10.1002/car.1083

Gallagher, B. (2000). The extent and nature of known cases of institutional child sexual abuse. *The British Journal of Social Work*, ***30***(6), 795–817. doi:10.1093/bjsw/30.6.795Pdf

Gavrilovici, O., & Groza, V. (2007). Violence in Romanian institutionalised children. Incidence, prevalence and trauma associated with exposure to violence in Romanian institutionalized children. *International Journal of Child and Family Welfare*, *3–4*, 125–138.

Gil, D. (1975). Unravelling child abuse. *American Journal of Orthopsychiatry*, *45*(3), 346–356.

Gil, E. (1982). Institutional abuse of children in out-of-home care. *Child & Youth Services*, *4*(1–2), 7–13. doi:10.1300/J024v04n01_03

Goffman, E. (1961). *Asylums: Essays on the social situation of mental patients and other inmates*. Garden City, NY: Doubleday Books.

Government of Romania. National authority for the protection of the child and adoption. (2001). Government Strategy Concerning The Protection of the Child in Difficulty (2001–2004).

Government of Romania. (2006). Governmental Decision 669 of 24 May 2006 for the approval of the National Strategy of Social Inclusion of Youth out of Care. Retrieved from http://www.mmssf.ro/pub/imagemanager/images/file/Legislatie/HOTARARI-DE-GUVERN/HG669-2006.pdf

Government of Romania. (2008). The National Strategy in the Domain of the Protection and Promotion of Children's Rights 2008-2013. Retrieved from http://legislatie.just.ro/Public/DetaliiDocument/97242; http://unpan1.un.org/intradoc/groups/public/documents/UNTC/UNPAN016039.pdf. Accessed on February 1, 2019.

Government of Romania. National Authority for the Protection of the Child and Adoption. (2014). National Strategy for the Protection and Promotion of Children's Rights for the Period 2014–2020. Retrieved from http://www.mmuncii.ro/j33/images/Documente/Transparenta/2014/2014-02-03_HG_Strategie_protectia_copilului.pdf. Accessed on February 12, 2019.

Greenwell, F. K. (2001). Child Welfare Reform in Romania: Abandonment and De-Institutionalization, 1987-2000, report prepared for the U.S. Agency for International Development (USAID) in Romania under Interagency Agreement ENI-P-OO-98-00009 between USAID and the U.S. Department of Health and Human Services, version 2003. Retrieved from http://www.crin.org/bcn/details.asp?id=9028&themeID=1001&topicID=1006

de Greiff, P. (2006). Justice and reparations. In P. de Greiff (Ed.), *Handbook of reparations* (pp. 451–477). New York, NY: Oxford University Press.

Kempe, C. H., Silverman, F. N., Steele, B. F., Dregenmuller, W., & Silver, H. K. (1962). The battered child syndrome. *Journal of the Medical Association*, *18*(1), 17–24.

Kim, D. H., Kim, K. I., Park, Y. C., Zhang, L. D., Lu, M. K., & Li, D. (2000). Children's experience of violence in China and Korea: A transcultural study. *Child Abuse & Neglect*, *24*(9), 1163–1173.

Larsson, N. (2016). Out of sight: The orphanages where disabled children are abandoned, *The Guardian*, September 26. Retrieved from https://www.theguardian.com/global-development-professionals-network/2016/sep/26/orphanage-locked-up-disabled-children-lumos-dri-human-rights. Accessed on February 15, 2019.

Macavei, E. (1989). *Familia şi casa de copii (The Family and The Children's home)*. Bucharest: Editura Litera.

Mathews, B. (2004). Queensland government actions to compensate survivors of institutional abuse: A critical and comparative evaluation. *Queensland University of Technology Law & Justice Journal*, *4*(1), 23–45.

Moffett, L. (2017). Transitional justice and reparations: Remedying the past? In C. Lawther, L. Moffett, & D. Jacobs (Eds.), *Research handbook on transitional justice. Research handbook in international law* (pp. 377–400). Cheltenham: Edward Elgar Publishing,

Retrieved from https://pure.qub.ac.uk/portal/files/122984908/Transitional_Justice_and_Reparations.pdf. Accessed on July 19, 2019.

Neagu, M. (2017). *Young adults' perspectives on their experiences of different types of placement in Romania* (PhD thesis). University of Oxford. Retrieved from https://ora.ox.ac.uk/objects/uuid:d1fe5a7a-bcbb-4482-b9f1-298904bf776d. Accessed on May 6, 2018.

Nunno, M. (1997). Institutional abuse: The role of leadership, authority and the environment in the social sciences literature. *Early Child Development and Care*, *133*, 21–40. doi:10.1080/0300443971330103.

Office of the SRSG on Violence against Children i. (2015). Toward a world free from violence Global survey on violence against children, United Nations, New York.

Onica-Chipea, L., Stanciu, S., & Chipea, I. F. (2008). *Efectele instituţionalizării asupra copiilor din România (Efects of institutionalization on children in Romania)*. Retrieved from http://www.upsc.md/wp-content/uploads/2017/03/cer_pub_ppsas_nr_13_-2008.pdf. Accessed on March 23, 2018.

Pettersen. (2010). Residential Institutions Redress Board 2010: 24.

Pinheiro, P. S. (2006). *Report of the independent expert for the United Nations study on violence against children, United Nations, General Assmebly session A/61/299*. Retrieved from https://documents-dds-ny.un.org/doc/UNDOC/GEN/N06/491/05/PDF/N0649105.pdf?OpenElement. Accessed on May 7, 2018.

Popwers, J. M., & Nunno. (1990). Institutional abuse: A review of the literature. *Journal of Child and Youth Care*, *4*(5), 81–95.

Porumb (Ciobriş), E.-M. (2010). *Traiectorii de viaţă ale tinerilor care au crescut în centre de plasament. (Life-course trajectories for young people out of residential care)*. Babeş-Bolyai University, Cluj Napoca. Doctoral thesis.

Roth, M. (1999). Children's rights in Romania: Problems and progress. *Social Work in Europe*, *6*(3), 30–37.

Roth, M. (2005). Copii ;I femei victim ale violentei. Editura Presa Universitara Clujeana, Cluj.

Rassenhofer, M., Spröber-Kolb, N., Plener, M. N., Kölch, M., & Fegert, J. M. (2017). Child Sexual abuse in religiously affiliated and secular institutions in Germany. In A. Rus, S. Parris, & E. Stativa (Eds.), *Child maltreatment in residential care* (pp. 169–179). Cham: Springer.

Rus, A. V., Parris, S., Stativa, E., & Popa, C. O. (2017). Child maltreatment in residential centers: Summing up. In A. Rus, S. Parris, & E. Stativa (Eds.), *Child maltreatment in residential care* (pp. 509–516). Cham: Springer.

Rus, A. V., Stativa, E., Pennings, J. S., Cross, D. R., Ekas, N., Purvis, K. B., & Parris, S. R. (2013, December). Severe punishment of children by staff in Romanian placement centers for school-aged children: Effects of child and institutional characteristics. *Child Abuse & Neglect*, ISSN 0145-2134, *37*(12), 1152–1162.

Rus, A., Stativa, E., Butterfield, M., Pennings, J., Parris, S., & Burcea, G. W. (2016). Peer exploitation: Findings from a Romania nationally representative sample of children living in long-term residential centres. *Child Abuse Review*. Retrieved from http://onlinelibrary.wiley.com/doi/10.1002/car.2464/pdf. Accessed on March 23, 2018.

Salomão, P. R., Wegner, W., & Canabarro, S. T. (2014). Children and teenagers living in orphanages victims of violence: Dilemmas and nursing perspectives. *Northeast Network Nursing Journal*, May-June; *15*(3), 391–401.

Silva, P. A., Lunardi, V. L., Lunardi, G. L., Algeri, S., & Souza, T. (2016). Reporting of violence against children and adolescents in a protective institution in southern Brazil. *Invest Educ Enferm*, *34*(1), 152–161.

Sköld, J. (2013). Historical abuse—A contemporary issue: Compiling inquiries into abuse and neglect of children in out-of-home care worldwide. *Journal of Scandinavian Studies in Criminology and Crime Prevention*, *14*, 5–23. Retrieved from https://www.tandfonline.com/doi/abs/10.1080/14043858.2013.771907?src=recsys&journalCode=scri20. Accessed on February 2, 2019.

Sköld, J., Sandin, B., & Schiratzki, J. (2018). Historical justice through redress schemes? The practice of interpreting the law and physical child abuse in Sweden. *Scandinavian Journal of History*, Special issue, December, doi:10.1080/03468755.2018.1555100. Retrieved from https://www.tandfonline.com/doi/pdf/10.1080/03468755.2018.1555100?needAccess=true. Accessed on February 3, 2019.

Sperry, D. M., & Widom, C. S. (2013). Child abuse and neglect, social support, and psychopathology in adulthood: A prospective investigation. *Child Abuse & Neglect*, *37*(6), 415–425.

Spröber-Kolb, N., Rassenhofer, M., Allroggen, M., Plener, P. L., Kölch, M., & Fegert, J. M. (2017). Research on child sexual abuse in institutions in German-Speaking countries: A summary. In A. Rus, S. Parris, & E. Stativa (Eds.), *Child maltreatment in residential care* (pp. 179–198). Cham: Springer.

Stănculescu, M. Ș., Grigoraș, V., Teșliuc, E., & Pop, V. (2016). *Copii din sistemul de protecție a copilului*. București: Alpha MDS. Retrieved from http://www.unicef.ro/wp-content/uploads/Copiii-din-sistemul-de-protectie-a-copilului_UNICEF_ANPDCA_BM_2016.pdf. Accessed on February 20, 2018.

Stativa, E., Anghelescu, C., Palicari, G., Stanescu, A., & Nanu, R. (2002). *Child abuse in residential care institutions in Romania*. Bucharest: Extrem Group.

Stativa, E., Rus, A. V., Parris, S. R., Pennings, J. S., Simion, B., & Wenyika, R. (2017). The prevalence of stunting among the Romanian institutionalized children placed in long-term institutional settings in the 1990s. In A. Rus, S. Parris, & E. Stativa (Eds.), *Child maltreatment in residential care* (pp. 111–126). Cham: Springer.

Tobis, D. (2000). *Moving from residential institutions to community based social services in central and Eastern Europe and the former Soviet Union*. Washington, DC: World Bank.

UNICEF. (2009). HIV and AIDS in Romania: Taking stock, *Unite For Children, The Quarterly Newsletter Of Unicef Romania - NR 3*, UNICEF, Bucharest. Retrieved from https://www.unicef.org/romania/United_for_children_3.pdf

United Nations. (2009). Guidelines for the alternative care of children, (A/64/434). Retrieved from https://www.unicef.org/protection/alternative_care_Guidelines-English.pdf

van der Kolk, B. A. (2014). *The body keeps the score: Brain, mind, and body in the healing of trauma*. New York, NY: Viking.

Winter, S. (2018). Redressing historic abuse in New Zealand: A comparative critique. *Political Science*, *70*(1), 1–25, doi:10.1080/00323187.2018.1483204

CONTRIBUTIONS AND LIMITS OF THE 'CHILDHOOD STUDIES' FOR THE RESEARCH OF THE CHILDREN'S AGENCY IN LATIN AMERICA

Rocío Fatyass

ABSTRACT

This paper recovers some theoretical elements of the sociology of childhood in the Anglo-Saxon field, to discuss their contributions, scopes and limits about child agency in children living in poor and urban contexts, in Latin America. The objective is to contribute to the debates within the field of childhood from a sociological perspective that accentuate the capacity of action and resistance of children even in the framework of structural restrictions, without assuming a decontextualized and ideal approach about the agency.

Keywords: Childhood Studies; agency; resistance; urban contexts; poverty; Latin America

INTRODUCTION

This publication recovers the theoretical and methodological contributions of the New Sociology of Childhood in the attempt to find limitations and challenges due to the relevance of the study of childhood 'in its own right' (Jenks, 1996), recognizing the multiplicity of experiences and analyzing the complexity of the agency in children in contexts of poverty. This point of view opposes the understanding of childhood in a normative, universal, romantic or miserabilist

Human Rights for Children and Youth: Sociocultural Differentiation, Resistance and Unity
Sociological Studies of Children and Youth, Volume 24, 133–149

ISSN: 1537-4661/doi:10.1108/S1537-466120190000024007

way (Grignon & Passeron, 1991), which has taken place in certain public treatments about childhood or in some approaches to social theory.

To understand children as social agents means to understand the difference between 'the subject position that childhood allows and contains and (how) people (boys and girls) can inhabit and configure discursively (and practically) in different ways (that position), being even possible not inhabit it or to do it in a very weakened way' (Ibarra & Vergara Del Solar, 2017: 61).

Under these conceptualizations about experience and agency, this work asks how the experiences of boys and girls (especially of popular classes in urban contexts) interpellate relationships and visions from which childhood is processed in the adult social order.

The organization of writing is as follows: first, it is pertinent to contextualize the intellectual climate that shaped the emergence of the New Sociology of Childhood. Second, the general dimensions of the Childhood Studies will be systematized. Third, some readings and postulates about children's agency will be proposed, emphasizing that the capacity of action in children includes specificities in the way of processing time, space and body in not evident relationships, in and between unequal groups.

Despite the undeniable contributions of the *Childhood Studies* as inaugural referents, it is pertinent to undertake new readings of these materials with lenses on their theoretical implications in particular contexts as in Latin America.

CONDITIONS OF PRODUCTION OF THE NEW SOCIOLOGY OF CHILDHOOD

The place of children in the social sciences has been, for a long time, secondary and fragmented, not considering children as agents and age as a category of social differentiation from which it is pertinent to explain the historical development.

Only at the end of the 1970s, from different disciplinary fields and in different contexts of academic production, conventional conceptions of childhood were questioned, especially the sense of 'protected childhood' that establishes that children are incomplete, innocent and malleable subjects (Ibarra & Vergara Del Solar, 2017).

From the field of psychology, studies based on notions about the individual and evolutionary child were discussed. The active role of boys and girls in human development was recognized, arguing that through social interaction children learn to internalize the skills and competencies they observed in others.

The classical contributions of anthropology manifested their own limits around the effects of the culture on the development of the child, since it appeared that productions showed that social life is not only ordained by others, but is also apprehended.

Within sociology, the social construction of reality was explored and the socially constructed character of childhood was recognized in dialogue with the thesis of Ariès (1987).

In addition, with respect to the sociology of socialization, there were critical and functionalist visions. Functionalist readings assume the existence of a given number of socially available roles for individuals. Socialization is considered the mechanism by which these roles are reproduced between generations. Thus, studies, research and interventions focus on the deficits and problems of social reproduction, giving rise to sociological considerations about deviance or anomie (Llobet, 2014).

From the critical sociology of education, Bourdieu and Passeron (1996) analyzed the homology between the field of the teaching system and the structure of the classes, through which school practices ensure the perpetuation of social hierarchies. Freire (2005), from another context of production, exposed the class logic from the concept of banking education. Puiggros (2003) contributed considerably to show, in a historical key and for the Argentine case, the processes of arbitrariness of teaching and how the State works from diverse devices and public policies as a guarantor of the processes of transmission of cultural capital. In a similar line, Tenti Fanfani (2010) exhibited in his works the relationships between the school, the State and the classes. This triad was highlighted by many investigations that analyzed the complicity between the official and hidden curriculums taught in schools, such as Tadeu Da Silva (1998) and Martin Criado (2010).

All these productions, to name a few, are inscribed in the line of critical sociology of education and in some way allow to connect the question of power and inequality with the processes of secondary socialization, in which children are shaped by the social order adult who acquires specificities within the school space.

At the micro-social level, the critical sociology of education also developed contributions on the institutional culture of the school and on how subjects inhabit these spaces, times and architectures (Bernstein, 1990; Brailovsky, 2014). Other studies refer to the links between teachers and students and how the relationship with knowledge is structured (Bolton, 2006). There are those who investigate grammars and school devices and the ways in which students make fun of them (Diker, 2014). In addition, there are several lines of work that interrogate the daily school, the experience of the subjects there, the unforeseen within the school routine, etc. (Noel, 2009; Rockwell, 2006).

Despite the fact that in these latest investigations the children's school experience emerges, boys and girls are defined only as students in a fairly passive relationship with adults or pedagogical agents, so the experience is not analyzed in itself, that is, a social experience of a particular group that exceeds the limits of the school.

In summary, the paradigm of socialization finds certain limits from the approach of the New Sociology of Childhood, since children appear mainly formed by adults. Affirming that children depend on adults has as one of its consequences their invisibility in historical and social analyzes.

According to Gaitán (2006), the birth of the New Sociology of Childhood as a sociological subdiscipline with its own entity can be found between the end of the 1970s and the beginning of the 1980s. It must be said that the anti-cultural movement of the 1970s, the emergence of the feminism and anti-colonial movements had challenged the hegemony of existing social and political relations, questioning the theory of traditional socialization.

The New Sociology of Childhood was mainly inspired by the theory of Giddens considering as a basic postulate that any act that contributes to the reproduction of a structure is also an act of production and, as such, can initiate the change altering the structure while reproducing it. If Giddens was right about the interaction between structure and agency, boys and girls, as well as adults, could be considered as active participants in society.

The New Sociology of Childhood, for Gaitán (2006), proposes to consider children as social agents and childhood as part of the social structure, and is divided into three types of approaches, in general terms:

Constructivist: childhood is a social construction and the culture of children should be studied in different dimensions, recognizing them as active subjects. It focuses on children's culture.

Relational: childhood is a social relationship that must be taken into account in accordance with the way in which children experience their lives, from intergenerational relationships and in peer groups. This approach gives importance to the analysis of the children's point of view and their daily lives.

Structural: childhood is a social, historical and cultural category, in whose framework children are a invisibilized minority and are subject to relationships of subordination.

During the 1990s, in Latin America, social research on children focused on the children's agency[1]. The firm of the International Convention on the Rights of the Child (CIDN)[2] in Latin America generated new debates about childhood and public policies directed to children.

The investigation of these topics in this period could also be classified, following Llobet, according to three currents: of cultural inspiration (influenced by the linguistic turn and the contributions of Raymond Williams around complex processes of construction of social identity); Foucault's perspective (regarding the concern for the tutelary device and childhood); and the approach that evaluates social policies (according to discussions on categories and forms of child protection) (Llobet, 2011).

In this way, the analytical axes of the New Sociology of Childhood are fruitful for the understanding of the mechanisms through which childhood is constituted as a category and social institution, introducing concern for the way in which boys and girls are related to society.

In these discussions present in the field of study of the childhood, from different theoretical references and production contexts, it is interesting to highlight the epistemic change that implies the investigation of the childhood assuming the multiplicity of children's experiences.

Later, the work focuses on some representatives of the New Sociology of Childhood who write from the Anglo-Saxon field and can be classified under the title of *Childhood Studies*, whose authors refer to James and James (2004, 2008), Prout (1997, 2003), Jenks (1996), Corsaro (2005) in the constructivist perspective,

Jens Qvrotrup, Corsaro, and Honig (2009) in the structuralist current and Mayall (2002) in the relational approach, being the closest to the analytical pretensions of this work.

CHILDHOOD STUDIES: CONTRIBUTIONS AND LIMITS

Since the 1980s and 1990s, the field of the New Sociology of Childhood has gradually been constituted; it arose in Europe, then expanded to the United States and more incipiently to Latin America. This work includes some pioneering productions of the Anglo-Saxon field, called *Childhood Studies*, to analyze dimensions of the children's agency.

The *Childhood Studies* establish a key differentiation for this work, that is, the distinction between childhood as an institution and as a social space configured with practices and discourses on children, and the boys and girls themselves as social agents; all this contribute to the reproduction and the transformation of childhood.

From the text of Jenks *Chilhood* (1996), the features of the paradigm of the New Sociology of Childhood are synthesized; to do so, Jenks is based on the work of James and Prout (1997):

> 1. Childhood is understood as a social construct, as such provides an interpretative framework for the first years of human life. Childhood, other than biological immaturity, is neither a natural nor universal characteristic of human groups, but appears as a specific structural and cultural component of many societies. 2. Childhood is a variable of society. It can never be completely divorced from other variables such as class, gender or ethnicity. This involves an intercultural analysis of children rather than a single or universal phenomenon. 3. The social relations and cultures of the children are worthy of study in their own right, regardless of the perspective and the concern of the adults. 4. Children should be seen as active in the construction and determination of their own social life, and of the societies in which they live. Children are not just passive subjects of social structures and processes. Ethnography is a particularly useful methodology for the study of childhood, which allows children a more direct participation in the production of sociological data which is usually possible through experimental or survey styles of research. (Jenks, 1996, p. 30)

Despite the potentiality of these constructions, as will be seen below, in some passages of the texts and references reviewed here are certain analytical limitations for research on the child agency in specific contexts of study, as in Latin America.

THE AGENCY AS REFLEXIVITY, FACE-TO-FACE INTERACTION AND DECISION-MAKING

James and James in *Key Concepts in Childhood Studies* (2008) define the agency from a series of ideas such as: (1) the ability of children and young people to make decisions about the things they do and to express their own ideas; (2) the possibility of having some control over the direction of their own lives and also to play a role in the changes that take place in society in a broad sense; and (3). the ability to act independently of social structures, institutions and value systems.

It is interesting to stop at the point which these authors analyze the agency as a possibility for children to use social markers to manage, with some relative autonomy, their social and cultural identities, highlighting that this child agency feature is on a reflective level:

> [...] How cultural ideas are articulated differently by different boys and girls in the context of the school that leads, for example, black boys to assertive masculinity, while black girls deliberately use the ideas of femininity to play with cultural stereotypes. (James & James, 2008, p. 11)

Qvortrup, Corsaro and Honig compile the book *The Palgrave Handbook of Childhood Studies* (2009) and start thinking that children, with their individual actions, can make a difference in a relationship or decision within the framework of structural restrictions. Thus, children are active participants in society and act as reflective interpreters of social life.

In one of the passages of the book mentioned is developed children's actions who are cancer patients and part of the reproduction and production of hospital life. This situation is conceptualized as a role play, reflective, which makes that every part of the interaction – children, parents and physicians – fulfill their role to support the expectations of others: children were aware of their illness, refused to perform other actions that were against their treatment and accepted to be cared for by the adults.

The previous theorizations are significant in that they emphasize the active and inventive character of the infantile practices, although they find certain limits since they register to the practice in functionalist frameworks, where they do not problematize relations of power (in the example of the hospital, who possesses the legitimate knowledge about the body to act on the other) and, in turn, the practice is anchored to a theatrical level, purely reflective, that does not let understand the complexity of the situation.

The *Childhood Studies* also express that the agency is a capacity that children have. In this way, the agency would be an attribute that children would activate or not, often reflexively, without connection with structural processes, because the dispositional does not appear as something significant in the explanation of the social: 'Thus [...] the agency [...] is an attribute of children. It is something that can or will not choose to exercise, and not a symbol of its social status minority' (Qvrotrup et al., 2009, p. 44).

The notion of agency expressed by of the *Childhood Studies* refers clearly to the fact that the agency means making decisions and, often, that agency does not imply going against the established order, but it does assure social interactions. Mason and Falloon (as mentioned in Qvrotrup et al., 2009) say that children can exercise agency when they do not want to reveal their experiences to maintain relationships with others and the status quo. However, can be say that reproduction is necessarily assured at the level of consciousness as these authors affirm, or rather works as a practical sense, incorporated and pre-reflective, to solve the situations?

Other references of the *Childhood Studies* not only conceive the individual agency but also the collective; this erupts around the idea of peer culture or interpretive reproduction of Corsaro (2005). The theory of interpretative reproduction holds that children do not simply imitate adult (dominant) culture but also certain aspects of the adult worlds in their own unique cultures. At the same time, children are actively contributing to cultural production and social change. Peer culture is defined as a stable set of activities or routines, artifacts, values and concerns that children produce and share in interaction with their peers. Peer culture becomes part of the adult culture and contributes to its reproduction and extension through its collective bargaining in the interactions with adults.

However, Corsaro (2005) does not stop to mention what dimensions of social life are reproduced or modified in the peer cultures and the causes of this. Nor does it appear in the notion of peer culture that the processes of social differentiation can operate as conflicts and tensions within the same groups of children.

THE DIMENSION OF THE BODY

Several authors of the *Childhood Studies* display conceptualizations about the body dimension, not biologically determined. This approach called incarnation presents an analytical plus within these studies, but finds other limitations by the way of understanding power.

The authors define the body as a variable that can be used in social interaction, again as a reflective practice. They express that children are based on their bodies in a creative way in social interaction. They mention that boys and girls are labeled based on their age and the capacities of their bodies. James and James finds that children are involved in body work, as they constantly negotiate the presentation of their body, the actions of their body and the appearance of their body. Christensen (as mentioned in Qvrotrup et al., 2009) finds that boys and girls experience their bodies in terms of the social consequences that the body has in their lives.

The body that these referents speak of is a body framed only in the condition of age, so it does not incorporate in the analysis of the other social ascriptions of the subjects, that is, it does not deepen the idea of a social body: a body which involves a social history incorporated in form of action, perception, disposition, feeling, depending on a position and social trajectory.

THE DIMENSION OF THE GAME

With respect to leisure and play, the *Childhood Studies* explains about the structural inequalities; since some authors admit that the participation and autonomy of children in recreational activities varies according to the social possession of the parents, they even mention that in contexts of poverty the game coexists or is suspended by the care or labour practices carried out by the children. In all cases, the game means an opportunity to mock or even reproduce material life, authority and relationships with adults.

This is linked to the thesis of Lareau (2011) who considers that children develop recreational, cultural and educational activities, according to the intersection between gender, race and possession of cultural, economic and social capital. The author addresses the forms of parenting, the use of language and the temporality of practice according to social groups. Lareau (2011) warns that the middle and upper classes in North America have a concerted and adult-regulated upbringing, while lower-class children have natural parenting, with less adult control in time organization, with a grid of less systematic cultural activities.

Lareau (2011), in line with the references of the *Childhood Studies*, understands the social practice in the division between structure and agency, so there is a marked difference between the possession of a capital and its activation, under certain circumstances. Therefore, they give relevance to the reflexivity, capacity, personality and the interactions of the subjects, as a condition of deliberately exercising the capital they possess.

THE DIMENSION OF TIME/SPACE

Jenks (1996) admits that the social construction of time can be crucial for the study of childhood. This time would be an individual time, typical of the age, psychological, based on emergencies and instinctive and emotional needs configured by children.

Hallett and Prout in their text *Hearing the Voices of Children: Social Policy for a New Century* (2003) analyze the possibilities of participation and representation of children in different social processes, deal with the images and devices of social policies for children, and work on changes in filiation and relationships with parents. Concerned about the transformations of contemporary society, they also examine the place of children in processes such as child labour, migration and school education, characterizing the forms assumed by the institutionalization of children in these contexts.

These variables of child practices involve successful analyzes about the multiplicities of childhood experiences in different contexts. The tension appears when Hallett and Prout (2003) state that the phenomenon of childhood is currently explained by 'domestication' to describe the progressive withdrawal of children from the streets and other public spaces and their accommodation in special and protected spaces; this would be a restriction on the possibilities of exercising children's citizenship.

These statements by Hallett and Prout (2003) are pertinent to thinking about childhood in a general level, that is, this way of conceiving space/time as individual, restricted, regulated use, they end up not being illuminating reflections to think about childhood in contexts of urban poverty, in Latin America, where children's practices are characterized by the circulation in the geographical space and the plastic use of time.

MAYALL'S PROPOSAL: ADVANCES FROM RELATIONAL POINT OF VIEW

The indicators of play and leisure in the practices of child agency lead to other interesting reflections on the temporality of the practice. In *Towards a sociology for Childhood*, Mayall (2002) understands that the generation, as a historical and social time, is a significant analytical key to comprehend the relationship between children and adults. For the author, the generation processes can take place on four levels: in individual transactions between children and adults; in group transactions, as between students and teachers; in individual relationships between subjects born at different points in history; in the social policies transmitted from a before cohort. In addition, Mayall (2002) recognizes three levels of generational affiliation: as subjects located historically and socially at a given time, as a real generation that participates in social events and as a unit that thinks and works together.

Childhood is then an intergenerational category. The weight of the past influences the capacity of the agency. Mayall (2002) understands the agency as a capacity to negotiate, improve or transform.

Mayall (2002) is located within the relational perspective of childhood, so it is the author that most closely links with the theoretical framework of this publication, particularly in relation to the theory bourdiana. Mayall (2002) admits that the generation involves not only the time of an age cohort, but that the generation is, reading Bourdieu, a social generation, since among the age groups positioned in the class structure are set up negotiations, conflicts and exchanges that are not explained only by the dimension of the age, although they cannot be understood outside of it. The use of social time by children (which is not reduced to a purely child time) means a central axis in the analysis of the agency in contexts of poverty.

Mayall (2002) operationalizes the relationship between experiences and agency, without losing sight of the notion of power, and considers that children make use of the knowledge they have of past experiences; say, social experience is condition of production to accumulate capacities, skills and practical knowledge that children can put into play in the social circumstances in which they are, altering the structural restrictions.

This activation is, for Mayall (2002), conscious, premeditated and desired, but it can also be dispositional and pre-reflective; it is explained according to relationships of strength and senses between different groups. The conditions of possibility of the agency will generate processes of dependence, autonomy and even inequality in the relations between social groups (of age, class, gender or other).

Mayall (2002) frames the idea of inequality as an explanatory component of the logic of the child agency, noting in cases such as work, care, the use of public space and overcoming the simple idea that children depend on adults. What is interesting to note here is that children are not only dependent, for example, on their parents (a question that should be relativized in the studies of children living in poverty), their practices are recorded in inequality relationships, naturalized and imperceptible, that in the same way can be questioned by the children themselves.

Under this line of thinking about power and disposition, Mayall (2002) defines boys and girls as moral agents:

> Children face problems of equity, fair distribution and exchange. Children adhere to the actions and feelings of others, and comply with the approval or disapproval of their own actions [...] Children are moral agents (more than premoral persons), who develop a practical knowledge of moral concepts and they do it through the consideration of the cases that they find [...] Reasonableness has an additional dimension: it is mainly a social disposition [...] It is not surprising that they often do not give credit for their own moral agency: this reflects the low moral status of children in our society. (Mayall, 2002, p. 88)

RECAPPING

In summary, the *Childhood Studies* pertaining to the Anglo-Saxon field, in some of its points of analysis and not in all cases, talks about a universal childhood that adopts a way of using time and space, a childhood that is dependent and autonomous but does not include in the examination the contexts of power. Many of the passages of the revised texts propose notions of individual agency, centred on the reflective and face-to-face level, where the agency refers to children making decisions about whether or not to carry out any daily activity, as if the agency were a device that is put into play or not. The practices of the children's agency are analyzed vigorously around the culture of peers and the relationships established with adults; however, the latter are not positioned in terms of class, they are adults in a general level.

The limits of the agency's approach to the *Childhood Studies* refer to the concept of agency that is informed from the conceptual frameworks of Giddens' theory. This publication problematizes the concept of action in Giddens, emphasizing that the author ends up closing the complexity of the practice given its instrumental and reflexive nature, without going deeply into the socio-historical processes of genesis of the social. For Giddens, the agent is in situation, so the practice develops in the interaction; highlighting the character of the situation is not the same as position the agent in the framework of multiple structural determinations. From the perspective of the agency focused on the face-to-face situation, it is acceptable that the level of consciousness seems significant and, in any case, what could be considered as practical awareness is conceptualized as a knowledge reserve that is reflexively updated when there are changes in the level of the interaction; there are no questions about the structuring of knowledge conditions, which would involve investigating why the world is known in one way and not another.

The concept of agency is similar in the *Childhood Studies* and in Giddens; the agency refers to the reflective record of the action in everyday life, the rationalization of the action and the individual motivation of the action, whose axes, although valid in the investigation of the agency, do not allow us to glimpse the complexity of the practices.

In the end, the discussion lies around the way of conceiving power. The concept of power articulated by the *Childhood Studies* could be synthesized in the following way:

> Power, fluid and constant change are a fundamental aspect of all social interaction. Power is both the ability to influence behavior than the ability to use resources to achieve the desired goals. For example, children and adolescents use the power to influence the opinions of others, to control the conversation and to increase their social status. They use resources such as the social status of their bodies and their knowledge to achieve their interaction objectives. (Qvrotrup et al., 2009, p. 217)

This publication moves away from this conception of power as a simple ability to use resources, and does not understand the conditions of existence of children as status, which involves a static notion and hierarchy of the position.

The conception of power that is interesting to be noted moves in a more relational analysis. Since relations between the different social adscriptions of the subjects are not evident, they are not reduced to the interactional, they are configured like relations of material forces (resources) but also symbolic (legitimizing certain capitals on others as principles of social distinction).

For this work, power, in brief terms, comprises a series of relationships between the positions occupied by the agents or institutions that are concurrent in a social space, in whose space it is disputed (according to the accumulation of capital and trajectories of the occupants) the principle of domination (Bourdieu, 2000).

The key is to situate the practices and experiences of the agents in multiple structural determinations, spaces and times, recognizing the possibility of change, as the *Childhood Studies* does, but also the conflict. In summary, this work comprehends the socio-historically positioned child experience, in order to explore how the age (from an intergenerational, class and gender perspective) enables the activation of new relationships, senses and practices.

CHILDREN IN POVERTY SITUATION AS SOCIAL AGENTS

The problem of social practices associated with the resolution of conditions of material, social and symbolic deprivation is related to the question of agency, which links structure and social action: how, despite structural constraints, do social agents reproduce their lives through the margins of freedom that allow the same deprivations?

González de la Rocha proposes the idea of resources of poverty to study the survival strategies of populations in conditions of inequality. He explains that 'My research on how the urban poor face poverty and economic crises led me to recognize their agency without ignoring intrafamily conflicts, unequal relationships and gender/generation differences within households' (Gonzáles De La Rocha, 2001, p. 76).

This present work recognizes that, within the framework of the processes of impoverishment in Latin America, the approach of the strategies of social reproduction under the bourdian logic, retaken by referents of the region as Gonzáles De La Rocha (2001), Gutierrez (2007) and Pavcovich (2011), allows to think about the practices of agency: (1) boys and girls, like other social agents, accumulate, use and activate capitals, under certain relationships of strength and senses; (2) children participate and make use of instruments of social reproduction, such as school, childhood policies, non-state cultural and recreational spaces, or others; (3) children are in contact with other social groups, whether boys and girls or adults from other social classes (dominant), with whom they maintain relationships of dependence, differentiation, exchange and negotiation; (4) the practices of children often involve a reasonableness that contains a reproductive and productive (inventive) sense of the social order; and (5) children can reconvert their capitals to sustain their material and symbolic reproduction.

The sociology of childhood should not 'close on itself' because children are social agents like the others, which requires a dialogue between different conceptual frameworks.

Following the contributions of Williams (1997) and Thompson (1981, 1995), the notion of experience, as a specific way of processing the relationships of forces and senses that 'are being', functions as a 'generative history' of the agency (Macnay, 2003), in other words, social experience is a condition for the production of agency possibilities. As some authors of the *Childhood Studies* have explained, in social experiences children are producing their social skills to activate in different contexts.

From the field of feminist studies, there are analytical clues to approach the agency (in the broad sense), discussing with other lines that also recovers this work, as is the case of Bourdieu (1994). For feminist authors such as Ortner (2016), Macnay (2003), Adkins and Berbeley (2003), among others, the agency means cognitive and emotional states in various levels of consciousness, and this demands to find out how the action is directed, cognitively and emotionally (Ortner, 2016).

According to the elemental structure of the agency, the intentionality of the practice can be: (1) explicit (according to the feminist readings, the subjects are defined as agents with moral capacity to intervene in the world, with narrative capacity to name it, with motivations); (2) hidden (as 'art of resistance' (Scott, 2003), which involves discourses and cultural practices that subordinate subjects elaborate on the 'backs' of the dominant and then enter the scene mocking the social order); (3) Pre-reflective (as in Bourdieu, given that the practical comprehension of the world, the habitus, is quite different from the intentional act of conscious deciphering, however, it is a strategic reasonableness that allows the subject to move in a field of possibilities).

Thus, for the case of children, the explicit can appear in their speeches and narratives (or counter-narratives), other times their practices involve ways of doing and solving what is played in the institutional spaces (resources, times, rules), and in almost every occasion children experience institutional contexts or even their territories of life from a practical and strongly corporal relationship, therefore, pre-reflective. In other words, all social agents – therefore, children – try to maintain or improve their social position and this involves a number of strategies (as capital accumulation) inherited and learned.

To operationalizing possible dimensions of the child agency, Rockwell's work (2006) on children's experience in school contexts (without falling into the classical perspectives of socialization) is retaken. Rockwell (2006) focuses her attention on everyday life as a space to reappropriate the experience, without neglecting structural analysis. The author performs ethnographic work in schools analyzing children's cultures, spaces, games and peer relationships with adults. She tries to detect in this scholastic dailyness how the resistance, the appropriation and the subversion are articulated; these three elements constitute some indicators of agency. These dimensions are activated in a different way, more or less intensive, creative and explicit (or not), according to the existing relations between children and with respect to adults, all of them unequally positioned in the social structure.

Thompson, Torres, Swanson, Blue, and Hernández Hernández (2017) try to overcome binary visions of childhoods in contexts of poverty in Latin America (boys and girls as victims or dangerous) to show the complexity of the experience and the child agency, recognizing the ability of boys and girls to make decisions about the course of their lives, according to their motivations and desires, which constitute a reflective indicator of the agency, as highlighted by several of the writings of the *Childhood Studies*. For their case of analysis, they find agency forms such as humour, irony, ingenuity and others that call pragmatic dependence and information protection.

These proportions are key since they allow to problematize how children use and appropriate the institutional times and spaces in which they participate, the resources, devices and rules that are structured there; they even make it possible to reflect on how children relate with authority, for example, by strategically elaborating social speeches expected by adults or by their peers, expressing in the same act their capacity for empathy, similar to the agency moral of Mayall (2002), pertaining to the relational current of the *Childhood Studies.*

On the other hand, the research work of Ibarra and Vergara Del Solar (2017), in Chile, examines children's speeches about play, children's time, memory, what boys and girls think about childhood and adulthood, how they relate to each other, the feelings that children attribute to their own body and the adult body, among other aspects. Under these analyzes, the authors find forms of discursive resistance in boys and girls that mean ruptures in stable discursive practices, putting into play absurd answers, the irony and the parody. Children are also able to develop counter-narratives in the face of social stigmatization processes that can suffer themselves or others, in tune with the use of social markers that were part of the logic of child agency according to the readings of the *Childhood Studies.*

From their age, children, with their linguistic resources, their ways of understanding the world question the experiences of the classes and the processes of social differentiation between unequal groups.

In opposition to counter-narratives, the construction of victimization stories can function as gears of the agency itself, particularly in the case of children of popular classes, since sometimes, explicitly and reflexively, they relate to adults and institutions and 'affirm' their presentation of themselves as 'poor'; available category that is used, to support from there certain affective bonds with adults (usually from other classes) or to access certain goods (materials and symbolic). However, this type of analysis does not support the notion of a culture of poverty but visualizes the strategies of the subjects to accumulate capitals in poverty from their social trajectories.

In any case, poverty is not always transformed into a 'theatrical practice', this is a point of tension with certain proposals of the *Childhood Studies*. The conditions of existence are lived from the body, as a disposition to act in one way more than another, according to the ways of speaking, doing, interacting, at home, in the street and in institutions. The experience and child agency involve a social body, committed to a practical sense, and it is not just an individual body marked by age regulations as postulated by the authors of the *Childhood Studies*.

Also significant are the contributions of De Certeau (2000) and his definitions of agency as vanishing point, ways of hunting the possibilities and use of resources, ways to reappropriate the organized space, in the words of the author, micro-liberties and micro-differences. Here the strategy distances itself from the idea of Bourdieu and prevails the tactic, more or less reflectively; because of its non-place, according to De Certeau (2000), the tactic depends on the time, attentive to catch the possibilities of profit.

This publication distances itself from the idea that the subordinate subject lacks a place of its own to capitalize its resources, since it can be said that the territories of life are a space, a place practiced by children of popular classes, a source of symbolic and material power that contains, in part, the reproduction strategies of these populations.

In this way, this work links the proposal of the 'logic of the hunter' of Merklen (2005) with some dimensions that can be visualized in the practices of child agency of urban popular classes, emphasizing the notions of time, space, use of resources, pre-reflexivity, in opposition to certain theorizations of the *Childhood Studies* described above.

The place of the 'urban hunter' is the territory, the neighbourhood and its main characteristic is to be skillful, astute. The 'urban hunter' knows the resources with which it counts, uses the resources available according to the opportunities presented, in an unplanned and immediate time. The 'hunter' is integrated into the society in two ways: (1) the most immediate according to personal relationships with neighbours, kinship or others; and (2) institutionalized relationships that allow access to society, the territory that provides a relational structure that serves as support, means a link with services and the city (access that, in situations of poverty, is marked by a class structure).

The 'hunter's logic' represents expressions of the child agency in the case of boys in poverty situation (and to a lesser extent in the case of girls). The boys of popular sectors make extensive use of the neighbourhood, circulate freely in the territory (less in the centre of the city), connect with others, friends and broad kinship groups, processing collective agency logics, use the institutions, combine strategies to obtain goods such as work, participation in family arrangements, ask for resources on the street, establishing affective and material bonds with other groups of other classes and ages and using the time pre-reflectively, temporality marked by the urgency of the resolution of life even from an early age.

It can be said that unlike the proposal of Merklen (2005) this work considers that the relation that the children establish with the institutions is not unstable (in opposition the figure of the 'hunter' the exchange with the institutions is insecure and eventual) since childhood is strongly institutionalized, however the boys (and in this case also the girls) find ways to be, to mean, to negotiate the rules and resources that circulate in the intuitions, although this does not abolish the relations of inequality.

Children, even in conditions of subalternity, know how to move in the world, although they often cannot explain why they know that way and not another, since social arbitrariness appears to them as natural (as to other social agents).

This accentuation of the dispositional in the practices of agency that is absent in the *Childhood Studies* does not imply to affirm that relations and strategies that establish the children in situation of poverty are reduced to the material resolution of their conditions of life. The agency also involves aesthetic forms, enjoyment, ways to build and manage identities that are defined from poverty and sometimes dispute and contradict that category.

Likewise, the social disposition structured from previous objective conditions is an antecedent and conditioning (not determinant) on the present and possible practice, because what is updated of the disposition is empirically verified from the experience socially situated. Particularly in the 'state of childhood' (Llobet, 2014) the processes of internalization are not closed since the schemes of perception and action of the boys and girls are in formation, and of here the possibilities of change.

The actions, relationships and interactions of children do not derive, therefore, from a universal analytical or hegemonic category about children; the children use, resist, resignify and update the social visions available regarding them. Children's practices are situated and their analysis requires introducing, necessarily, the theme of the action, their experiences and their possibilities of agency.

FINAL REFLECTIONS

In conclusion, revising all these works and questioning certain constructions of the *Childhood Studies*, it can be said that the child agency involves different modalities in the practices and meanings (tactics, strategies, counter-narratives, expected speeches, presentation of itself as 'poor', 'logics of hunting', among others), according to spaces, times and situations (in the family, in the territory, within the framework of the State or non-state institutions, etc.).

The agency means to produce a particular practice in relation (not determined) to a field of possibilities and repertoires of action. The agency expresses what the subjects do in the structural restrictions, how they accumulate and activate capitals (according to relationships of strength and sense), develop strategies, build visions and social divisions, produce moralities and classifications in the relationships they establish with others. The agency is that set of practices and relationships lived and activated in a particular way, by means of which the subjects, mainly children, rehearse other ways of being in the world, therefore, the age it is a category of social differentiation in relation to others (such as class and gender), but in the experience of the children themselves is permanently renewed.

NOTES

1. It can be said that the question for the agency of children in other contexts of production, as in the United States, arises in the 60s.
2. The CIDN proposes a fundamental transformation: "the best interests of the child" as the maximum satisfaction, integral and simultaneous of their rights and guarantees, trying to reconfigure the role of the State (and to a lesser extent of the family) in opposition to the previous paradigm, which is based on the idea of "minor in moral and material risk" to guarantee the absolute and discretional power of the judge.

While the advances made by the adoption of the CIDN in the discourse of the various actors operating in the field of childhood are undeniable, this does not mean that the rights of children are fully assured, since the practices of state agents remain anchored to a large extent under the old paradigm.

Faced with a present of greater weakness in the application of public policies and social guarantees, it is necessary to recover critically the available instruments, such as international normative agreements and local mechanisms for the construction of rights in childhood and adolescence, to support the achievements historically conquered as those of the Convention, advancing, in turn, in the dialogue between the rights approach and the participation of children and adolescents.

REFERENCES

Adkins, L., & Berbeley, S. (2003). *Feminism after Bourdieu*. Chichester: Blackwell.

Ariès, P. (1987). *El Niño y la Vida Familiar en el Antiguo Régimen*. Madrid: Taurus.

Bernstein, B. (1990). *La estructura del discurso pedagógico. Clases, códigos y control (Volumen IV)*. Madrid: Ediciones Marota S.L.

Bolton, P. (2006). *Educación y vulnerabilidad: experiencias y prácticas del aula en contextos diferentes*. Buenos Aires: Editorial Stella, CELADEC, La Crujía.

Bourdieu, P. (1994). *El Sentido Práctico*. Madrid: Taurus.

Bourdieu, P. (2000). ¿Cómo se hace una clase social? Sobre la existencia teórica y práctica de los grupos. Poder, derecho y clases sociales. Recuperado de http://es.scribd.com/doc/24675078/Bourdieu-Como-Se-Hace-UnaClase-Social

Bourdieu, P., & Passeron, J. C. (1996). *La reproducción. Elementos para una teoría del sistema de enseñanza*. México: Distribuciones Fontamara, S.A.

Brailovsky, D. (2014). Los objetos escolares en la infancia. *Clase X, Diploma Superior Infancia, Educación y Pedagogía*. Argentina: FLACSO Virtual.

Corsaro, W. (2005). *The Sociology of Childhood*. Newbury Park, CA: Forge Press.

Criado, M. E. (2010). *La escuela sin funciones. Crítica de la sociología de la educación crítica*. España: Bellaterra.

Da Silva, T. (1998). Cultura y currículum como prácticas de significación. *Revista de Estudios del Currículum, 1*(1).

De Certeau, M. (2000). *La invención de lo cotidiano. I artes de hacer*. México: Universidad Iberoamericana, Instituto Tecnológico y de Estudios Superiores de Occidente.

Diker, G. (2014). ¿Qué hay de nuevo en las nuevas infancias? *Clase VIII, Diploma Superior Infancia, Educación y Pedagogía*. Argentina: FLACSO Virtual.

Freire, P. (2005). *Pedagogía del oprimido*. Buenos Aires: Siglo Veintiuno Editores.

Gaitán, L. (2006). La nueva sociología de la infancia. Aportaciones de una mirada distinta. *Política y Sociedad*, *43*(1), 9–26.

Gonzáles De La Rocha, M. (2001). From the Resources of Poverty of the Poverty of Resources: the erosion of suvival model. *Latin American PerspectiveSage*, *28*, 72–100.

Grignon, C., & Passeron, J. C. (1991). *Lo culto y lo popular. Miserabilismo y Populismo en sociología y literatura*. Buenos Aires: Nueva Visión.

Gutierrez, A. (2007). *Pobre como siempre. Estrategias de reproducción social en la pobreza*. Córdoba: Ferreyra Editor.

Hallett, C., & Prout, A. (2003). *Hearing the voices of children: Social policy for a new century*. London: Routledge.

Ibarra, P., & Vergara Del Solar, A. (2017). *Ser niño y niña en el Chile de hoy. La perspectiva de sus protagonistas acerca de la infancia, la adultez, y las relaciones entre padres e hijos*. Santiago de Chile: CEIBO.

James, A., & James, A. L. (2004). *Constructing childhood. Theory, policy and social practice*. New York, NY: Palagrave Macmillam.

James, A., & James, A. L. (2008). *Key concepts in childhood studies*. London: Sage.

James, A., & Prout, A. (1997). *Constructing and reconstructing childhood contemporary issues in the sociological study of childhood*. Basingstoke: Falmer Press.

Jenks, Ch. (1996). *Chilhood*. London: Routledge.

Lareau, A. (2011). *Unequal childhoods. Class, race, and family life*. Berkeley, CA: University of California Press.

Llobet, V. (2011). Las políticas para la infancia y el enfoque de derechos en América Latina: algunas reflexiones sobre su abordaje teórico. *Revista de Psicología*, *23*(3), 447–460.

Llobet, V. (2014). Infancias, políticas y derechos. *Clase III, Diploma Superior Infancia, Educación y Pedagogía*. Argentina: FLACSO Virtual.

Macnay, L. (2003). Agency and experience: Gender as a lived relation. In Adkins & Berbeley (Eds.), *Feminism after Bourdieu*. Oxford: Blackwell.

Mayall, B. (2002). *Towards a sociology for childhood*. Buckingham: Open Univerity Press.

Merklen, D. (2005). *Pobres ciudadanos: las clases populares en la era democrática, Argentina, 1983-2003*. Buenos Aires: Gorla.

Noel, G. (2009). *La conflictividad cotidiana en el escenario escolar: una perspectiva etnográfica*. San Martín: UNSAM EDITA de Universidad Nacional de General San Martín.

Ortner, S. (2016). *Antropología y Teoría Social. Cultura, Poder y Agencia*. San Martin: Universidad de San Martín Edita.

Pavcovich, P. (2011). *El barrio. Lo social hecho espacio*. Córdoba: Eduvim.

Puiggros, A. (2003). *¿Qué paso con la educación argentina? Breve historia desde la conquista hasta el presente*. Buenos Aires: Galerna.

Qvrotrup, J., Corsaro, W., & Honig, Ms. (2009). *The Palgrave handbook of childhood studies*. London: Palgrave Macmillan.

Rockwell, E. (2006). Los niños en los intersticios de la cotidianeidad escolar: ¿resistencia, apropiación o subversión? *Centro de Investigación y de Estudios Avanzados*. Buenos Aires: Conferencia presentada en el XI Simposio Interamericano de Etnografía de la Educación.

Scott, J. (2003). *Los dominados y el arte de la resistencia*. México: ERA.

Tenti Fanfani, E. (2010). *Sociología de la educación*. Buenos Aires: Ministerio de Educación de la Nación.

Thompson, A., Torres, R. M., Swanson, K., Blue, S. A., & Hernández Hernández, O. M. (2017). Re-conceptualising agency in migrant children from Central America and Mexico. *Journal of Ethnic and Migration Studies*, *2*(45), 235–252. Retrieved from https://www.tandfonline.com/doi/full/10.1080/1369183X.2017.1404258

Thompson, E. P. (1981). *Miseria de la teoría*. Barcelona: Crítica.

Thompson, E. P. (1995). *Costumbres en común*. Barcelona: Crítica.

Williams, R. (1997). *Marxismo y Literatura*. Barcelona: Editorial Península.

LIFE EXPERIENCES OF CHILD MINERS IN PARACALE, CAMARINES NORTE, PHILIPPINES: TRADICIÓN, INSPIRACIÓN, EXPLOTACIÓN Y ASPIRACIÓN

Noel R. Rafer

ABSTRACT

This study aimed to document the life experiences of child miners (CMs) engaged in small-scale gold mining system (SSGMS) in Paracale using qualitative and ethnographic approaches. Findings revealed that the SSGMS started even before the Spaniards came in 1572. Pagbibitâ *(underground mining), and* pagkocompressor *(underwater mining) were identified as types of SSGMS (*pagkakabod*) with common organizational structure and CMs. Their differences were in the nature of work, roles, costs, income, equipment, and processes. Majority of the CMs are males, out-of-school youth, eldest children, and have worked from two months to nine years. Altruistic factors, a source of* inspiración, *motivated them to engage on mining. They view their families as poor, and mining as their primary means of livelihood and family* tradición. *Their life threatening or work-related risks and impoverished living conditions unquestionably infringe their children's rights. Their* aspiración *include having permanent employment, better family life and community, finishing their studies, and sending their siblings to school. Perseverance and hard work are their means to realize them.*

Their experiences of labour explotación *and destitution are indeed social issues. Espousing social development and community organizing frameworks,*

Human Rights for Children and Youth: Sociocultural Differentiation, Resistance and Unity
Sociological Studies of Children and Youth, Volume 24, 151–179

ISSN: 1537-4661/doi:10.1108/S1537-466120190000024008

good governance, holistic alternative livelihood and learning system may minimize their plight as child miners.

Keywords: Children's rights; child miners' working and living conditions; life experiences; practice theory; small-scale gold mining system; basic social development framework

INTRODUCTION

'*Bella esperanza de la patria mia*' (The youth is the hope of my fatherland) – such is the famous dictum of the Philippine's national hero, Jose Rizal (1879), regarding the Filipino youth. The same sentiment is embodied in the United Nations' (UN) 2030 Agenda for Sustainable Development, which vows to provide children with a nurturing environment to enjoy their full rights and potentials (UN Department of Economic and Social Affairs, 2015). However, in the Philippines, some of the children are not considered as such and are not provided with the said nurturing environment. Instead they do hard labour and live in worst conditions to earn a living. Ericta and Johnson's study on the 2011 Survey on Children, sponsored by the National Statistics Office (NSO) and the International Labour Organization (ILO), showed that an estimated 5.492 million children (aged 5 to 17 years) were working for at least one hour in 2011; 54.5% (2.993 million) of whom were working in hazardous environment in which 30% (897, 900) of them were working in the mining sites (Ericta & Johnson, 2012, para. 1 & 4). Because of this, children may be considered dehumanized. Having their own inherent dignity taken away from them makes them vulnerable as objects of exploitation. As such, their issue becomes part of social development discourse, being themselves devoid of a quality life or general well-being. In short, it is evident that one of the common social development problems pertaining to children in the Philippines is child labour and their inhumane conditions.

In the southern part of the Philippines alone, particularly in the Bicol Region, other forms of child labour exist such as *kargador* (baggage boys) and female vendors either on the streets (Magayanes, 2009), or at the market site (Longasa, 2009), (garbage) scavengers (Manzanillo, 2012; Zulueta & Liwag, 2001), workers at quarrying sites (Mujar, 2009), and most significantly as miners at mining sites in Masbate (Reluao, 2008).

As further published in print and broadcast media and in the internet (Arumpac, 2012; Bayanihan, 2012; Perez, Appel, & Koester-Rasmussen, 2007; Soltes, 2012), child labour, specifically child mining, exists in the same region, more so in Paracale, Camarines Norte. This is due to the presence of a lot of small-scale gold-mining activities in which the London-based Philippines Mineral Syndicate's first professional attempts was done in the 1890s (Australasian Institute of Mining and Metallurgy, 1987).

International Labour Organization's (2006b) study in the Philippines also vouchsafed the said existence. Specifically, it presented the major factors why communities engage in small-scale mining and quarrying such as 'the presence of shallow veins of high grade gold bearing ores and the lack of other livelihood opportunities and ample spare time during off seasons for farming and fishing' (International Labour Organization [ILO], 2006b, p. 168). It also highlighted the fact that 'parents do not put much the value of education' due to the high cost of 'packed lunch, basic school supplies, uniforms, shoes, and slippers', and because 'teachers do not report regularly' as a result of the difficult terrain. As a result, many families considered a school diploma as a waste of time, money, and effort (ILO, 2006b, p. 169).

Likewise, the study showed results that provided a general context to this study by presenting the extent of child labourers in the Philippines, that is 23,922 out of 86,104 who provided their working status, and in which 977 were involved in mining – 556 of whom are from Camarines Norte (ILO, 2006b, pp. 31–37). See Table 1 for the summary. However, the specific distribution of child miners per municipality was unknown. Only the percentage or actual numbers of child labourers per municipality was specified (ILO, 2006b, p. 37). See Graph 1 for more details.

Table 1. Specific Numbers of Child Labourers in the Philippines, particularly in Relation to Camarines Norte and Mining.

Category	Number
Number of Total Child Respondents in the Philippines (N)	102, 933
Number of those who provided working status out of N (n)	86, 104
Number of those reported to be working out of n (n_1)	23, 922
Number of those who are mining out of n_1 (n_2)	977
Number of those who are mining from Camarines Norte out of n_2 (n_3)	556 or 57% (Highest in Camarines Norte, followed by Compostela Valley, i.e. 409)

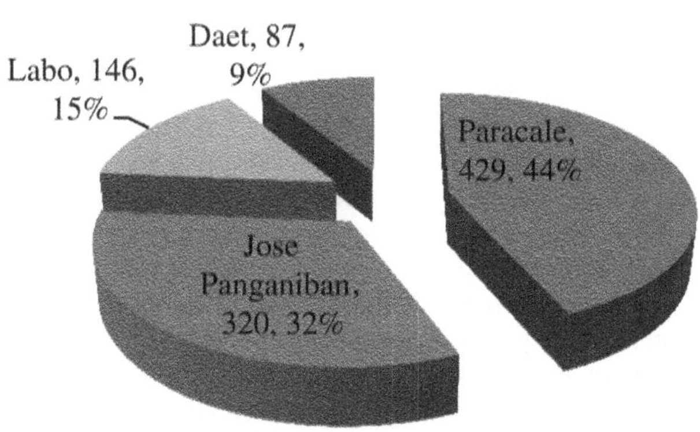

Graph 1. Distribution of All Types of Child Labourers in Camarines Norte Per Municipality (982 Out of n1).

Child labourers in Camarines Norte as referred to in Graph 1 belong to the following categories: those who are working in the sugarcane, other agricultural sector, deep-sea fishing, forestry and manufacturing sectors. Likewise, the study presented that out of 977 children working in the mining sites, 77% were boys and 23% were girls (ILO, 2006b, p. 41). Most of these children are from Camarines Norte (566) and Compostela Valley (409). However, the study failed to identify the actual numbers of child miners (CMs) in every municipality, and their specific experiences and living conditions, which this study hopes to provide.

In any case, by attempting to know, document, present and validate CMs' existence in Paracale, this paper may generally and eventually help all major stakeholders in our society working for the protection of children and their rights understand their participation's dynamics in the said activity, and hopefully forge activities, projects or programs that may help and protect them from the dehumanizing living conditions and exploitative participation in mining activities. In this regard, this will hopefully contribute to the discourse on social development.

PRACTICE THEORY: EXPLAINING THE EXISTENCE OF CHILD MINERS

Various specific and grand theories may explain CMs' existence. Family expectations that everybody should contribute to the family income (Panopio & Raymundo, 2004); subsistence poverty and income inequality, and parental characteristics like lack of education (Fors, 2008; Rogers & Swinnerton, 2002); and community factors such as 'poverty and breakdown of social systems (like marital separation) are thought to be responsible for driving children out of their house and into the streets leading to their exploitation' (ILO, 2007, p. 10). Merton's Modes of Adaptation (as cited by Appelrouth & Edles, 2012), Durkheim's Division of Labor and Solidarity, Weber's idea of rationality, and Homans' exchange cum rational choice theory (Macionis, 2007; Peet & Hartwick, 2009) may also give explanations to their existence.

However, this chapter is anchored more on Ortner's practice theory, which 'seeks to explain the relationship(s) that obtain between human action, and some global entity which we may call "the system,"' (Ortner, 1984, p. 148). The system refers to organizational schemes like 'social relations, economic arrangements, cultural categories, norms, values, ideals, emotional patterns, and so on', which are considered as 'an integral whole in reference to practice', and which also acknowledges 'specific realities of asymmetry' (Ortner, 1984, pp. 148–149). In this context, the involvement of child miners will be considered as part of the entire Paracale small-scale gold mining system. Likewise, practice is considered as 'all forms of human action' done by 'acting units' or 'individual actors'. This practice is largely viewed 'in terms of pragmatic choice or intentionality of acting' in relation to structure (Ortner, 1984, p. 150).

Apart from the discussion of system and human action, she also asserted that the above theory 'requires some sort of theory of motivation', which include 'need, fear, suffering and desire', among others. These could be categorized into three, that is, interest theory, strain theory, and developmental perspective (Ortner, 1984). Under the interest theory, she regarded actors as 'essentially individualistic [...] rational, pragmatic [...] rationally go after what they want [...] (which) is materially useful for them within the context of their cultural and historical situations [...]' (Ortner, 1984, p. 151). For the strain theory, she cited Geertz that 'actors in interest theory are always actively striving for gains, (while) actors in strain theory are seen as experiencing the complexities of their situations and attempting to solve problems posed by those situations' (Ortner, 1984, pp. 151–152). And lastly, as for developmental perspective, which is 'long-term tactical "moves", as opposed to "short-term" in the interest approach', action is 'shaped not only by problems being solved, and gains being sought, but by images and ideals of what constitute goodness – in people, in relationships, and in conditions of life' (Ortner, 1984, p. 152). In short, any human action or 'practice' may be interpreted as being done by a free-willing agent in the context of a 'system', as motivated by either interests, social forces, or ideals of goodness.

Using the said contexts, this chapter theorizes that the CMs' existence in mining activities in Paracale maybe explained as something created by a 'system' or structure, that is, the Paracale small-scale gold mining system considered either as a family tradition, or a sole means of livelihood. Personal gains (under the interest theory), a means to solve social problem – poverty (under the strain theory), and altruism or love of the children for their family (under developmental perspective) motivate this structure.

Similarly, this chapter argues that the Paracale SSGMS, while it permits the children to realize their possible motives of any sort, has elements of 'asymmetry' (Ortner, 1984, p. 149), that is, exploitation in this case, since CMs are underpaid for their hard labour, while the gold is sold for exorbitant prices. Taking into consideration ILO's definition of child labour as a form of economic exploitation, children's employment in the system may also be deemed exploitative because they are 'compelled to work on a regular basis to earn a living for themselves and their families; their work is damaging to their health, physical and mental development; and they are separated from their families, often deprived of educational and training opportunities' (ILO-IPEC as cited in Philippine-ILO, n.d., para. 4) that make mining as hazardous for children, and one of the worst forms of child labour (ILO, 2005). As such, CMs may be deemed inevitably as a case of human and social development issue that needs to be addressed.

FINDING THE CHILD MINERS: METHODOLOGY

In searching for CMs' life experiences, qualitative research with the use of ethnographic approach was employed. It relied much on the actual statements of the key informants (KIs), who were the main sources of data. Participant-observations, focus group discussions (FGDs) and in-depth interviews (Schutt, 2004) were primarily used in documenting their stories. The secondary data, which provided the background of the study and facilitated in analyzing the results of the study, were taken from books, unpublished theses, and the internet.

The Municipality of Paracale, particularly Barangays Casalugan, Tawig, and Malaguit, was the locale of the study. The presence of small-scale gold mining (SSGM) activities in their area and CMs was the main reason for purposively and conveniently choosing the said barangays.

Choosing the Miners and Ethical Considerations

There are two types of KIs in this study: adult miners, or CMs' family members who provided the mining industry's background in Paracale, and the CMs (12–17 years old) of the said locale. They were chosen based on their willingness to participate in the study. Aside from the CMs' consent, their parents or guardians' approval was also obtained, without which interviews were not conducted. Informed consent and assent forms were prepared and tried to be obtained as recommended by an Ethics Review Committee. However, considering that their activities are illegal based on Philippine Laws, such as Republic Act (RA) 7610 – An Act Providing For Stronger Deterrence And Special Protection Against Child Abuse, Exploitation And Discrimination, or also known as the 'Anti-Child Abuse Law of 1992', and RA 7658 or An Act Prohibiting the Employment of Children, it was hard to get a signed written informed consent form, notwithstanding the possibility of self-incrimination for signing a document pertaining to a consent or participation in an illegal activity. This was considered a risk for joining the study. Nevertheless, the KIs who verbally consented to be interviewed, but did not sign the consent/assent form, were assured that any information that they provided will not be used in any legal proceedings. Hence, interviews were still conducted and pictures/videos were taken, as long as verbal consent was given, and after the objectives, significance of the study, the nature of their involvement, and their rights and privacy were explained.

Their surnames and exact addresses were not provided to protect their identities. They were also assured that when either their videos or pictures will be shown or printed, their faces will be covered, or not completely shown, unless otherwise given authorization, which all of them consented.

In obtaining the number of key informants and in getting their informed consent, other factors were also considered such as (a) there should be no conflict of interest, especially between them and the principal investigator (PI) or the researcher – in this study, it is assured that there was no conflict of interest, because the PI has no business, relatives or connection with any person, agency or organization involved in the mining industry in Paracale; (b) the PI all had a courtesy call and sought permission from the concerned LGU authorities (like the Municipal Mayor) to conduct the study; and (c) both the parent and the child must give their consent, after proper explanation about the purpose of the study. The PI either went to the actual mining site, or to their house to get their consent, prior to the interview and observation.

Once KIs' consent was obtained with their parents or guardians, they were interviewed using the prepared instrument. Their participation in the study were only limited to (a) answering questions pertaining to the above topics; (b) taking of their pictures/videos, not showing their faces or covering them in the event of printing, publication or public presentation as mentioned above; (c) to show the processes of their activities; and (d) showing their actual mining sites and the processes involved. The KIs were not subjected to any social experiments that may include physical, financial or psycho-emotional harm.

As for community consideration, even if the three Barangays were named to be the locale of the study, specific sites were not divulged to protect the privacy of the key informants, and in no way that the Barangays' names were maligned in writing the results of the research. The study's benefits are generally non-material, such as understanding the dynamics of CMs' participation in mining activities, and hopefully creating bases for developing appropriate policies or strategies for the promotion of their safety and welfare, proposing local/national programs, ordinances or laws and developing a fair and sustainable small-scale gold mining system, and for creating simple and practicable projects like creating an alternative learning system for the out-of-school youth (OSY), once submitted to concerned stakeholders. No monetary compensation or anticipated payment was given.

The KIs were chosen through non-probability sampling, particularly the purposive and snowball sampling. The KIs were chosen based on their willingness, other KIs' referral, and just to complete at least 10 CMs to give a picture of their situation.

There were 26 identified CMs, which is not its absolute or total population, with the following ages: 11 years – 1, 13 years – 1, 14 years – 3, 15 years – 5, 16 years – 6, and 17 years – 10. However, only 22 were luckily found and conceded to be interviewed. Out of the 22, six came from Barangay Casalugan, six from Barangay Tawig, and ten from Barangay Malaguit. But only ten major stories, with almost complete data set or very significant and in-depth answers, are presented in this study. The rest, with very short answers, were just used as supporting data in order to validate the 10 CMs' claims.

Three separate adult miners, two from Barangay Casalugan and one from Barangay Malaguit, were also interviewed. Two groups of adult miners (with four and six members in each group) were also met by chance during the field immersion, and agreed to be interviewed as a group. Hence, two FGDs of adult miners were also conducted upon the members'approval. Additional bits and pieces of information related to mining in the locale were also gathered from the three respective Barangay Offices' guides, the chief of police, and some residents.

The duration of the study was eight months, inclusive of five-month preparation, library research, proposal writing and submission for institutional research proposal evaluation and ethics review, and three-month gathering and writing the results of the data, after the Institutional Review Board approval. As for the direct involvement of the participants, it was between one to two hours each, or depending on their willingness to show their humble abode, share or how lengthy their answers were, and in showing the actual mining sites (in the mountains) and processes, which normally take the whole day for the underwater mining, and days to months for the underground mining activities that are being done.

Drawing and Making Sense of Their Stories

To capture their own thoughts, the KIs were asked open-ended questions, using two interview guides, which were finalized after its pre-testing, and translated into Filipino. The first guide, which dealt with the mining system in Paracale, was for the adult miners. The second one focused on the CMs' life experiences.

All gathered data were analyzed using Schutt's qualitative analysis framework (2004, pp. 421–430, & 462–468) – documentation of the data and the process of data collection; organization/categorization of the important data into concepts; connecting the identified and categorized important concepts to their possible relationships or explanations; corroboration/legitimization, or evaluating alternative explanations and disconfirming evidence using the KIs' responses, and secondary sources of data, such as related literature, studies and theories; and writing or reporting the findings.

PAINTING THE WHOLE PICTURE: THE PARACALE SMALL-SCALE GOLD MINING SYSTEM (SSGMS) AND THE LIFE EXPERIENCES OF CHILD MINERS

The Paracale Small-scale Gold Mining System

SSGM as a Means of Livelihood and as a Family Tradition

The numerous mining sites' existence in Barangays Malaguit, Tawig and Casalugan, which started before the Spaniards came in 1572 in the Bicol Region (Philippine Statistics Authority-National Statistical Coordinating Board (PSA-NSCB), n.d.), correlates with the Paracale Chief of Police's statement that almost 75% of the residents do SSGM as their primary means of livelihood and a family tradition. If this is the case, shutting SSGM in the locale would be a difficult ordeal for the local officials.

Nowadays, the search for gold still continues, having more or less 2,400 holes at Barangay Malaguit, about 300 ones at just one site in Barangay Tawig, and around 100 holes at solely one area in Barangay Casalugan. Apart from dreaming to have a better life, especially if they hit a large quantity of gold, it appears that such factors are the very reasons that the SSGM activities in the locale exist. The five interviewed CMs (namely Mario, Gilbert, Ronald, John Erick, and John-John), two groups of adult miners during the two FGDs conducted, and two individual adult miners (Arsel and Michael) validated these, which were also featured in major media networks, like the Philippine Daily Inquirer (Soltes, 2012) and GMA Network (Arumpac, 2012).

Even if SSGM activities are quite difficult and hazardous, miners are quite enticed with the idea that if mother nature will let them find free gold, as adult KIs and CMs averred, they could become instant millionaires, and would no longer work as team players or miners. Such adult and child miners' dream of having a better life could be illustrated in Elliot's Patterns of Poverty in the Third World (as cited in Manalili, 2012, pp. 127–129). He avers that just like the fishes at the bottom jar that wish to be at the large part of the upper jar, and whose fate depends on the opportunity and bigger fishes' permission to open the passage, the miners also hope that one day, they will no longer be at the bottom jar. This could only happen with the current financiers' help. Nonetheless, this hope keeps them from mining, despite its difficulty and hazards.

The SSGM is also considered as a family tradition, specifically by Mario, Gilbert, Paolo, Ronald, John Erick and John-John, just like the members of the second conducted FGD. On one hand, the members of the first FGD hold that they do not allow child miners at their site because it is illegal. But at some sites, children are employed. They were also giving some leeway to very young children to wander around with their parents, and to those as young as 12 years old to work or help at the site. However, a mother of a CM stressed that they only allow their children to work on weekends just for them to earn money for their school allowance, and for as long as they take extra precautions. As observed, the presence of girls or women, that is, either children or wives of the miners, are quite obvious particularly for the *pagkocompressor* (underwater mining) as compared to *pagbibitâ* (underground mining). They are either helping or just waiting and looking at their family members doing mining. But still in general, there are more men and boys in both types of mining.

In other words, since SSGM is seen as a family tradition, seeing children in a mining site is a usual occurrence, thus accepting SSGM activity and having child miners as a natural activity. The above dream has even seemed to already permeate into the very young minds of the children roaming around the mining sites, playing and simulating small-scale gold mining activities. If this is the case, shutting SSGM in the locale would be a very difficult ordeal to face, especially for the local officials.

With the above contexts, they may eventually result to the CMs being trapped in the cycle of poverty and the SSGM system, as implied in Elliot's illustration of poverty in the Third World, and that of the Ortner's idea of a system with asymmetry. On a lighter side, taking into consideration the same contexts, the mining's practice in Paracale, may then be considered as a result of its historic and systemic SSGM activities, motivated by the miners' dream of having a better life, as two adult miners achieved. In this regard, Ortner's practice theory is then substantiated.

The Types of SSGM and Its Risks

Pagbibitâ (underground mining), and *pagkocompressor* (underwater mining) were identified as SSGMS's general types (*pagkakabod*) with common organizational structure and CMs. Their differences were in the nature of work, roles, costs, income, equipment, and processes.

CMs' health and safety is always at stake due to non-formal training in mining, and absence of state-of-the-art equipment. In fact, the local government closed the mining sites at Barangay Palanas when tunnels collapsed on January

29, 2012. A lot of people were believed to be buried alive. However, only two were officially reported.

With the said risks, adult miners claimed that they usually practice the 'safety first' policy. But in case of accidents, miners do not have any insurance. The financiers will just voluntarily help the concerned miner, in case he gets sick or injured. Adult miners also acknowledged that bankruptcy is their biggest problem, since gold is not always abundant. Hence, they also have to find other jobs, as one KI revealed.

The Cost and Income

The cost and income in *pagbibitâ* as compared to *pagkocompressor* may be bigger, because more equipment and materials are used for the former activity, and more members are involved in the long term mining and shifting mode. The bigger income is also due to the possibility of extracting more quantity of gold by digging deeper and wider.

However, since there are more players in *pagbibitâ*, greater expenditures shall be deducted from their gross income, and more people have to share the net income. For example, if they earn Php 60,000 per week as they claimed less Php 15,000 mining costs, then their net income is only Php 45,000. It is divided among 20 players, for example 8 per group, multiplied by 2 (since they do shifting by group), equals 16, plus the financier who usually owns the compressor, the land and the generator set, that makes him eligible to get four shares. Thus, the Php 45,000 shall be divided into 20 shares, which is equal to Php 2,250 (US$ 41.67) per week or Php 375 per day (US$ 6.94) – still within the income range of the underwater miners Php 50 to Php 700 (US$ 0.92 to US$ 12.96, based on US$ 1 = Php 54 exchange rate as of September 12, 2018), see Table 2.

Having the above figures, it shows that the miners may still generally be considered poor, as per World Bank's (2015) standard. This is because their minimum income per day, that is, Php 25–50 or US$ 46–92¢, is below the poverty threshold. For a family of 5 members to survive daily, it should have at least a

Table 2. Sample Computation of the Actual Net Income of Adult Miners Doing *Pagbibitâ*.

Items	Income
A. Gross Income per Week	Php 60,000/group
B. Less Expenses per Week	Php 15,000
C. Net Income per Week	Php 45,000.00
D. C divided by the Number of Shares, i.e. Players (16) + Shares of the Financier, Owner of the Land, Compressor and Generator Set (4) = 20	Php 2,250/player or share Per week *(USD41.67)*
Actual Net Income Per Day	Php 375/day (US$ 6.94)*

*As compared to the actual net income of child miners doing pagbibita or pagkocompressor, i.e. between Php 25–Php 50 to Php 700/person per day (US$ 46–92¢ to USD12.96; with US$ 1 = PhP 54 exchange rate as of September 12, 2018).

daily income of US$ 9.5 or equal to Php 513 (i.e. US$ 1.90 × 5 members = US$ 9.5 or Php 513, based on World Bank's poverty threshold, i.e. US$ 1.90).

In addition, miners' exploitation may be experienced when financiers, or gold buyers sell the same at a higher price, and they only get few hundred pesos in exchange of their hard labour.

The Life Experiences of Child Miners

Their Socio-demographic Background

Most of the 10 CMs, who are predominantly males with one female, are of 15 (Paolo, Jr, Aljun, and Francis) and 17 years of age (Mario, Gilbert, Ronald and Carlo). The rest (Carlito and Veron) are 16 years old. They started mining from eight years old to 15 years old. In addition, five of them (Veron, Ronald, Jr, Carlo, and Aljun) are the eldest children in their respective families. The number of their siblings ranges from two to nine, with highest concentrations on four, seven and nine siblings (Ronald and Aljun, Carlito and Carlo, and Mario and Gilbert respectively), followed by two, three, five and six siblings (with one CM each). Only seven CMs gave their years of experience – three KIs (Gilbert, Ronald and Veron) for two years, two KIs (Paolo and Carlo) for four years, and two KIs (Carlito and Mario) either six or nine years. The remaining three KIs (Jr, Aljun and Francis) had no response.

Their Educational Background

All 10 major KIs are OSY. Six (Gilbert, Paolo, Carlo, Carlito, Mario and Jr) had some elementary education, and the rest (*Ronald, Francis, Aljun* and *Veron*) reached secondary education. They preferred to work at the mine sites rather than study. In fact, four of them, namely Jr, Carlito, Aljun and Joshua, would say without batting an eye lash that there is no money in education, and they just learn their classmates' bad influences, which may be reckoned as a serious concern. Besides, they also asserted that if they stay at school, they would not be able to help their families, and would have nothing to eat. This reasoning upholds ILO's (2007) findings that the quality of schooling and enrolment is considered having very low returns for the family. In this regard, Merton's adaptation, Homans' social exchange theory (Peet & Hartwick, 2009) and actor's motivation in Ortner's Practice Theory (1984) in explaining the CMs and their parents' choice are quite in place.

Their Living Conditions

The CMs' living conditions are disheartening. Their houses are made up of extremely light materials – the roofs are of *nipa* (a kind of native palm tree) leaves with either none or very few old galvanized iron sheets; most walls are dilapidated, also made from *nipa* or from very old pieces of wood, with few concrete hollow blocks as in Fig. 1a and 1b. One does not even have walls, but with only one-sided roof that touches the ground and simultaneously acts as a wall as in Fig. 1c. Their foundations, especially for the underwater miners, do not follow the legal easement (three-metre wide in urban areas and 20-metre wide in

(a) (b) (c)

Fig. 1. (a) Sample CM's House. (b) Another Sample CM's House. (c) Sample CM's Dwelling with One-sided Roof cum Wall (CM with the Author).

agricultural areas along the river banks, streams, and shores) set by the government as stipulated in Article 51 of the Water Code of the Philippines (or Presidential Decree No. 1067 of 1976). As for the underground miners' houses, they are constructed in the mountains or near the underground mining sites. Aside from having murky and polluted water, their physical surroundings could usually be seen with piles of garbage around the house, which is usually closely constructed with their neighbours without the necessary distance or fire wall.

With such impoverished conditions, evidenced by lack of proper waste disposal, sanitary toilets, potable water supply, and nutritious food, the CMs may be prone to depression, having low self-esteem, malnutrition, pulmonary/skin and other water-born illness, breach of personal/physical security, loss of personal properties, and exposure to wild life and hazards like fire, flooding, soil erosion, and strong typhoons. In the above regard, the CMs are devoid of the rights to privacy – protection from attacks against their way of life, good name, families, and homes (Article 16); health and health services – best health care possible, safe water to drink, nutritious food, a clean and safe environment, and information to help them stay well (Article 24); social security – help from the government, if they are poor (Article 26); and adequate standard of living – food, clothing, a safe place to live, and to have their basic needs met (Article 27) as embodied in the UN Convention Rights of the Child (UNICEF, n.d.a).

Their Reasons for Working as Child Miners

The CMs' main reason for working is something cultural and predictable in Filipino families. The eldest children are always expected to help meet their families' needs, especially when their parents are already separated, or if they are left by themselves as reflected in their stories. This corroborates with ILO (2007) and Ericta and Johnson's (2012) findings respectively that children are driven out of their house to find work to the point of exploitation, due to the following: community factors, like marital separation and death of their fathers as the seven CMs (*Gilbert, Francis* and *Aljun*, as supported by the information given by Mark Angel, Raymond, Mark John, and Almark) explicitly experienced; to supplement their family's income, or generally for their well-being and most especially for their siblings in the case of eight CMs (Ronald, Mario, Gilbert, Paolo, Carlo, Jr, Carlito, and Francis), which the 10 other KIs (Ronald, Mario, Gilbert, Paolo, Carlo, Jr, Carlito, and Francis) validated, and for their personal consumptions as two CMs (Aljun and Veron) and two other KIs (Joshua and Arlan) claimed and maintained respectively.

Their stories also clearly reveal that their families' economic impoverishment, which substantiates studies of Panopio and Raymundo (2004), ILO (2006a), Basu and Van (as cited in Rogers & Swinnerton, 2002), Fors (2008) and ILO (2007), is a major reason for working, aside from considering mining as their primary means of livelihood, or as a family tradition.

All these confirm Ortner's Theory particularly on the three types of motivations for an actor's practice, namely strain vis-à-vis the community factors, developmental vis-à-vis for the CMs' family welfare, and interests vis-à-vis the CMs' personal motive.

How They Become Child Miners

Listening to the CMs' stories on how they become miners themselves, the social learning theory (Michener, DeLamater, & Schwartz, 1990) considerably applies to them. They acquire skills in mining from their parents, families or other community members (ILO, 2006a, p. 14) through imitation, socialization or training in order to value work (Panopio & Raymundo, 2004), and reinforcement, that is, monetary rewards, notwithstanding their noble reasons. This is quite true as 17 out of the total 22 interviewed CMs (Mario, Gilbert, Paolo, Ronald, Francis, Jr, Veron, Carlito, Carlo, as well as Vince, Arlan, John Erick, Raymond, John-John, Joshua, Maing and Vincent) revealed.

Their Work

Their engagement's differences in any SSGM could be readily explained due to mining sites' locations. The ones mining on top of a mountain in Casalugan and Malaguit (Carlito, Carlo, Jr, Aljun, Veron, as well as Mark John, Mark Angel, John-John, Arlan, Joshua, and Vincent) definitely do *pagbibitâ*. Those in Tawig and some parts of Casalugan and Malaguit (Mario, Gilbert, Paolo, Ronald, Francis, as well as Vince, Almark, John Erick, Raymond, Maing and Norman) do *pagkocompressor*, because the mining sites are either located at the rice paddies, near a foot of a mountain, or along the sea shore. Actually, it is difficult to find the same CMs at a similar spot, because they hop from one site to another after exhausting the gold in a particular site.

Their underwater mining roles include digging underwater, cooking/heating gold particles, pulling a heavy bag filled with mud, crushing and sifting it, gold panning, covering the hole after mining and buying food. Their underground mining roles consist of digging and going through tunnels, being a mocker, bagger, runner or porter, timber man, being puller or tagger, manual blower operator, runner, fetching water, searching for other precious stones, buying and cooking food, grinding stones, gold panning and heating gold particles, most of which correlate with ILO's (2006a, p. 14) findings.

Likewise, getting inside the tunnel exposes the CMs to greater risks, such as getting suffocated for lack of oxygen, if the compressor malfunctions, poisoned by gases emitted from the decomposing materials like wood, being buried alive just in case the tunnel collapses when it rains hard, and if there are bombings done to break thick layers of rock, having an accident in going up and down the pit via a pulley, in case the rope snaps out, and being electrocuted due to faulty electrical wirings. Melting gold particles is also dangerous because of being exposed to mercury, borax, and nitric acid, and being burned, if the gas tank and the blower explode. On one hand, the lighter ones include gold panning, grinding stones, *tagagaragad* (puller or tagger), or getting out of the tunnel by being pulled through a rope tied on one's waist, *taga-blower*, being a runner, fetching water, searching for precious stones, cooking and buying food.

Despite the said risks, CMs are employed because they are 'quicker and agile' than their adult counterparts (ILO, 2006a, p. 14). And to use Ortner's Theory, their activities may not necessarily be exploitative, but the most practical response in relation to their experienced strain or socio-economic problem – poverty, in the cases of Mario, Gilbert, Paolo and Aljun.

In *pagkocompressor*, most of the above risks are not evident, since the said functions are assisted by adult miners. The following hazards may also happen: as *bosero* (underwater miner), being drowned or buried as well if the hole collapses, and not getting enough oxygen, if the long hose that supplies oxygen is disconnected. As *tagapatnaw* (crusher) and *taga-akaw* (sifter), they could get wounded on the hands and feet, as some CMs showed. As *tagabanton* (puller), not having enough strength to pull the heavy *lasdok* (bag) may result to dislocated arm or shoulder, and possibly being pulled down into the well and drown. Melting gold particles also has the same risks as that of *pagbibitâ* CMs.

With regard to their working hours, most of them worked from eight to fourteen hours and beyond. See Table 3 for more details. This would further endanger their health and well-being (safety and security), and ultimately exploit them by being paid minimally, considering the mining activities' rigors and dangers. Similarly, this may retard their personal and emotional development (Philippine-ILO, n.d., para. 14).

Table 3. Working Hours of the 10 Child Miners.

Number of Hours	Frequency
5 hours (11am–4pm)	1 (Veron)
8 hours (8am–4pm)	3 (Mario, Gilbert and Paolo)
9 hours (8am–5pm; 7am–4pm)	3 (Carlo and Carlito; Ronald)
10 hours (7am–5pm)	1 (Jr)
14 hours (5am–7pm)	1 (Francis)
Stay-in	1 (Aljun)

Their Income

Having also interviewed adult miners on different occasions as regards their income, it may be said that CMs were undoubtedly quoting their real income per day or week, i.e. Php 25–Php 700 per day or Php 150–Php 4,200 per week, and not just making up stories. As mentioned above, the variation of their income is dependent on the amount of gold collected for a particular day (for the *pagkocompressor)* or week (for the *pagbibitâ)*, and on the price of gold per gram (like Php 1,300–Php 1,360) that also changes from time to time, less the costs incurred for the day or week. With the irregular volume of gold collected and its price, and more so with their minimum income (Php 25–Php 50 or US$ 46¢–92¢), almost all of them (21 out of 22 generally interviewed CMs) are indeed considered poor, based on the minimum daily earning of a person per day, i.e. US$ 9.5 or equal to Php 513 (i.e., US$ 1.90 × 5 members = US$ 9.5 or Php 513), as measured by the World Bank (2015). Please see Tables 4–6 for more details.

The only one with income of Php 700 per day may still be considered poor considering that the excess of his income, that is, Php 187 (from Php 700 less 513) in relation to the minimum income for a family of 5, is quite meagre to finance a family's other basic needs. In this regard, just like the adult miner's case, they may also be trapped in the cycle of poverty, thereby losing their precious human potentials, especially in case their dream of hitting free gold will not be realized as mining now becomes highly competitive with the existing thousands of SSGM holes.

Implicitly, their income vis-à-vis the selling price of gold may be deemed an aspect of exploitation, precisely because of the following scenarios:

- The CMs' income is not commensurate to their hard labour. The processes involved in mining gold (from getting the *bitâ* to melting the gold particles to produce gold nuggets) are quite dangerous as revealed by the miners, and as presented and discussed above.
- The selling price of gold is way beyond the actual buying price or income of the miners. For example, as in Fig. 2, where a pair of locally made gold earrings and an internationally purchased gold pendant are more or less 48% and 65% respectively higher than the actual buying price. Hence, unless the CMs actually hit free gold in large volume, they remain poor, while the seller becomes richer.

Table 4. Summarized Child Miners' Net Income per Day or per Week with the Other 12 CMs.

Income per Day	Income per Week*	Frequency
Php 25[a] – Php 250	Php 150 to Php 1,500	1 (Mark John)
Php 50 – Php 200	Php 300 to Php 1,200	3 (Mario, Gilbert, Paolo)
Php 83.33 – Php 116.67	Php 500 to Php 1,000	2 (Carlito, Carlo)
Php 83.33 – Php 416.67	Php 500 to Php 2,500	1(Mark Angel)
Php 100–Php 300	Php 600–Php 1,800	1 (Maing)
Php 150	Php 900	3 (Norman, John-John, John Erick)
Php 166.67–Php 250	Php 1,000–Php 1,500	1 (Jr)
Php 200	Php 1,200	1 (Raymond)
Php 250	Php 1,500	2 (Arlan, Aljun)
Php 300–Php 400	Php 1,800–Php 2,400	1 (Vince)
Php 333.33	Php 2,000	1 (Veron)
Php 500	Php 3,000	3 (Joshua, Ronald, Francis)
Php 500–Php 700[b]	Php 3,000–Php 4,200	1 (Almark)
Income Varies	–	1 (Vincent)
Total		22

*Notes: *One week is only equivalent to 6 days, because Sunday is their rest day.*
[ab] Equivalent to US$ 0.46 to12.96; with US$ 1 = Php 54 exchange rate as of September 12, 2018. The bold ones are the 10 major CMs.

Table 5. Child Miners' Net Income per Day or per Week in *Pagbibitâ.*

Income per Day	Income per Week	Frequency
Php 25–Php 250	Php 150–Php 1,500	1 (Mark John)
Php 83.33 – Php 116.67	Php 500 to Php 1,000	2 (Carlito, Carlo)
Php 83.33–Php 416.67	Php 500 to Php 2,500	1(Mark Angel)
Php 150	Php 900	1 (John-John)
Php 166.67–Php 250	Php 1,000–Php 1,500	1 (Jr)
Php 250	Php 1,500	2 (Arlan, Aljun)
Php 333.33	Php 2,000	1 (Veron)
Php 500	Php 3,000	1 (Joshua)
Income Varies	–	1 (Vincent)
Total		11

Their Income Utilization

CMs' income is greatly utilized for their families' needs. See Table 7 for more details. Eight out of 10 major KIs (Ronald, Mario, Gilbert, Paolo, Carlo, Jr, Carlito, and Francis) revealed that they entirely give their income to their parents for hog's feeds, buying food and clothes, his siblings' school needs/

Table 6. Child Miners' Net Income per Day or per Week in *Pagkocompressor*.

Income per Day	Income per Week	Frequency
Php 50–Php 200	Php 300–Php 1,200	3 (Mario, Gilbert, Paolo)
Php 100–Php 300	Php 600–Php 1,800	1 (Maing)
Php 150	Php 900	2 (Norman, John Erick)
Php 200	Php 1,200	1 (Raymond)
Php300–Php400	Php 1,800–Php 2,400	1 (Vince)
Php 500	Php 3,000	2 (Ronald, Francis)
Php 500–Php 700	Php 3,000–Php 4,200	1 (Almark)
Total		11

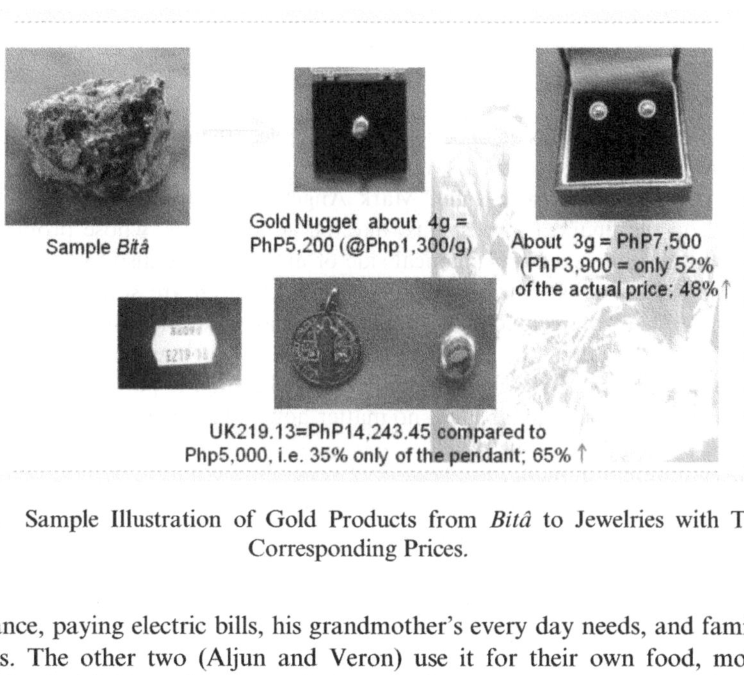

Fig. 2. Sample Illustration of Gold Products from *Bitâ* to Jewelries with Their Corresponding Prices.

allowance, paying electric bills, his grandmother's every day needs, and family's savings. The other two (Aljun and Veron) use it for their own food, mobile phone load, drinking, cigarettes, clothes, playing computer games, and buying a bike.

While the CMs' experiences may reveal their exploitation, it also unfolds the unquestionable altruistic side of the Filipinos, that is, to always help their families during hard times. Similarly, it also validates that Filipino children are expected to help earn income for their family's needs, or to help support their siblings' or their own educational needs (Panopio & Raymundo, 2004). This is quite obvious for poor Filipinos in which raising a family becomes a shared responsibility among all its members – something to be considered as a noble cause.

Table 7. Income Utilization of the 10 Child Miners.

Utilization of Income	Frequency
1. *For the entire family only*: gives entirely to their parents (for hog's feeds, buying food and clothes, and for his siblings' school needs/allowance) (*Ronald, Mario, Gilbert, Paolo, Carlo*)	5
2. *Both for the family and themselves*: gives to their parents (for food and paying electric bills) and grandmother (for every day needs), and saves some, i.e. either Php 60 or 100 to 200, for themselves (for their own food, mobile phone load, drinking, cigarettes, and clothes; for playing computer games; for buying a bike) (*Jr, Carlito, Francis*)	3
3. *As savings either for one's self or for the family*: saves it, and either lends it to his mother, if needed, or voluntarily gives Php 1,000–Php 2,000 weekly to his mother (*Aljun*)	1
4. *For personal consumption*: personally handles or budgets it (*Veron*)	1
Total	10

Their Difficulties

If one has to analyze their experienced challenges, their responses are more on personal safety and health, as recognized by Mario, Gilbert, Paolo, Aljun, Vincent, Jr, Joshua, Mark John, Mark Angel and Ronald. Only one (Veron) focused on the financial aspect, just like the adult miners, whose problems are more on the technical or mechanical side of mining, while also looking into the personal safety of its team players. However, children are still more prone to danger for lack of technical or mechanical materials and aspects of mining. Hence, they should not be forced or even asked to work as miners in the name of family's welfare. Besides, it is the responsibility of the parents to raise their family, not the other way around, no matter how noble their cause might be.

Their Day-to-day Activities

Although the child miners could still do some activities, like hanging out with their friends at their plaza, playing basketball, computer games, and billiards for few hours, drinking with them, or just exchanging text messages with them, their activities reveal that they only have very limited options and time to do something leisurely after engaging in the SSGM for six days in a week and almost eight hours and beyond a day. This further means that for working at mining sites, CMs are not able to fully enjoy their basic right to leisure, play and culture (Article 31, UN Convention on the Rights of the Child, UNICEF, n.d.a) and undergo the usually accepted psychosocial development of a child as pointed out by Erikson (Matlin, 1999), especially that of the play and school age, wherein they are expected to develop their sense of industry, curiosity and learning in the right context and avenue.

Their Views on Being Child Miners and About Their Families

One CM considered their involvement as plain and simple work, although they also acknowledged that it is quite dangerous and tiresome. He and his companions did not mind its difficulty, because they deemed it as their way of contributing to their family's welfare, as discussed above.

On a sad note, their work's exploitative nature is not in any way within their consciousness. For them, mining is always an easy means of earning money to help their family, thereby making them dependent on it. They, except for a few who have long term aspirations in life, were only concerned with the present without much regard for their future. Without them knowing it, they are slowly being trapped in the cycle of poverty and mining, and may be used by financiers to gain more capital at their own expense, having no insurance, security or protection from the dangers in mining, and being cheaply paid for their hard labour.

When asked to compare their families with other families without CMs, only a few responded by saying that the families of the latter have children who could go to school, have good jobs, no financial problem, need not worry to earn for a living, and have a good life, while they have not. Hence, they need not mine, while their families, who are generally considered poor, should. Two other KIs even added that life for them is difficult, and that their families are never equal, in contrast to them. This perception is quite obvious, with their kind of family background. In this instance, one's social interaction is a strong influence to a person's life and perception, as symbolic interactionist theory emphasizes.

Their Aspirations in Life

It is noteworthy that only a few CMs have aspirations in life, particularly for themselves. Two out of the 10 major CMs wanted to be an agriculturist (Francis) and a well-educated person (Mario). Only seven out of the remaining 12 CMs dreamed of having a career in the future either as a basketball player (Vince), a seaman (Vincent), policemen (Maing and Almark), a soldier (Arlan), an information technologist (Mark Angel), or a company worker (Raymond). As such, it may be posited that they could still see the importance of education, which they consider as one of their means to achieve them, and which Filipino parents and teachers usually inculcate in their children or students.

Looking into their aspirations, one may see both positive and negative aspects. On a positive note, a truly Filipino character, that is, children being family oriented and having a strong determination, really stands out among the child miners. Another one is the social awareness of the children, despite their age, having concerns for their physical and social environment, and wishing for a better community. On one hand, their aspirations also imply family disorganization, environmental destruction, presence of conflicts, and lack of basic social services.

Espousing a Basic Social Development Framework

To address the plight of the child miners, a simple but primordial human and social development framework may be espoused. As in the illustration in Fig. 3, such framework asserts that any development efforts start from the *individual level*, in the case of CMs themselves. Individuals are deemed to have a *reservoir*

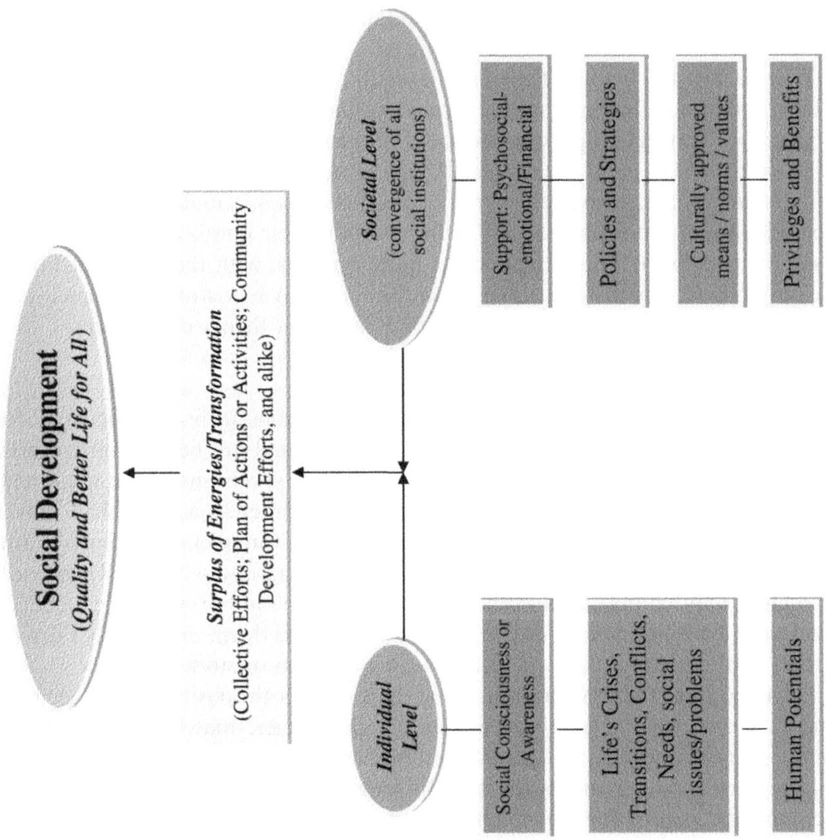

Fig. 3. A Basic Social Development Framework.

of human potentials, have the capacity to be, to create and plot their own destinies. These potentials come to the fore when individuals are met with *life's crises* (like death in the family, calamities that destroyed their families and properties), *conflicts* (personal such as identify crises, conflict with the law and the community), *emergent needs* (need for food, shelter and clothing, for education, for justice, equal access to opportunities and privileges in the society, for jobs, and alike), *transitions* (migration, single parenthood, marriage, adulthood), and *various social issues*, be it in the personal or societal contexts. They also have to have *individual and social consciousness* that they have to do something with regard to the challenges that they face. Otherwise, no necessary actions may arise, or no development plan of actions may happen. On one hand, once there is awareness on their part as individuals try to address any of the aforesaid challenges, they will only become successful once they are met with *support by the society or the community* they belong. However, once they are met with societal contradictions, like they are not being given access to the socially approved means to achieve their goals, then they will not prosper, as illustrated in Elliott's patterns of poverty and as stressed by Manalili (2012).

Development on their part will start in the *societal level* when their families, peer groups, or the community in general are very supportive of their goals or plan of actions. The *society's support* may be in any of the various forms: *financial and psychosocial–emotional support, policies and strategies* (like the ones suggested under the recommendations sub-section) that may allow them to legally work on their plans, *socially approved means* that are in place, privileges and benefits are within one's reach, and *social or cultural values, norms* that are also permissible to their development plans. Once all these are in place, the individuals may now proceed with their plan of actions.

Now, when there is a convergence of individuals and society, the result will be *surplus of energies and social transformation activities*, specific examples of which in relation to this study are also given under recommendations. These would be the actual realization of the individuals' or collective plan of actions, like studying for one's advancement, their families', as well as their community's welfare, doing community development efforts, and other activities that individuals and society in general collaboratively organized. All these will result in the betterment of one's life, family and community, if collectively and seriously implemented.

In short, all individuals, like the CMs, in a given society, should always have the individual and social consciousness with regard to their situations, whether they are exploited or not, and to have that belief and trust in their human potentials and the drive to work not only for one's self and family, but also for the good of their community. It is only when such consciousness is ever present, as triggered by their life's challenges, like the CMs' experiences, and when individuals conversely collaborate with the society and its major social institutions and stakeholders (like the church, educational institutions, government, economic system, health care system and non-governmental agencies) in doing their roles and functions, and vice-versa, that successful activities will be well-thought of, organized and implemented, just like the ones recommended by this study to eradicate, if not minimize CMs' incidence. Consequently, such surplus of activities will catapult any human and social development, and in this regard, the realization of child miners' aspirations.

CUTTING THE CHASE: POSSIBILITIES AND EVOCATIONS

Based on the foregoing results of the study, the following possible statements may be said about the Paracale SSGMS:

The mining system has existed since time immemorial as residents' primary means of livelihood. It is likewise considered as a *tradición*, particularly of the miners' respective families. Having both 'historic and systemic character' (Elliott, as cited in Manalili, 2012, p. 129), banning the SSGM without any alternative and sustainable means of livelihood may be a difficult ordeal.

The miners' income, which falls below WB's poverty threshold, is also not directly proportional to their hard labour considering all the involved processes and dangers involved in mining. Hence, miners' exploitation is evident. But looking deeper into their personal perspectives, their mining activities are not regarded as exploitative in nature, but rather as means to an end.

Similarly, the following may be inferred about the child miners:

Poverty, curiosity, influence of their parents, particularly their fathers, relatives and friends, and being the eldest, with a strong sense of helping their families, left by their father with several siblings to take care of and assumed the role of breadwinners – all correlate why they work as CMs. Significantly, the latter reason denotes both the altruistic values of the CMs and their source of *inspiración* for working as such.

Working as CMs may not be fully deemed as they truly value mining over studying. In fact, they still see studying as one of the means of realizing their aspirations. The CMs' love for their families is revealed in the study, having given almost all their income to their parents for their basic needs, siblings' educational needs or allowances, electric bills, and so on. On one hand, it may be said that they are forced to engage into mining, considering that they have no other economic alternatives, as should be provided by the State. In this regard, it may really be considered as a failure of the state (or concerned agencies) to deliver basic social services, as ILO (2006b, p. 5) argues.

CMs are likewise employed because of their 'agility' (ILO, 2006a, p. 14), as required by their additional tasks like running to and fro the mountain and the town centre to do some errands, like bringing the sacks of *bitâ* (ore) for grinding and gold extraction with the use of ball mills and *pabirik* (gold pan).

Their actual roles and functions could be arranged from the most dangerous to the least ones, based on actual observations and experiences inside and outside several mining sites. In *pagbibitâ* for one, getting inside the tunnel, either as a *tagabitâ*, mocker, timber man, or just digging or widening a tunnel, exposes the CMs to great risks, even if some claimed that they did not encounter any problem.

Even the least dangerous ones, which include getting out of the tunnel by being pulled through a rope tied on one's waist, and being a runner to fetch water and buy food, may also involve risks. Considering the possibility of a rope snapping out in the process of the child miner being pulled out from the tunnel, the child miner might either die or severely wounded with dislocated bone structures upon falling into a deep well, as experienced and shared by a KI. Running up and down the mountains, and passing by steep slopes and bushy areas might also put their lives at risk by either falling from the slope, or possibly being bitten by snakes.

In *pagkocompressor*, most of the above risks are not quite evident, since most of the said functions are also done by adult miners. Overall, whether it is in *pagbibitâ* or in *pagkocompressor*, working in mining, which seriously endangers their health and security, is always hard labour and hazardous, hence, it is regarded as one of the worst forms of child labour (ILO, 2006a, p. 1).

The entire interviewed CMs, similar to adult KIs, will always be considered poor, taking into consideration their number of siblings and daily income, in relation also to WB's poverty threshold.

The CMs' challenges, in relation to adult miners', focused more on their personal safety and health, with only one stressing on financial difficulty. None of them disclosed about any technical or mechanical problems in mining. This implies their lack of professional knowledge on SSGM, which may put them into greater danger as compared to the adult ones. One could make a conjecture that they have not shared their real challenges for fear of exposing the imminent dangers they face every time they work at mining sites. Hence, they may think that authorities would apprehend and strictly prohibit them from working as miners, knowing that their activity is indeed illegal. However, authorities claimed that they only give them due consideration for them to earn something for their basic needs. That is why they are not being apprehended.

Working at mining sites from Monday to Saturday for longer hours leaves the CMs with very limited time to rest, play and socialize with their families and friends, and most especially, to study, except for a few (6 CMs), who would only work part-time and still go to school on weekdays. This means that CMs are generally deprived of the usually accepted psycho-social development as children, as pointed out by Erikson (Matlin, 1999), and of their basic right to leisure, play and culture (Article 31, UNICEF, n.d.a).

Their views of working as CMs may imply several concerns. One, they are not really and fully aware of its hazards. If they are, its rewards, like being able to help their family, put food on the table, and earn money to buy their identified wants, outweigh them. This perception may eventually create false hopes, because they do recognize gold's limited quantity. Two, the strenuous nature of their work, not being paid commensurately with their hard labour, and not having any insurance, protection or security, is not in any way in their consciousness. Thus, they may unconsciously be trapped in the cycle of poverty and SSGMS, and used or abused by financiers to gain more capital at their own expense. Hence, the CMs' situation may really be a case of *explotación*.

Their perceptions of families without CMs are quite understandable considering their circumstances. Such perceptions may be considered as products of their interaction with other people in their community, and not just simple responses to stimuli, expressions of biological drives, profit maximization or conformity to social norms, as symbolic interactionist perspective upholds.

It is alarming that only nine out of 22 interviewed KIs do have *aspiraciónes* for themselves. This may be because of their perception that it is difficult for poor people to dream, because the means to achieve them are not always readily available for them, as some KIs expressed. Nevertheless, their aspirations may be simply influenced by their thought of helping their families to be uprooted from poverty, or by their truly altruistic nature seeing their circumstances.

Corollary to the findings of the study, the CMs' circumstances shall always be a case of human and social development and a classic interplay between a system, that is, the Paracale SSGMS and the failure of the state to provide decent choices for the CMs to better off their lives, actor's practice, that is, the CMs' involvement in mining, and actor's motivations, that is, CMs' reasons for mining – based on their personal interests, practical response to their poor socio-economic condition and separation of their parents, leaving them without much choice but to engage in mining, and altruism or ideals of goodness to help their families, as exemplified in the 'Modern Practice Theory' (Ortner, 1984).

The CMs' case, despite the nobleness of their reasons for working in the mining sites, are still in violation of some of the basic rights of the child such as rights to privacy, parental responsibilities and government assistance, health and health services, social security, adequate standard of living, education, leisure, and protection against child labour and exploitation (UNICEF, n.d.b). It may also be deemed inhumane and not developmental, considering the illegal, hazardous and exploitative nature of their work, being not fully and truly developed and protected as they work at mining sites, and sacrificing their human potentials by dropping out from school to the detriment of their well-being.

The very fundamental concerns in the Paracale SSGM as seen, heard and experienced are the eminent destruction of the environment, and the need for CMs to earn money due to poverty. The latter concern may eventually result to their exploitation, dependency on the SSGM, and negligence of their personal and social development. These are more problematic than the revealed difficulties, and more costly than the actual costs of the SSGM operation, because the future generation is at stake.

The CMs' life experiences truly reveal the Paracale SSGMS' contradictions. While it is valued as a *tradición* for having been practiced for a long time, it may also be a source of both *inspiración* of having a better life, and *explotación* due to the factors presented above, particularly the failure of the concerned stakeholders to provide both equitable economic and educational alternatives. Inspite of these, they still remain positive and hopeful as expressed in their *aspiraciónes*.

Lastly, espousing a simple but primordial social development and community organizing framework that considers individuals' consciousness and potentials (coming from their life's crises, conflicts, emergent needs, life's transitions and various social issues) to create their own destinies, and societal or community's support whether financial or psycho-social–emotional, coupled with good governance, policies and strategies, socially and culturally approved means with due privileges and benefits, holistic alternative livelihood and learning, may uplift the conditions and minimize, if not end, the plight of child miners.

In relation to the aforementioned findings and possibilities, the following evocations are made for consideration of concerned stakeholders:

For National and Local Government Unit's (LGU) Social Policy Makers and Leaders

- They should practice good governance, as one child miner aspires, addressing the social problems correlated with the child miners' existence and the basic social services or needs of the people, and work collaboratively with their families and leading government and non-government agencies (NGAs), like the LGU of Paracale, Department of Education (DepEd), DSWD, Department of Labor and Employment (DOLE), Technical Education and Skills Development Authority (TESDA), Health Centres and Population Commission, Social Action Center (SAC) of the Diocese, and alike, in addressing or meeting them, using either of the ILO-IPEC's two-pronged approach: '*upstream*, i.e. action to create a policy environment conducive to regularization of small-scale mining operations, and *downstream*, i.e. activities to monitor children in the mining areas, withdraw those found to be working and place them in school or training' (ILO, 2006a, p. 4).

  They may also use the above proposed basic social development framework in conjunction with the community development framework espoused by Manalili (2012) in his book *Pag-oorganisa ng Pamayanan Tungo sa Kaunlaran na Mula Tao Para sa Tao*, wherein community development focuses on the analysis of the economic, social and physical realm of the powerless, building their communities to be self-reliant through *Productivity, Equity, Access, Employment* and *Popular Control*, and eventually their empowerment.
- In addition, they may implement due rules and guidelines to warrant the safety and well-being of the miners. Part of the rules and guidelines are standard salary scale to guarantee proper and just compensation of the miners, prescribed working hours, safety measures and use of necessary gadgets or materials for miners' protection. Violators should be severely sanctioned.
- Moreover, they should provide sustainable alternative means of livelihood. This should be forged based on the needs of the residents, as well as that of the municipality's human and material resources, and after due consultation with them, together with the line agencies like the LGU of Paracale, DSWD, DOLE, TESDA, Department of Trade and Industry (DTI), Department of Agriculture (DA), Department of Science and Technology (DOST), National Irrigation Authority (NIA), and other concerned non-governmental agencies (NGAs) like the Social Action Center of the Diocese and partner institutions having a strong socio-economic development program (SEDP) to combat the

economic impoverishment of the town and its people that is considered as the main reason for involving in SSGM.

- To ensure the sustainability of whatever forged projects or alternative means of livelihood in addition to or in lieu of small-scale mining industry, they should not only provide financial assistance to the residents, particularly the CMs' families, but also a holistic system of support, that is, from making feasibility studies of their proposed projects, its production, marketing, networking, financial management, and other related support requirements.
- Furthermore, miners should be provided with alternative learning system (ALS) through the DepEd so that they could still continue with their studies while helping their families, as well as formal and intensive professional training thru TESDA and other concerned agencies, having only learned the trade from their parents and friends, to avoid most, if not all, possible dangers that they are facing and would be facing in the future.
- They may institute the following activities together with the aforesaid agencies: (f. 1) summer camps on education, its relevance and impacts on personal life and community for the out-of-school youths or children (OSY/C) to instill in them the importance of education for themselves and the future of their community; (f. 2) intensive seminar or campaign on responsible parenthood for the parents, young couples and adolescents stressing parents' obligations and children's rights, and making it as a compulsory subject in secondary and tertiary education; and (f. 3) environmental protection and conservation campaign and activities to address the community's environmental degradation, and link them as well to any community programs and educational activities and requirements at all educational institutions across levels.

For the Parents, Children and Concerned Individuals

- Educate them to take part in solving the existing problem. For example, they should be made to understand the significance of financial readiness in raising a family to guarantee their children's future, as well as decent lives, which include not letting them work at mining sites.
- They should be made aware when financiers or other people may try to exploit them through basic training in entrepreneurship, business relations and fair labour practices. They should also not look down on themselves (even if they are 'only' miners, as some children would say), but rather tap and trust in their skills and human potentials that they could break from the chain of poverty. This is also an important step towards self-actualization and development.
- They should also be encouraged to actively and seriously participate and cooperate both individually and collectively in all government or non-governmental activities or programs, just like the ones proposed above, and more importantly the ones that they themselves would propose, and that would surely benefit them and their children towards their very own human and social development.

ACKNOWLEDGEMENTS

My heartfelt gratitude to the following agencies and/or persons:

- *Mga Batang Ginto* (child miners) and their parents, all the *adult miners* for sharing their stories, and Local Government Unit and Barangay Officials of Paracale, Camarines Norte, Philippines for giving us the permission and the guidance in gathering data for this book;
- *Mr. & Mrs. Jeffrey Miralles & Family* of Paracale, Camarines Norte for letting us stay in their abode for weeks, and for providing us food and security during our stay;
- my former professors, *Dr. Ramon Felipe Sarmiento*, Research Director of Catanduanes State University and Philippine Women's University (PWU) PhD in Social Development Program Professor, and *Dr. Angelito Manalili*, PWU PhD in Social Development Program Coordinator, Professorial Lecturer and former Dean of University of the Philippines (UP) – Diliman College of Social Work and Community Development, for all their heartfelt and invaluable suggestions, efforts, assistance and resource materials; and *Dr. Raul Pertierra*, Professor of Anthropology, UP Diliman, and *Dr. Kristina A. S. Benitez*, PWU Vice-president for Academic Affairs, for all their significant inputs;
- my *Department of Sociology*, College of Social Sciences and Philosophy, Bicol University Family, especially *Prof. Glenton Guiriba*, for the financial and moral support and *Prof. Katherine Evasco*, for helping me write the stories;
- my research assistants and students, *Alvie Belesta, Rogel Christian Capili, Jeyson Miralles, Rachel Balbalosa, Mikee Baria, Joyce del Rosario, Rose Ann Letada, and Rea-Lyn Pria*, for all the research assistance;
- my surviving family members, *Mr. Aino Balce Rafer*, my father, and *Agnes*, my sister, as well as my departed loved ones, *Mrs. Leticia Tijam Rosana-Rafer*, my mother, and *Joel*, my brother (may they both rest in peace), for being the 'wind beneath my wings'; and to my ever dearest loving partner, *Go*, for all the moral, emotional, spiritual, physical and financial support during my entire research; and
- most of all, to *God*, for giving me all the blessings in life, more particularly the opportunity to write and complete this chapter, and for keeping me, *Go*, and my research assistants safe all throughout our journey to and fro Paracale, Camarines Norte, Philippines.

REFERENCES

Appelrouth, S., & Edles, L. (2012). *Classical and contemporary sociological theory: Text and readings* (2nd ed.). Thousand Oaks, CA: Pine Forge Press.

Arumpac, A. (2012, July 3). Paracale's real treasurers are not gold. *GMA Network*. Retrieved from http://www.gmanetwork.com/news/story/263976/publicaffairs/iwitness/paracale-s-real-treasures-are-not-gold

Australasian Institute of Mining and Metallurgy. (1987). *Beginning of Gold Mining in the Philippines*. Retrieved from http://www.onemine.org/search/summary.cfm/Beginning-of-Gold-Mining-in-the-Philippines?d=123456789012345678901234567890123456789012345678901234567890123419680 2&fullText=paracale

Bayanihan. (July 25, 2012). *MGB maintains mining ban in gold-rich Paracale town*. Retrieved from http://bayanihan.org/2012/07/25/mgb-maintains-mining-ban-in-gold-rich-paracale-town/

Ericta, C., & Johnson, L. F. (2012). *The number of working children 5 to 17 years old is estimated at 5.5 million (Preliminary Results of the 2011 Survey on Children)*. Retrieved from https://psa.gov.ph/content/number-working-children-5-17-years-old-estimated-55-million-preliminary-results-2011-survey

Fors, H. (2008). *Child Labor: A Review of Recent Theory and Evidence with Policy Implications*. Gothenburg, Sweden: School of Business, Economics and Law, University of Gothenburg.

International Labour Organization. (2005). *A load too heavy: Children in mining and quarrying*. Retrieved from http://www.ilo.org/ipecinfo/product/download.do?type=document&id=880

International Labour Organization. (2006a). *Minors out of mining! Partnership for global action against child labour in small-scale mining*. Retrieved from http://www.ilo.org/ipecinfo/product/download.do?type=document&id=2519

International Labour Organization. (2006b). *Philippines: Time-bound Programme Baseline Survey - Integrative Report*. Retrieved from http://www.ilo.org/ipecinfo/product/download.do?type=document&id=8530

International Labour Organization. (2007). *Explaining the demand and supply of child labour: A review of the underlying theories*. Geneva: ILO.

Longasa, S. A. (2009). *Incidence of child labor in market site, Daraga, Albay: Its economic implication* (Undergraduate thesis). BUCBEM, Daraga, Albay.

Macionis, J. (2007). *Sociology* (11th ed.). Upper Saddle River, NJ: Pearson Education, Inc.

Magayanes, L. M. (2009). *Child laborers in selected Urban Barangays in Legazpi City* (Undergraduate thesis). BUCSSP, Daraga, Albay.

Manalili, A. (2012). Pag-oorganisa ng Pamayanan Tungo sa Kaunlaran na Mula Tao Para sa Tao. UP Diliman, Quezon City, Philippines: Sentro ng Wikang Filipino.

Manzanillo, R. B. (2012). *Child scavengers in Peñafrancia, Daraga, Albay* (Undergraduate thesis). BUCSSP, Daraga, Albay.

Matlin, M. (1999). *Psychology* (3rd ed.). Fort Worth, TX: Hartcourt Brace College Publishers.

Michener, A., DeLamater, J., & Schwartz, S. (1990). *Social Psychology* (2nd edn.). Orlando, FL: Harcourt Brace Jovanovich, Inc.

Mujar, A. M. (2009). *Child workers in the quarrying industry in selected barangays of Daraga, Albay* (Undergraduate thesis). BUCSSP, Daraga, Albay.

Ortner, S. (1984). Theory in anthropology since the sixties. *Comparative Studies in Society and History*, *26*(1), 126–166. Retrieved from http://www.jstor.org/stable/178524

Panopio, I., & Raymundo, A. (2004). *General sociology: Focus on the Philippine setting* (4th ed.). Quezon City, Manila: KEN Inc.

Peet, R., & Hartwick, E. (2009). *Theories of development* (2nd ed.). New York, NY: The Guilford Press.

Perez, E., Appel, P., & Koester-Rasmussen, R. (2007). *Training of small scale miners and their families in safe handling of mercury during extraction of gold in the Philippines. Improving access to social services: Health services and income opportunities for small scale miners and their families*. GEUS. Retrieved from http://www.geus.dk/program-areas/common/geus_rep_2007-35.pdf

Philippine-ILO. (n.d.). *Philippine child labor laws and legislation*. Retrieved from http://ipecphils.tripod.com/phillaws/intro.htm#DEFINITION

Philippine Statistics Authority-National Statistical Coordination Board. (n.d.). *Historical background (Municipal Profile-Daet, Camarines Norte)*. Retrieved from www.nscb.gov.ph/ru5/overview/profiles/daet/history.htm

Reluao, B. (2008). *The child miners in Aroroy, Masbate* (Undergraduate thesis). BUCSSP, Daraga, Albay.

Rizal, J. (1879). *A La Juventud Filipina*. Manila, Philippines: Manila Lyceum of Art and Literature.

Rogers, C., & Swinnerton, K. (2002). *A theory of exploitative child labor*. Washington, DC: US Department of Labor.

Schutt, R. (2004). *Investigating the social world: The process and practice of research* (4th ed.). Thousand Oaks, CA: Sage Publications, Inc.

Soltes, J. (2012, July 11). Paracale mining: A way of life, death. *Inquirer*. Retrieved from http://newsinfo.inquirer.net/227467/paracale-mining-a-way-of-life-death

UN Department of Economic and Social Affairs. (2015). *Transforming our world: The 2030 agenda for sustainable development*. Retrieved from https://sustainabledevelopment.un.org/post2015/transformingourworld

UNICEF. (n.d.a). *Fact sheet: A summary of the rights under the Convention on the Rights of the Child.* Retrieved from https://www.unicef.org/crc/files/

UNICEF. (n.d.b). *UN convention rights of the child in child friendly language*. Retrieved from https://www.unicef.org/rightsite/files/uncrcchilldf

World Bank. (2015). *World Bank forecasts global poverty to fall below 10% for first time; Major hurdles remain in goal to end poverty by 2030*. Retrieved from www.worldbank.org

Zulueta, F. M., & Liwag, D. B. (2001). *The social problems and issues in the Philippines.* Navotas, Manila: Navotas Press.

CHILD'S PLAY IN AND OUT OF SCHOOL: BODIES CONTROL OF SLUM CHILDREN

Letícia Mendonça Lopes Ribeiro

ABSTRACT

This study aimed to analyze the most common child's play of students (approximately seven years old) both during the playtime and the time they are not at school, also considering the teacher's interpretation of the child's play practiced in the school, located in a small slum of the metropolitan area of Belo Horizonte. In this way, the analysis considered the issues that involve the recognition of the essentiality of childhood (Dahlberg, Moss, & Pence, 2003; Sarmento, 2007), in the context of the reality and affectivity of children in the place called slum (Coelho, 2007; Perez & Jardim, 2015, Tuan, 1983), as well as in aspects that demonstrate the control of their bodies through the child's play performed in the school (Brighente & Mesquida, 2011; Foucault, 2009). As a methodological basis, participant observation was chosen because it was believed that from this practice it was possible to extract important experiences and reflections from the research participants, know our actions and, by observing these people, their behaviours and attitudes in routine situations (Lüdke & André, 1986). The results suggested that the slum children's play, both in school and outside, are different among boys and girls. In the open areas of the slum, the boys explore more spaces than girls, who prefer child's play in the domestic sphere. At school, educators try to censure some behaviours and attitudes of children, suggesting the pursuit of obedient postures and disciplined bodies. In this context, it is crucial that educators do not convert the school into a place of censorship of the child's play that resides in the slums and thus transforming the school into

Human Rights for Children and Youth: Sociocultural Differentiation, Resistance and Unity
Sociological Studies of Children and Youth, Volume 24, 181–192

ISSN: 1537-4661/doi:10.1108/S1537-466120190000024010

a space that reinforces the domestication of bodies from the earliest stages of childhood.

Keywords: Child's play; children's bodies; slum children; teacher practices; identity; childhood

INTRODUCTION

When the child is recognized as a subject of rights, which is in particular a developing person, it is also important to recognize the right of the child to play, believing that this activity is fundamental for their development.

Based on these ideas, the present study aims to analyze the most common child's play[1] of students during the playtime and when they are not at school, also considering the teacher's interpretation of the child's play practiced in the school. It is noteworthy that the children referred to in this study are in Elementary School (approximately seven years of age) and are students of a municipal school located in a small slum[2] of the metropolitan area of Belo Horizonte.

In this sense, it is believed in the seriousness in recovering aspects that involve the recognition of the essentiality of childhood (Dahlberg, Moss, & Pence, 2003; Sarmento, 2007), in the context of the reality and affectivity of children in the place called slum (Coelho, 2007; Pérez & Jardim, 2015; Tuan, 1983). Thus, it will be possible to describe not only the relevance of most common child's play practices by children during playtime in childhood but also the importance of developing certain games/practices among the children who live and study in the slum.

Another issue, which will be important in the text, is the strategies that demonstrate the control of children's bodies through child play carried out (or censured by educators) in school (Brighente & Mesquida, 2011; Foucault, 2009), aspects that relate to the docility that is imposed on the infant body, through the guidance of certain behaviours valued by adults. Such behaviours are essentially linked to the recriminatory attitudes that teachers maintain when children have actions that contradict them or awaken them to prejudice.

In this context, consistent with the theoretical basis of the text, the study was based on the analysis of data from two moments – more specifically, from two days when playtime was observed, in June 2018 – that children (study participants) played and three educators observed the practices/plays. It is important to note that this observation, dedicated on the analysis presented here, focused on only two days, which facilitated the production of data and its study. However, this analysis is in a broader context, because the researcher responsible for the collection and interpretation of the data was part of the institution's work team for three years. Therefore, it is suggested that the researcher knows, with a critical and in-depth view, the data produced in this research. Therefore, the effectiveness of this data collection is realized with participant observation, in which the researcher was a member of the group and became part of the activity and the research object. This allowed to extract experiences and important reflections of the subjects of research and also to observe the behaviors and attitudes of the people in daily situations (Lüdke & André, 1986). Thus, the analysis of the collected data interpreted the main points of the observation and some indications made by the students (with the intervention of the researcher) and by the educators (who emerged without any intervention of the researcher).

Therefore, for the better understanding of the study, the following text is presented: after this introduction, the following section named 'Childhood, slum and children's bodies: Necessary reflections' will indicate the theoretical basis to understand the subject; the next section, 'Child's play practices in school and in the open area of the slum', will show the analysis of the results considered as most important; Finally, the final section, 'Final Considerations', will present a preliminary conclusion that will provoke the reflection on the perspectives of this research for the understanding of childhood in school spaces and slums.

CHILDHOOD, SLUM AND CHILDREN'S BODIES: NECESSARY REFLECTIONS

For Sarmento (2007), childhood is a complex process, resulting from historical conceptions about children and their modes of coexistence in social images – these images may have transparency, but may also hide the reality of the child's social and cultural worlds. Thus, childhood is usually represented in an 'adult-centred' perspective, which allows one to escape from the actual experiences, cultures and representations of the children themselves about their multiple universes.

In fact, it is already possible to recognize that 'childhood is in the process of change, but it remains a social category with its own characteristics' (Sarmento, 2004, p. 19). This finding of childhood disregards the paradigm of the fragile, innocent child, who is unable to decide for himself, starting to consider the conception of the strong and autonomous child, capable of constructing his or her identity and culture, which makes it possible to recognize the identity of the child and associate it as an 'active, competent individual with potential to be developed from birth; individual that learns and builds knowledge in the process of social interaction' (Andrade, 2010, pp. 66–67).

In this sense, the identity of the child must be associated with the identity of a social actor, equally important to society as any other members of different age groups. As Dahlberg et al. (2003, p. 71) describe, it must be recognized that:

- children are social actors, participating in the construction and determining their own lives, [...] they have activity and function; the social relationships and cultures of children are worthy of study by law;
- children have their own voice and to be heard in order to be taken seriously by involving them in dialogue and democratic decision-making, and to understand childhood: children contribute to the resources and the social production, not being simply a cost and a burden;

These indications are fundamental for the realization of the child's vision as a social actor. However, while having their rights legally recognized, there are still several challenges for children, their cultures and their actions to be studied and valued. Instead, there is a devaluation of the child's play universe. This was shown in the work by Rodrigues and Reis (2018), who presented a critical analysis on the play and the body in the processes of knowledge construction by children in contemporary education. According to the authors, several times the use of the body and the playful are seen as an element of alienation of the subject in school. That is, they can be considered by the educators as a loss of time, because they are moments that differ from the routine imposed by the institutionalized formative dynamics. Therefore, there is a clear intention to show how insignificant the great learning that comes from the playful opportunities with the body is, besides its cultural representativeness, reducing the body to an object that does not allow possibilities for the exercise of the creative imagination. All this scenario reinforces that the 'right to education refers directly to the difference between legality and legitimacy, that is, the presence of the subjects in the school field does not presuppose the right of access to the field of school culture' (Rodrigues & Reis, 2018, p. 28). Therefore, this framework reinforces that children's actions represent demarcated forms of living and being in childhood, meaning collective representations in a historical and social context. It is fundamental to emphasize that 'the child brings a proper knowledge, marked by its history, so, 'they cannot be seen only as a receptacle that receives images in an uncritical way' (Pereira et al., 2005) and passive' (Pérez & Jardim, 2015, p. 495).

The child's way of playing is associated with his or her life history. If the child's life history consolidates into a slum, for example, his or her way of playing is associated with this slum. For Perez and Jardim (2015), the practice of child play in the favela allows children to give meaning to the place where they live by establishing relationships and opinions about this place. Thus, in a collective dimension, "action causes the child to change, enabling the consolidation of the feeling of being part of that place" (p. 499).

In a similar sense, Coelho (2007) shows that the identities of children are built in the innumerable child's play practices that they perform in the slum. Thus, child's play guard the sense of the domain of space, and self-knowledge that associates the child with that place. As a participant in the place where he or she lives, plays and identifies himself or herself, the child of the slum is able to establish relationships interpreted as affectionate.

The affection that the child feels with the slum is understood when it is possible to admit the uniqueness of the slum space – and especially when there is recognition of the difference between this space and the place that the slum has in the interpretation of the young people who live there. Silva (2014), when mentioning the work of Tuan (1983), makes an important and easily understood conceptual distinction among space and place.

> It is from the idea of threat, associated with the unfamiliar one, that a difference among space and place is established. In this way, space, by being endowed with value and by acquiring definition and meaning, becomes a place. In the author's words, "[...] what begins as an undifferentiated space becomes a place as we know it better and give it value" (Tuan, 1983, p. 6). It is understood that familiarity with space transforms it into a place that, then, becomes a concretion of value linked to feeling. (Silva, 2014, p. 56)

Recognizing the importance of this place leads us to recognize and interpret also the meaning of topophilia: the creation of an affective bond among person and place, according to Tuan (1980 cited in Lopes, 2013). The topophilia established among the child and the slum is also established between the child and the school. However, the relations of affection are very distinct in the meaning of these two places, as Martins (2018) instigates us to think from a fictitious account – and, at the same time, very real.

> André was always turned off. In class, in religious services, at family lunches. He was always far away, fantasizing everything with the same passion and urgency. Only on vacation did not feel the need to daydream. He preferred to keep his feet on the ground, to run fast, to feel his heart beat. However, this time, he could not imagine his debut at the new school. Even with the kite, the marbles and the pimps during the day and the little joke gathering the whole group in the late afternoon, he took a moment in his thoughts to dream about the near future (Martins, 2018, p. 46).

The excerpt, written by Geovani Martins in his work *The Sun in the Head* ('O sol na cabeça', in Portuguese) shows the anxiety of the young André, who at approximately 11 years, will attend Middle School in a new educational institution, a little further away from where he lives (and plays): the Vidigal slum, in the Rio de Janeiro, Brazil.

A very interesting point of the book written by Martins (2018) is the mention of the many practices that the child, resident in the slum, can carry out in his spare time, although this place is marked by a 'social forces game' (Perlman, 1977, p. 40), with its own cultural laws and codes. However, it is undeniable that slum imposes itself on the identity of the individual 'slum dweller' – especially if that individual is a child.

Unfortunately, the interpretation of people, who are not residents of the slums, in the face of the identity of the children living in slums, disregards the grandeur and importance of this construction. On the contrary, prejudice and the intention to impose a new infantile identity are common characteristics of the educator's behaviour. Longo (2012), in her work on the stigma surrounding teenagers who are 'poor, black, and peripheral', – most common characteristics for describing slum residents – expresses how teachers form stereotypes of their students by pasting them in a marginalized position, usually associated with condemnation that will never achieve any social and/or intellectual ascent. The words of Hasenbalg (1997, p. 65 cited in Longo, 2012, p. 5) describe this marginalization with evidence:

> The stereotypes of teachers regarding the education of black and poor children function as self-actualizing prophecies. These stereotypes are the basis of a messaging system that helps to shape children's self-esteem.

However, while educators themselves believe that slum students are condemned to marginality, they also hold that they can 'mold' these students, and then they will have some chance worthy of a different future. They usually do this by controlling the bodies of children in school institutions. In this way, the docilization of bodies, which is not necessarily linked to physical violence, such as punishment and pounding, but is consolidated by 'a "symbolic violence", as described by

Bourdieu (2002, p. 50). There is a look of disapproval, as well as the deprivation of the word, the prohibition of the expression of thought, the requirement of good conduct' (Brighente & Mesquida, 2011, p. 2392).

It is important to emphasize that the imposition of docile bodies implies an important form of disciplinary power, to then 'train' the 'confused and useless crowds of bodies', and to set up obedient individuals (Foucault, 2009, p. 164). Discipline, capable of constructing modes of thinking, feeling and acting, is required in classrooms – and outside them in all spaces of the school, such as where the playtime is spent, for example. This discipline is, therefore, a type of power that intends to transform individuals into objects of easy conduction (Brighente & Mesquida, 2011).

In this aspect, it is interesting to establish a dialogue between the intention to reduce the child's body to an object of obedience, as proposed by Foucault (2009), and the 'adult-centred' view that disregards the child's play activities for the benefit of the disciplinary activities (without body use) at school, as Sarmento (2007) indicates. In these two views, the intention is repeated: the devaluation of childhood culture and the valorization of obedience, of the so-called 'institutionalized formative dynamics' (Rodrigues & Reis, 2018, p. 25). Thus, it is essential that the culture of childhood be able to overcome this process that is secondary to it, being considered not only as a prescribed right, but also as a duty of school practice.

The following section will present the association among childhood, slum and children's bodies from the results obtained in this study. This association will allow a more in-depth reflection on how children living in slums have their childhood interpreted in a contradictory way by teachers who impose control of their bodies with child's play that they (adult educators) value most.

CHILD'S PLAY PRACTICES IN SCHOOL AND IN THE OPEN AREA OF THE SLUM

As indicated in the previous section of this text, participant observation was carried out in two days during playtime. In this, the children approximately seven years of age – belonging to the elementary school of a municipal education institution – played and were supervised by three educators. It is also important to point out that the educational institution is located in a small slum and, therefore, all the children of the school live in this slum or in its surroundings.

On the first day, the research focused on identifying the main child's play practices of the 23 children during the playtime, without any scheduled intervention. Boys (10 children) and girls (13 children) chose to divide into groups that did not mix, although there is a seemingly quiet relationship among boys and girls. Some boys played soccer in a very small area (less than $30m^2$), others exchanged cards for the Soccer World Cup album and two boys ran across the schoolyard in a child's play resembling the notorious 'police and thief', very common in Brazil. As for the girls, most of them played with the dolls L.O.L Surprises®, which two girls had taken to school; two others wore lipsticks and other make-up.

It was possible to see that the three educators observed the schoolyard with attention and that all of them tried to warn the students (mainly the boys) to avoid getting hurt or doing some damage to the school's yard areas. However, the pedagogical coordinator was more exalted and dedicated to censoring the actions of boys who practiced soccer and, especially, of the pair who played as 'police and thief', a game that 'a group of children, representing the police, goes out looking for other hidden children, who represent the bad guys' (Oliveira & Fux, 2014, p. 267). She reinforced her opposition to this activity with these following phrases: 'I don't like you to play this!', 'You know that playing that is wrong, okay?', 'Let's stop it!'. In spite of her devoted pursuit of disciplining the students, in constant vigilance (Foucault, 2009), at times she became distracted by the call of an educator and the boys managed to proceed with the game, almost hidden. The purpose of preventing the play of 'police and thief' presupposes the intention of the educator to disassociate the activities of children from actions that refer to marginality (Coelho, 2007).

Regarding the girls' plays, although they do not suffer from the misery of the educators, they deserve to be emphasized in the aspects that associate the option for certain activities, which value maternity, for example, to the detriment of others. For Whitaker (1995), play brings with it a perspective of sexist socialization, influenced by the adult universe. Thus, girls are encouraged to play in restricted spaces and at the same time practice tasks supposedly attributed to women, such as care for appearance and appreciation for motherhood, very present in contact with dolls. Meanwhile, boys are encouraged to play with more autonomy and in larger spaces, enabling the development of a better spatial orientation, in activities that require strength and agility.

The second day of observation was the observation of the play-child once again, which were very similar to those performed the previous day. There were 24 children: 11 boys and 13 girls. On this day, some interference was established by the researcher who questioned the children about child's play practices within the school and in the open slum spaces. This small talk happened at the end of playtime, with the permission of the class teacher, just before the students returned to the classroom.

The first question ('what do you most like to play when you are in school, during playtime?') had different answers among boys and girls – as was already expected by observation. The boys cited soccer, the practice of trading cards from the World Cup card album and other child's play that required movement and racing. The girls talked about their preferences in playing with their little dolls, and they liked to dance and also to talk. These male and female gender differences in child's play may presuppose a difference in the 'gender role according to the society and culture in which they are inserted' (Wanderlind et al., 2006, p. 264).

That same difference, among boys and girls, was also noted with the answers given to the second question: 'what do you most like to play with when you are not in school?' Several boys responded cheerfully about how much they enjoyed playing soccer, in a field near the slum, or dropping kites on the outskirts of their houses. Among the child's play performed by the girls out of school, dance and dolls/accessories were once again remembered as activities of interest to be practiced at home. They also remembered 'little house play' that involved fantasy and characters from children's films. This play is a very common child's play in Brazil. In this, girls assume, in an imaginary way (as in a play), the role of mother, father, children and other family members. An imaginary family can also be interpreted with the use of dolls.

It is interesting to note that while two girls indicated their preferences for little house play, one of the boys made a pout, showing disgust for this child's play. Once again, a gender distinction has been found for many of the child's play practices, with girls tending to focus more on domestic and affective performs, but boys enjoy more agitated child's play and more space exploration (Wanderlind et al., 2006).

An important exception concerns in 'hide-and-seek', a game in which 'a group hides from a child in order to dispute who is hidden for the longest time' (Oliveira & Fux, 2014, p. 256). According to the students, both boys and girls play hide-and-seek together, between the alleys of the slum. This is an example of a child's play that allows children, living in the slum, to experience all the space that is within their reach, identifying with it (Coelho, 2007). This information can also be corroborated by the researcher, responsible for collecting and interpreting the data presented in this research. In their slum walks, girls and boys are occasionally seen together in 'hide and seek' jokes. However, boys are often seen running around playing kites and playing soccer.

Another important exception is the use and appreciation that all children, from this research, demonstrated by the electronic games of the mobile devices. One of the girls mentioned: 'It's bad here (at school) because the directress forbade us to bring in cell phones. [...] In my house, I use yes (the cell phone). There's my mother's and my sister's. It's good!' Actually, since 2017, the use of any electronic device by the students in the areas of this school has been prohibited. However, the great appreciation of children for gaming also raises a concern: it is possible that activities involving greater social interaction and physical activity are less frequent when compared to virtual games and the use of apps, which the child doesn't interact (Santos, Simões, & Gonçalves, 2017).

Although the main focus of this study is the child's play practices and the reflections of the children about playing inside and outside the school, it is very convenient to present two moments that can demonstrate, again, the censorship practiced by educators, in the face of children's behaviour on this second day of observation. The first is the insistence of one of the educators (the teacher) to persuade the girls to stop playing with the L.O.L Surprises® dolls and opt for the old-fashioned 'jump rope' play. Even without being questioned by the researcher, about the reason for this interference, the teacher decided to verbalize: 'to waste time with crap is silly, because it is much better to do something more useful!' The teacher's speech and interference suggest that the children's desire was disrespected by the adult, since she didn't seek to know the reasons that led the children to choose that child's play and only imposed their opinion and action (Martins Filho, 2008).

The other moment when the children were again censured by the teacher during playtime can also be described as one of the most interesting situations in the whole observation. On this second day, the playtime was presented with a sound box that played funk songs, from the musical programming of the cell phone of one of the educators. Many children – especially the girls – played choreographies of well-known and recent songs. However, the excitement increased gigantically when the song 'Só quer Vrau'[3] was played. Most of the children knew melody and lyric with primacy. The animation was unanimous while the children sang and danced (mainly the girls) the song – which presents, in their lyric, the exaltation to the space of the slum, especially with the mention 'the way slum likes'.

Seeing the explicit excitement of the children, the pedagogical coordinator interrupted the reproduction of the music before its end and shouted to the professional of the secretary of the school: 'Oh God! Get something you can get these kids to hear! No such crap!' Immediately, the professional changed the songs played by her cell phone and everyone heard another song: gospel. Initially, the children complained about the change. Soon afterwards, however, they began to sing gospel music, which repeated the expression 'Lord Jesus' relentlessly.

It is important to emphasize that the lyric and choreography of 'Só quer Vrau' (as with most funk music) is, according to Lopes (2017, p. 2) marked by 'pornographic aesthetics, in which the female figure appears deprecated or sexually objectified'. However, again according to Lopes (2017), it is very important to note that funk is a musical rhythm that maintains a stance that subverts socially imposed standards and presents itself as an element of important cultural resistance for slum's residents.

This context suggests that the educator wanted to *protect* her students from the lyrics and their content, believing that the lyric and choreography of the song were inadequate for them. However, at the same time, it is also possible to suggest that the educator made the same interference as a way to control the children's bodies and make them obey their commands (Foucault, 2009). In view of the scenario that has been designed, with the substitution of funk music for gospel music, it is based on the belief that the attitude of the educator is more related to the control of the bodies and the attitudes of the children (and also to the prejudice with the funk music) than the children's shelter, protecting them from hearing inappropriate lyrics for their age group.

It is possible to state once again that this situation is important to promote thoughts about the teaching practices and the prejudices maintained by the educators when they work with students living in slums. Strategies to keep the children disciplined and disciplined bodies in school (including playtime) became consistent with the pedagogical practices consolidated by educators (Brighente & Mesquida, 2011). Therefore, it is convenient to analyze the repercussions of these strategies for the life of children in and out of school.

FINAL CONSIDERATIONS

The results of this study suggest that despite the similarity among child's play practices chosen by children in and out of school, slum spaces offer more freedom and autonomy so that children can, in fact, develop activities consistent with their real interests.

Most child's play practices chosen by boys are different from those preferred by girls. Boys opting to play with greater space exploration, while girls opted for activities with primarily in domestic settings. However, there are two exceptions: the hide-and-seek – practiced together by boys and girls – and the use of electronic games, available on mobile devices. Regarding electronic games, it is possible to consider that many children prefer solitary games of mobile devices when compared to interactive child's play practices without any digital resources.

Concerning the interference of educators in child's play practices, two situations were observed in which the children were censured by their teachers, when they judged the behaviour of the students as inadequate. These situations were suggestive of teacher bias and stigma as to the student's practices – especially when boys played 'police and thief' and girls danced funk. These are activities that, converted into child's play practices, interfere in the construction of the identities of children living in slums (Coelho, 2007).

Denying children's play can become a way of denying children's identities, especially when behaviours that value the control of children's bodies, by educators, are constantly reinforced. It is essential that children are not seen, in an adult perspective, as passive objects of socialization (Martins Filho, 2008).

Childhood in slums needs to be estimated in its large context and, for this to really happen, slum children need to have their child's play practices respected and valued by educators and other adults involved in their development.

NOTES

1. The expression 'child's play' describes all the plays practiced by the children, participating in this study, without being restricted to describing the most common childhood games.
2. In this text, it was chosen to designate 'slum' as synonymous with 'favela', a term very common in Brazil to characterize a set of precariously built and unpopular housing. However, the expression 'shanty town' can also be termed a synonym for 'favela'.
3. The Italian song 'Bella Ciao' meant the resistance of the Italian workers against the fascist regime of Mussolini, in the context of the Second World War (Antonicelli, 2004). This song was adapted into a popular Spanish series (Netflix®) in 2017 and, then, transformed into a funk parody in Brazil in 2018, named 'Só quer Vrau'. This parody was exhaustively reproduced in the Brazilian radios.

REFERENCES

Andrade, L. B. P. (2010). *Educação infantil: discurso, legislação e práticas institucionais*. São Paulo: Editora UNESP; São Paulo: Cultura Acadêmica. Retrieved from http://books.scielo.org/id/h8pyf/pdf/andrade-9788579830853-06.pdf. Accessed on August 29, 2018.

Antonicelli, L. (2004). Linguagem das músicas italianas em respeito à época. In: XX Jornada Gelne, João Pessoa. *Anais*... (pp. 1371–1386). Retrieved from http://gelne.com.br/arquivos/anais/gelne-2004/PDF/Leonardo%20Antonicelli.pdf. Accessed on January 8, 2019.

Bourdieu, P. (2002). *A dominação masculina*. Rio de Janeiro: Bertrand Brasil.

Brighente, M. F., & Mesquida, P. (2011). Michel Foucault: corpos dóceis e disciplinados nas instituições escolares. In X Congresso Nacional de Educação – Educere. Curitiba. *Anais*... pp. 2390-2403. Retrieved from http://educere.bruc.com.br/. Accessed on January 8, 2019.

Coelho, G. N. (2007). Brincadeiras na favela: a constituição da infância nas interações com o ambiente. In V. M. R. Vasconcellos & M. J. Sarmento (Orgs.), *Infância (in)visível* (pp.173–203). Araraquara, SP: Junqueira & Marin.

Dahlberg, G., Moss, P., & Pence, A. (2003). *Qualidade na educação da primeira infância: perspectivas pós-modernas*. Tradução Magda França Lopes. Porto Alegre: Artmed, 2003.

Foucault, M. (2009). *Vigiar e punir: nascimento da prisão*. Rio de Janeiro: Vozes.

Hasenbalg, C. (1997). O contexto das desigualdades raciais. In J. Souza (Org.), *Multiculturalismo e racismo: uma comparação Brasil - Estados Unidos* (Vol. 15, pp. 63–68). Brasília: Paralelo.

Longo, I. S. (2012). O estigma dos três ps: pobre, preto, da periferia: a visão de adolescentes da Comunidade Heliópolis. In: Colóquio Internacional Culturas Jovens - Afro-Brasil América: encontros e desencontros, São Paulo. *Anais*... Retrieved from: http://www.proceedings.scielo.br/pdf/cjaba/n1/17.pdf. Accessed on January 8, 2019.

Lopes, J. J. M. (2013). Geografia da Infância: contribuições aos estudos das crianças e suas infâncias. *Revista de Educação Pública*, Cuiabá, *22*(49), 283–294, may/aug. Retrieved from: www.periodicoscientificos.ufmt.br. Accessed on August 30, 2018.

Lopes, M. L. (2017). *Glamourosas: funk, feminismos e direito*. Trabalho de Conclusão de Curso – Pós-graduação Lato sensu em Gênero e Direito. Escola de Magistratura do Estado do Rio de Janeiro (EMERJ). Retrieved from: http://www.emerj.tjrj.jus.br/revistas/genero_e_direito/edicoes/1_2017/pdf/MarianaLoubackLopes.pdf. Accessed on January 8, 2019.

Lüdke, M., & André, M. E. D. A. (1986). *Pesquisa em educação: abordagens qualitativas*. São Paulo: EPU.

Martins Filho, A. J. (2008). Práticas de socialização entre adultos e crianças, e estas entre si, no interior da creche. *Pro-Posições*, *19*(1), jan./abr., 97–114. Retrieved from: http://www.scielo.br/pdf/pp/v19n1/a14v19n1.pdf. Access in: 08 jan. 2019.

Martins, G. (2018). *O sol na cabeça*. São Paulo: Companhia das Letras.

Oliveira, H. M., & Fux, J. (2014). Considerações psicanalíticas sobre os jogos de esconder: do puti ao esconde-esconde. *Ágora*, Rio de Janeiro, 17(2), 255–269. Retrieved from: http://www.scielo.br/pdf/agora/v17n2/07.pdf. Accessed on April 5, 2019.

Pereira, R. M. R. et al. (2005). Ladrões de sonhos e sabonetes: sobre os modos de subjetivação da infância na cultura do consumo. In S. J. Souza (Org.), *Subjetividade em questão: a infância como crítica da cultura* (pp. 99–116). Rio de Janeiro: 7 Letras.

Pérez, B. C., & Jardim, M. D. (2015). Os lugares da infância na favela: da brincadeira à participação. *Psicologia & Sociedade*, *27*(3), 494–504. Retrieved from: www.scielo.br/pdf/psoc/v27n3/1807-0310-psoc-27-03-00494.pdf. Accessed on August 30, 2018.

Perlman, J. E. (1977). *O mito da marginalidade: favelas e políticas no Rio de Janeiro*. Rio de Janeiro: Paz e Terra.

Rodrigues, R., & Reis, M. (2018). O lúdico e o corpo nos processos de construção de conhecimentos na escola. *Em Aberto*, *31*, 23–36. Retrieved from: http://emaberto.inep.gov.br/index.php/emaberto/article/view/3549. Accessed on April 5, 2019.

Santos, V. B., Simões, M. M., & Gonçalves, C. M. (2017). Os desafios de desenvolver-se na era digital. *Revista Científica Eletrônica de Psicologia*, *28*(1), 60–65, May. Retrieved from: http://faef.revista.inf.br. Accessed on January 8, 2019.

Sarmento, M. J. (2004). As culturas da infância nas Encruzilhadas da 2ª Modernidade. In M. J. Sarmento & A. Cerisara (Eds.), *Crianças e Miúdos: perspectivas sociopedagógicas da infância e educação* (pp. 9–34). Porto: Edições Asa.

Sarmento, M. J. (2007). Visibilidade social e estudo da infância. In V. M. R. Vasconcellos & M. J. Sarmento (Orgs.), *Infância (in)visível*. (pp. 25–52). Araraquara, SP: Junqueira & Marin.

Silva, E. M. P. (2014). *Representações socioespaciais da cidade de Cuiabá-MT, segundo crianças*. Dissertação (Mestrado em Educação) – Universidade Federal de Mato Grosso. Cuiabá, 2014, 247 fl. Retrieved from http://ri.ufmt.br/bitstream/1/290/1/DISS_2014_Eliza%20Moura%20Pereira%20da%20Silva.pdf. Accessed on August 30, 2018.

Tuan, Y.-F. (1980). *Topofilia: um estudo da percepção, atitudes e valores do meio ambiente.* São Paulo: Difel.

Tuan, Y.-F. (1983). *Espaço e lugar: a perspectiva da experiência.* São Paulo: Difel.

Wanderlind, F. et al. (2006). Diferenças de gênero no brincar de crianças pré-escolares e escolares na brinquedoteca. *Paidéia, 16*(34), 263–273. Retrieved from: http://www.scielo.br/pdf/paideia/v16n34/v16n34a14.pdf. Accessed on January 8, 2019.

Whitaker, D. C. A. (1995). Menino-Menina: sexo ou gênero? Alguns aspectos cruciais. In R. V. Serbino & M. A. R. L. Grande (orgs.), *A escola e seus alunos: estudos sobre a diversidade cultural* (pp. 31–52). São Paulo: EDUNESP.

ECONOMICALLY, CULTURALLY AND POLITICALLY DISADVANTAGED: PERSPECTIVES ON, AND EXPERIENCES OF, SOCIAL JUSTICE AMONGST WORKING-CLASS YOUTH IN MAINLAND SCOTLAND'S SMALLEST COUNCIL AREA THROUGH THE LENS OF NANCY FRASER

Charlotte McPherson

ABSTRACT

Young people are widely known to have poorer outcomes, social status and political representation than older adults. These disadvantages, which have come to be largely normalized in the contemporary context, can be further compounded by other factors, however, and are particularly amplified by coming from a lower social class background. An additional challenge for young people is associated with place, with youth who live in more remote and less urban areas at a higher risk of being socially excluded (Alston & Kent, 2009; Shucksmith, 2004) and/or to face complex and multiple barriers to employment and education than their urban-dwelling peers (Cartmel & Furlong, 2000).

Human Rights for Children and Youth: Sociocultural Differentiation, Resistance and Unity
Sociological Studies of Children and Youth, Volume 24, 193–220

ISSN: 1537-4661/doi:10.1108/S1537-466120190000024011

Drawing upon interviews and focus groups in a qualitative project with 16 young people and five practitioners, and using Nancy Fraser's tripartite theory of social justice, this paper highlights the various and interlocking disadvantages experienced by working-class young people moving into and through adulthood in Clackmannanshire, mainland Scotland's smallest council area.

Keywords: Young people; social justice; rurality; social class; youth transitions; place

INTRODUCTION

As members of the future generation, young people are subject to intense scrutiny and intervention. Governments and policymakers continue to idealize and prefer that young people make speedy, linear transitions between education, employment and training (EET), despite extensive research demonstrating that such trends are increasingly rare and incompatible with the more flexible, unpredictable nature of moving into and through adulthood in the contemporary context (Furlong, Woodman, & Wyn, 2011; Yates, Harris, Sabates, & Staff, 2011). Particular attention is devoted to those young people who are deemed most likely to become 'not in education, employment or training' (NEET), and who therefore present as 'risks' rather than 'assets' to the economy of today and tomorrow.

Typically, those that felt most likely to deviate from the idealized route into/through adulthood are young people from lower social class backgrounds, who often face a complex myriad of barriers in and around education and employment that are either absent or considerably ameliorated for more affluent youth (Duckworth & Schoon, 2012; Thompson, 2011). Working-class youth are significantly more likely to achieve no or low qualifications in school (Goodman & Burton, 2012; Strand, 2014), to drop out of school entirely (Maguire, 2013; Thompson, 2011), and to become and remain unemployed or underemployed than young people from more affluent backgrounds (MacDonald, 2009, 2011; Nayak, 2006).

In addition to social class, place has also been demonstrated to play an influential role in the transitions of young people. Specifically, research has found that young people who live in more rural, remote and less populated areas are at an enhanced risk of social exclusion, unemployment and disengagement from education and training as compared to youth who live in urban cities and towns (Abbott-Chapman, 2011; Corbett, 2007). These outcomes are often associated with there being fewer as well as narrower education and employment opportunities in these places, with limited access to qualify further and higher education (Irvin, Byun, Meece, & Farmer, 2012; Roscigno & Crowley, 2001), minimal availability of local jobs (Abbott-Chapman, 2011) and poor, fragmented or prohibitively expensive transport facilities to major urban centres, all disproportionately affecting youth (Farrington & Farrington, 2005; Meek, 2008).

However, while there has been an abundance of research on young people's transitions, the transitions of young people of low socioeconomic status (SES), of inner-city young people and of youth living in deeply rural or remote locations, there has been significantly less research exploring the lives and experiences of working-class youth who live in areas that are neither stereotypically rural or urban but fall somewhere ambiguously in between. In their research on youth unemployment in rural areas, Cartmel and Furlong (2000) acknowledged this problem, and adapted a typology originally developed by Stern and Turbin (1986) to differentiate between the four different rural sites under their analysis of youth unemployment in rural Scotland. There has been a tendency to simplify and homogenize non-urban areas, which encompass a broad variety of geographic situations, a problem which has been exacerbated by the lack of a clear definition surrounding the concept of 'rural' (Cartmel & Furlong, 2000).

Clackmannanshire, the case site for the current study, is best defined as both an 'urban fringe' area – 'in which employment is affected by proximity to more densely populated areas' (Cartmel & Furlong, 2000, p. 1) – and an 'ex-industrial' rural area, 'in which the withdrawal of manufacturing or extractive industries has declined significantly in recent years' (Cartmel & Furlong, 2000, p. 2). These traits help to distinguish Clackmannanshire from the more obviously or traditionally remote rural contexts of, for example, the Scottish Highlands or the Scottish Borders, while acknowledging its difference from urban hubs like Glasgow and Edinburgh. Indeed, that Clackmannanshire is difficult to place in normative categories of rural and urban, and that it is surrounded by major cities has meant that it has often been overlooked at the policy level, with a recent audit finding that Clackmannanshire was one of three Scottish council areas set to use up their cash reserves within three years in the wake of substantial cuts to their budget (Audit Scotland, 2017).

Equally missing from most research focused on young people's lives and journeys into/through adulthood is an engagement with issues of social justice. Notions of justice are typically invoked in research with young people when they are oriented towards their experiences of, and presence within, the criminal justice system (e.g. Johns, Williams, & Haines, 2017; Mendes, Baidawi, & Snow, 2014; Muncie, 2006), and the much more general, everyday understanding of justice as expressed in discourses of human rights is very rarely applied to youth. In this paper, I argue that this is highly problematic, given the acute vulnerability of many young people, and particularly those from low SES backgrounds and less populated or urban areas. Using Nancy Fraser's (1998) three-part model of social justice, I demonstrate that young people, and especially the low income and more rurally situated young people as in my study, are victims of injustice culturally and politically as well as economically, and that each dimension of injustice interlocks with and enables the other. Drawing upon qualitative interview data with 16 young people and 5 practitioners in Clackmannanshire, this chapter demonstrates the role of place, social class and age in their experiences of social (in)justice and argues that urgent attention is required to counter these problems at the levels of both policy and practice.

YOUTH TRANSITIONS AND SOCIAL CLASS

Most research and policymaking around youth has coalesced around the terminology and notion of 'youth transitions', with an extensive literature focused on the pathways taken by young people between education and employment (Aaltonen, 2013; Serracant, 2012). Recently, it has become widely acknowledged that transitions are not straightforward, universal or singular, but rather can be multiple, fluid, overlapping, complex and unpredictable from person to person (Punch, 2015; Woodman & Wyn, 2011). However, the main critique levelled at youth transitions research is its under-acknowledgement of the structural forces that continue to complicate and constrain many young people's trajectories from 'youth' to 'adulthood' (Harris, 2015; Woodman, 2009). In their rush to correct the largely deterministic and reductive constructions of young people as advanced in much previous youth research, some scholars have arguably gone too far in casting young people, regardless of their backgrounds, as agentic and emancipated from social structure in the contemporary, late modern context, obscuring the constrained nature of this agency and the continued vulnerability of working-class youth in the process (Cote & Bynner, 2008; Walther, 2006).

Specifically, young people of low SES have an enhanced risk of social exclusion, long-term unemployment and early disengagement from education, all of which place major constraints on their adult outcomes and cause governments and policymakers major concern (Bivand, 2012; Gregg & Tominey, 2004). They are more likely to live in deprived neighbourhoods, to have poorer health and to attend under-resourced schools, with implications for their attainment, development and 'employability' in the neoliberal sense of amassing credentials and experience that are desirable for employers seeking high-skilled workers (Benjet et al., 2012; Bynner & Parsons, 2002). Low SES youth also come from, and typically still live in, deprived households, where it is more likely that their parents will have low or no qualifications or employment themselves, and where they may be living in challenging conditions (Ashby & Schoon, 2010; Cavanagh & Fomby, 2012).

Young people of low SES also fare significantly worse than their more affluent peers in terms of employment, where they are the least likely to be hired, the most likely to be fired and are the most likely to experience in-work poverty and underemployment because of their overrepresentation in precarious sectors with poor pay and working conditions (Biletta & Eisner, 2007; Krestos, 2010). Further, according to MacDonald (2009, p. 173), because of profound transformations to the labour market, and in particular the decline of traditional industry and job security, working-class young people are overwhelmingly engaged 'in precarious, poor work [that] *reflects* and *adds* to class-based disadvantage'. While working-class youth's, and young people's more generally, increasingly marginal position in the contemporary labour market has been framed and effectively justified by some as a temporary and natural predicament, resolved by the young person simply maturing into adulthood and working their way 'up' a hierarchy of increasingly secure jobs (Auer & Cazes, 2003; Quintini, Martin, & Martin, 2007), MacDonald (2009, p. 174) argues that 'precarious, poor work has now become constitutive of lasting economic marginality and emblematic of longer-term processes of downward social mobility', which disproportionately disadvantages youth of low SES.

YOUTH TRANSITIONS IN A RURAL CONTEXT

In the last 20 years, increasing attention has been paid to the differences between 'urban' and 'rural' contexts when it comes to youth outcomes and experiences. This spike in interest largely derives from the recognition that young people in rural contexts face amplified as well as altogether different challenges and factors when transitioning into and through adulthood versus those who live in more urban areas (Alston & Kent, 2009;Farrugia, Smyth, & Harrison, 2014a; Panelli, Punch, & Robsen, 2007). Heightened scrutiny around young rural lives has also occurred in response to critiques of the 'metrocentric' focus of youth studies, where there has been an overemphasis on the experiences and transitions of urban, inner-city youth (Ansell & Van Blerk, 2007; Farrugia, 2014). This skewed focus has also served to prioritize and make ubiquitous urban lives and experiences, and to consign rurality to the past, where it is conflated with notions of traditional, stagnant and fundamentally pre-modern forms of social life (Cloke, 2005; Farrugia, 2014; Thomas, Lowe, Fulkerson, & Smith, 2011).

As a result of this overemphasis on urban young lives, comparatively little is known about rural youth, who are often either simplistically subsumed within this metrocentric focus or are marginalized and overlooked entirely. As more recent research has begun to address this gap in knowledge (e.g. Haukanes, 2013; Leyshon, 2008) and the sociology of youth has become increasingly 'spatialised' (Alston & Kent, 2009; Farrugia, 2014), the important role of place in young people's transitions has emerged. Like most young people born since the 1980s, young people in rural locations have been impacted by the same seismic social and economic shifts that have transformed youth transitions for most young people, whereby the labour market has deindustrialized, destabilized and fragmented and social life is felt to be characterized by risk and choice rather than certainty and predictability (Cuervo & Wyn, 2012; Jentsch & Shucksmith, 2017). In the last few decades, there have been significant changes to labour markets in the minority world that have impacted everyone, but particularly young workers. Deindustrialization and the concomitant rise of the service sector has led to an intense casualization of the labour market, where labour, and particularly youth labour, is devalued and unstable, with it now increasingly the norm for (mostly young) individuals to maintain multiple jobs, involuntarily work on part-time or fixed-term contracts, and to cycle in and out of unemployment and underemployment (Fenton & Dermott, 2006).

This shift from traditional industry and patterns of working to the precarious service sector has been felt particularly significantly in the rural context, however, with youth in these areas typically dependent on work in agriculture or small, local manufacturing outfits for employment, both of which are sectors that have seriously declined in recent decades (Cartmel & Furlong, 2000; Thissen, Fortuijn, Strijker, & Haartsen, 2010). There are considerably fewer employment opportunities open to young people in rural communities than are generally available in urban areas (Cuervo, 2011; Cuervo & Wyn, 2012), and this has resulted in not only higher levels of youth unemployment in some rural places relative to urban ones, but also in high levels of out-migration or 'brain drain' (Corbett & Forsey, 2017; Forsey, 2015). Research exploring young people leaving their rural communities for urban areas has revealed that this exodus is largely driven by a lack of local opportunities (Alloway, Gilbert, Gilbert, & Muspratt, 2004; Cuervo, 2014). Other research has found that young people are also motivated to leave by their construction of rural environments as socially and culturally isolated and inferior to the lifestyle they perceive to be available in metropolises (Cuervo, 2014).

In addition to often having fewer employment opportunities open to young people, rural areas are also associated with reduced and more complicated access to quality further and higher education. Access to post-compulsory education (PCE) is not inevitable nor equal for young people, and much of a young person's access to these opportunities is heavily patterned by both class and place. There are widely acknowledged barriers to participation in PCE for young people of low SES, for whom the considerable financial costs associated with such a decision may be prohibitively or impossibly expensive (Raffe & Croxford, 2015). Participation in PCE is further complicated by the matter of place, with young people living in rural areas less likely to have access to quality further or higher education due to tertiary institutions typically being situated in more urban contexts and requiring substantial, complex and/or expensive commutes (Abbott-Chapman, 2011; Alloway & Dalley-Trim, 2009; Stewart & Abbott-Chapman, 2011).

The limited, pricey and poor availability and connectivity of public transport in rural spaces has been widely commented upon in the literature (Mackett & Thoreau, 2015; Meek, 2008), where it has increasingly been delineated as a key aggravating factor in the social exclusion of rural youth. Moreover, where educational institutions are locally proximate, they are typically under-funded and can be more limited in their offering compared to courses and institutions delivered in urban settings. For example, in Clackmannanshire's only PCE college, provision is highly regional in that courses are limited in their focus on construction, salon skills, care work, and access and progression (read: employability) (Forth Valley College, 2018). Finally, rural youth are less likely to be accepted into, or apply for, PCE courses due to both inadequate school qualifications or because of the low status of their schools, but also because they are less likely than their more affluent peers to be versed in the forms of social and cultural capital that make 'playing the game' of PCE remotely possible (Bathmaker, Ingram, & Waller, 2013).

While it is important to be careful not to submit to simplistic, pejorative binaries that conflate rurality with disadvantage and urbanity with advantage, it is equally important to acknowledge and highlight the often amplified disadvantage that exists in rural areas, and how this can have immediate and long-term effects on the youth who live there (Cuervo, 2014; Wierenga, 2009). This is particularly important when considering the transitions of working-class young people, who are especially vulnerably proximate to the frontiers and effects of socio-structural change (Cote & Bynner, 2008; Evans, 2007), and whose vulnerability in this and other regards is rarely considered in research or policy in proportion with its scale and enduring impact.

YOUNG PEOPLE AND SOCIAL JUSTICE

This study aims to address this gap by adopting a social justice lens. Social justice is necessarily broad and complex, as well as arbitrary and fiercely contested. Like all that is socially constructed, justice is not a universal, fixed notion and is not evenly experienced by everyone. Rather, conceptions, applications and responses to it vary widely across time and space, acknowledging and protecting certain groups or actions in one place or time, while evading or overlooking others. In its simplest form, justice is about giving people what they deserve (Bragues, 2006), throwing up complex questions about 'what people are due and why' (Sandel, 2009, p. 19). Scholars of social justice examine the role of, among other things, the economy, political structures and other institutions of power in shaping how justice or injustice is meted out and experienced, and by whom, where and at what point in history (Charmaz, 2011).

The relevance of such an approach, and its focus on the connections between power structures, individuals and ideas of virtue and 'deservingness', for young people, who are typically low on power, status and representation, and who are routinely negatively socially constructed as variously undeserving, is clear. There has been a surprising lack of in-depth engagement with social justice frameworks within youth studies. While social justice arguments are routinely advanced by youth scholars and practitioners, who highlight and condemn the oppression and structural disadvantage of young people, in-depth theoretical discussions of youth and social justice are relatively scarce compared to research on the lives and experiences of more recognized minority groups (LGBTQIA + individuals, women, ethnic minorities, the disabled, and so on).

There are a few exceptions, however, with Hernan Cuervo (2014) heavily focused on social justice in his research with rural young people in Australia. Using notions of equality and inequality as a proxy for justice, Cuervo (2014) not only highlights rural youth's constrained access to opportunities, but also critiques the neoliberal emphasis on personal rather than social responsibility for achieving equality, pointing to the powerful role of structural forces in the young participants' disadvantage which fell far beyond their control. Most work, however, has drawn attention to how young people experience injustice in their interactions with the criminal justice system (Hurst & Frank, 2000; Murphy, 2015).

More recently, justice has been framed generationally in youth studies, with a growing body of research focused on perceptions of justice between generations (McKee, 2012; Woodman & Wyn, 2015a, 2015b). As noted earlier, there have been profound changes to the nature of youth transitions in recent decades. A complicated nexus of economic, societal and political shifts has made transitions into and through adulthood more complex for young people, who, in the last 30 years, 'have slumped from being a well-remunerated cohort able to buy property, settle down and start families, to being the poor relation of society' (Malik & Barr, 2016). Young people's struggles to buy homes, attain job security, start families, contribute to good pensions, and amass savings has seriously disturbed the notion that has historically defined British society and social mobility, which is that succeeding generations should, and do, outperform previous ones, producing research which foregrounds a distinctly justice-oriented approach (Hoolachan, McKee, Moore, & Soaita, 2017; Ng, Lyons, & Schweitzer, 2017). In the main, however, there has been a significant lack of work exploring young people's access to, and perceptions of, social justice, outside of the criminal justice system. There have been even fewer studies that have adopted this approach when exploring young lives in a rural context, which research has widely indicated to often be a challenging environment in which to transition into and through adulthood.

NANCY FRASER'S TYPOLOGY OF SOCIAL JUSTICE

Social justice claims have historically been associated with matters of *distribution*, and the notion that societies distribute their most prized assets – income, wealth, opportunities and resources – unfairly (Sandel, 2009). In her approach to social justice, however, Nany Fraser argues that, in line with various socio-structural shifts, this unilateral focus on distribution no longer applies and is no longer adequate when conceptualizing and measuring social justice. Instead, she proposes that social justice needs to be considered as three-dimensional, encompassing the original structural focus on redistribution, cultural issues of recognition and misrecognition, and, thirdly, a political consideration of representation and participation (Fraser, 1998, 2000, 2007).

The first two pillars in Fraser's theory of social justice are *redistribution* and *recognition*. As noted, historical and contemporary discussions of social justice have tended to emphasize the problem of 'maldistribution', where there is an unequal and uneven distribution of a society's opportunities, resources and assets, leaving some highly advantaged and others unjustly disadvantaged. Recently, however, Fraser argues that this historical, enduring fight for distributive justice has been increasingly accompanied by a consideration of *recognition*. These justice claims prioritise individuals and groups being treated equally and given the same rights and respect as one another, where the goal is to sustain a 'difference-friendly world, where assimilation to majority or dominant cultural norms is no longer the price of equal respect' (Fraser, 1998, p. 3).

In the case of this second and more cultural dimension, justice hinges upon being appropriately recognized; your individual or group identity being culturally acknowledged and given equal respect as that of others. By extension, injustice here occurs when a group or individual is *misrecognised*; their identity or their socioeconomic characteristics are not understood or appreciated, and are culturally devalued in a way that prevents them from accessing broader social justice. Fraser (1998) argues that, in recent decades, the original emphasis on the egalitarian quest of redistribution has shifted more towards a focus on injustices of recognition, misrecognition, with increasing attention devoted to improving the cultural standing and rights of, in particular, minority groups.

Despite her considering them in symbiosis, Fraser (1998, p. 4) notes that the tendency has been to perceive these two realms and problems of social justice – redistribution and recognition – as practically and intellectually distinct from one another, leading to 'effectively [being] presented with what is constructed as an either/or choice'. According to Fraser, these are false binaries, which present skewed and inevitably incomplete accounts of two equally important and heavily interlinked dimensions of justice. The presence of both is required to achieve social justice in the contemporary context where cultural traits and perceptions of 'difference' can have a significant bearing on how a society distributes its resources. Simplistic, dichotomous understandings of both the politics of redistribution and the politics of recognition fail to account for the nuances within and between them, and the implications of these nuances for social justice (Fraser, 1998).

Joining redistribution and recognition as the third and final pillar in Fraser's typology of social justice is *representation.* Within this dimension, injustice arises as a result of certain individuals or groups being denied the right to political representation, participation or voice within their society, which Fraser (2008, p. 278) declares to be a fundamental 'matter of social belonging'. Fraser's discussion of political injustice, or *misrepresentation*, probes why and how some groups are denied the ability to effectively participate in wider society or to express their politics or voice. While the dimension of representation, which could also be termed participation in that it not only refers to a group's representation by others but also to their ability to represent themselves, came to Fraser's work later than redistribution and recognition, it is envisaged as equally critical to the achievement of social justice:

> [...] no claim for justice can avoid presupposing some notion of representation, explicit or implicit [...] representation is always already inherent in all claims for redistribution and recognition. The political dimension is implicit in, indeed required by, the grammar of the concept of justice. Thus, no redistribution or recognition without representation. (Fraser, 2008, p. 282)

Crucially, then, according to Fraser, efforts to redress injustice for virtually any oppressed group will either fail or remain incomplete if attention is not paid to *both* a politics of recognition and a politics of redistribution, as well as to issues of representation and participation. The three are intertwined and co-dependent. Culture is a legitimate terrain of struggle, where injustice is legitimated and interwoven with economic inequality (Fraser, 2000). Moreover, a lack of visibility, voice and representation causes groups to 'cease to exist', to experience 'political death', and significantly constrains opportunities for, and the feasibility of, progress towards social justice. Without all three, 'parity of participation' in social life, Fraser's ultimate yardstick of social justice, is impossible. Parity of participation, which Fraser describes as the 'normative core' of her theory, requires a society to foster social conditions that enable all adult members within it to engage with one another as peers (Fraser, 1998). For this to occur,

Fraser (1998, p. 5) argues, two conditions, involving all three of her analytical dimensions, must first be in place:

> First, the distribution of material resources must be such as to ensure participants' independence and voice. Second, the institutionalised cultural patterns of interpretation and evaluation express equal respect for all participants and ensure equal opportunity for achieving social esteem. Both these conditions are necessary for participatory parity. Neither alone is sufficient.

Fraser's theory of social justice has been widely applied to many different groups and in many different fields, including in education (Keddie, 2012), social work (Holscher, 2014), and disability rights (Knight, 2015). However, it is yet to be applied, in-depth or in totality, to young people. This omission, and the lack of a social justice focus in youth policy and some fields of research more generally, is likely due to the lack of acknowledgement of young people as a vulnerable, oppressed group. Indeed, there has been a deliberate rejection of the use of notions and terminologies of vulnerability around youth, with policymakers and politicians keen to emphasize the agency, and thus the responsibility, of young people rather than their vulnerability (Gray, 2007; Yates & Roulstone, 2013). However, in line with Catherine Robinson (2018), I argue that young people, and particularly those of low SES can, and in many cases should, be considered highly vulnerable, living under a set of often chaotic and damaging conditions associated with both youth and poverty that need to be better understood rather than ignored.

Detracting attention away from this vulnerability, which I suspect to be part of the reason why there is a lack of justice-focused research on young people, is to turn a blind eye to the harsh realities of many young people's lives. Adopting a social justice lens, which focuses on highlighting not only the presence or absence of injustice, but the nuances within it, is an important and underused tool in the sociology of youth's repertoire, and one that can draw attention, without apology, to the challenges facing one of society's most disadvantaged, and most important, groups. This study applies all three pillars of Nancy Fraser's social justice framework to interpret and analyze the experiences and perspectives of working-class youth as they move into and through adulthood in an overlooked rural area of Scotland.

THE STUDY

This chapter is based on part of a broader qualitative project that was conducted with 42 young people of low SES in Scotland in 2017–2018, which focused on a comparison between the transitions and perspectives of young people in both an urban and a rural Scottish context. However, this paper is concerned exclusively with the experiences of the 16 rural participants from this study, who all lived in disadvantaged neighbourhoods within Clackmannanshire, mainland Scotland's smallest council area. The participants were recruited to the study through either gatekeepers (schools and youth organizations) or word of mouth, with the only sampling stipulations guiding recruitment being that the young person be between the ages of 14 and 30, allowing for a broad range of experiences and stages of youth, and that they live in one of several listed neighbourhoods of deprivation as identified from Scottish Index of Multiple Deprivation (SIMD) data. Of the 16 participants, nine were male and seven were female, and the mean age of the sample was 21, with the youngest participant aged 15 and the oldest aged 29. In addition to young people, five relevant practitioners were also recruited to this study – a guidance teacher, a council employee, and three employees of local youth organizations – in order to gain their insight into the nature, and potential challenges, associated with journeying into and through early adulthood in rural Scotland.

Fieldwork consisted of in-depth, semi-structured interviews and three focus groups. Most of the interviews were carried out in person in Clackmannanshire, but a minority were conducted online over a social media messenger service at the participants' request. All three of the focus groups were conducted as online 'group chats', also at the convenience of the participants. While the focus groups were focused on broader themes of youth justice and injustice, as well as on what young people feel is needed to assist the current cohort of youth in their transitions into/through adulthood, the interviews engaged with more detailed, personal accounts of social justice in how it has been distributed to, or how it has eluded, the participants. The 5 practitioners were all interviewed in person. All participants have been provided with pseudonyms in this paper for anonymity.

As discussed, this study focuses on the experiences and perspectives of young residents of Clackmannanshire, a rural council area of approximately 61 square miles with a population of 51,500 that is located in the countryside and hills of Central Scotland. For a rural location, it is reasonably well connected to major cities and roads, bordering the council areas near Stirling, Fife and Perth & Kinross, as well as being in commuting distance of Scotland's two biggest cities, Edinburgh and Glasgow. With respect to Cartmel and Furlong's (2000) adapted typology of rurality in Scotland, Clackmannanshire can therefore be described as an 'urban fringe' area, in that it is geographically situated closely to busier and more populated areas. This close proximity is widely perceived to be an asset to rural communities, with urban fringe areas found to possess higher numbers of labour market opportunities than other, more traditionally remote rural contexts (Cartmel & Furlong, 2000).

However, Clackmannanshire can also be categorized under another dimension of Cartmel and Furlong's typology, as an 'ex-industrial rural area', which are associated with having the *lowest* quantity, quality and availability of job and education opportunities for young people. Ex-industrial rural areas are so-defined because their labour markets have suffered significantly from the impact of deindustrialization in recent decades. This is highly applicable in the case of Clackmannanshire, which was historically a hub for a range of traditional manufacturing and industry, spanning from weaving to ship-building. As these industries have declined or folded altogether, the retail and service sector, characterized by precariousness, low pay and low status, has replaced them as the main source of income and jobs, greatly reducing the quantity and quality of jobs available in the local area.

NOMIS (2018a) data reports a job density rate of just 0.50 for Clackmannanshire, which means that there are 0.50 jobs available per resident aged 16–64, which falls below the Scottish (0.80) and UK (0.84) averages. This is also reflected in the out-of-work benefits claimant count figures for Clackmannanshire, where 8.1% of claimants are aged 16–24, over double the Scottish and UK averages, and 8.7% are aged between 18 and 21 (NOMIS, 2018a, 2018b). To put these figures into perspective, in Edinburgh, an hour's drive away from Clackmannanshire, only 1.1% of benefits claimants are aged between 18 and 24, an eighth of the figure in Clackmannanshire, and far below the Scottish and UK averages (NOMIS, 2018b). In terms of education, there are three secondary schools and just one further education college in Clackmannanshire, with the closest university located in Stirling, roughly eight miles away. Finally, with regard to deprivation, five areas in Clackmannanshire fall into the 5% most deprived areas in Scotland according to the SIMD map, with most of these neighbourhoods clustering in and close by to the town of Alloa, which is where most of my participants were recruited from.

While this research is focused on social justice, the complexity and ambiguousness of this term and concept meant that it had to be explored in different and sometimes indirect ways in the study. This included using terminologies of fairness as a proxy and, less directly, by probing different aspects of the young participants' experiences for evidence of possible justice and injustice. As a result, much of the initial discussion with participants was centred around their current and previous EET status, their long-term aspirations, their confidence or lack of confidence in the future, and whether they felt supported by, or identified as participating members of, wider society. This chapter will now discuss some key findings that emerged from the research around the overlapping themes of social justice, rurality and social class. It will consider each of Nancy Fraser's three pillars of social justice in turn, with the role of both place and social class considered throughout.

INJUSTICES OF MALDISTRIBUTION: UNEMPLOYED, UNDEREMPLOYED AND OUT OF OPPORTUNITIES

Most of the participants possessed very low levels of educational qualifications and work experience, and had quite poor structural outcomes, with five NEET, three long-term unemployed and four underemployed on part-time or insecure job contracts, with only one of the participants in permanent, full-time employment. Two were current high school students and a further two were engaged in PCE at the local college.

The participants seemed to put their position in – or out of – the labour market down to a combination of factors, much of which they felt were out of their control. Most significantly, many cited a concrete lack of opportunities in Clackmannanshire, in terms of both education and employment, as the reason behind their difficulties. As noted previously, Clackmannanshire's labour market has transformed since deindustrialization, resulting in not only a sharp decrease in the availability of jobs, but also in their perceived quality and status. Faye, an employee of a youth volunteering organization, described Clackmannanshire's labour market as being 'a shadow of its former self', and felt that the decline of traditional industry and job quality in the area was a 'real challenge for young people in poor families'.

It is worth underlining that low job availability and quality is a problem that is not limited to Clackmannanshire, and much has been written about how working-class jobs have changed since deindustrialization. In his work, Roberts (2012) traces the intergenerational decline in job quality, availability and pay experienced by working-class youth to the deindustrialization of local and national economies since the 1970s, which eradicated swathes of relatively skilled, secure and higher paid jobs from the labour market (Goos & Manning, 2003). What constitutes a working-class job today – a customer service worker or cleaner, for example – is less likely to be able to protect a person, or household, from poverty than the occupations previously available to early school leavers or those with typically low qualifications and capital (Birdwell, Gist, & Margo, 2011; Roberts, 2012). As a result, young people with low skills, qualifications and resources are finding it significantly more difficult to gain and sustain a meaningful foothold in the labour market or, by extension, to attain economic security and independence.

Many of the participants were in desperate financial straits. Steven, 25, had been unemployed on and off for almost seven years and had literally no access to money at the time of interview, having just been sanctioned by the job centre for being late to an appointment. His back story was a familiar one for many of my participants, beginning with a difficult home life, followed by a challenging and ultimately unproductive school career and leaving school at 16, with very little qualifications. For Steven, this was followed by a year of unemployment, before he was taken on as an informal apprentice by the friend of a neighbour, who taught him basic skills in construction and carpentry, and paid him a small wage. After a year and a half of this arrangement, Steven's neighbour's friend told him that he could no longer afford to keep him on, but helped him apply for an entry level engineering course at a local college. Steven was doing well at the course, but his girlfriend found out that she was pregnant a few months in and he dropped out, with the view to finding work to help pay for the baby. A job never materialized and he has been unemployed ever since, unable to return to college because of the money he owes them on the incomplete course. Steven described feeling like he was stuck in a limbo, with no idea how to get out:

> I literally apply for jobs for hours and you just hear nothing back. At first I was doing it every day, but now there's not enough jobs to keep that up even. But I do look every day and it's always the same, like, cleaning jobs sometimes but no information on the hours or the pay, but you know it'll be shit, or jobs that are far away, and I can't obviously because of my wee son, or jobs that are way too, like, advanced, and I can't go get the qualifications for them because I'm in debt to the college already. So, what do I do?

Steven's experiences of EET after school hint at the difficulties young people of low SES backgrounds can have in attaining distributive justice. They are also a reminder of the continued influence of structural forces, including social class and economic inequality, on how the lives and outcomes of young people in vulnerable situations are stratified, despite rhetoric – and research – that increasingly foregrounds the existence and possibility of agency over structure in youth contexts, and which argues that education is a meritocracy that levels the playing field.

Those participants who *did* have jobs at the time of the study were almost all underemployed. Underemployment occurs when there is a mismatch between the job a person holds and their human capital, expectations and/or preferences (Peiro, Hernandez, & Ramos, 2015). This mismatch can be based on an employee being over-qualified for their job, working in a job that is irrelevant to their training and experience, or, as was the most common case in this study, comes down to being involuntarily employed in a part-time, temporary or otherwise intermittent capacity when you in fact wish and need to work full-time. As economies have started to recover since the 2008 global financial recession, governments have been keen to celebrate rising employment rates. However, hidden in these statistics is the *nature* of employment that people are increasingly engaging in, and particularly young people, who are highly overrepresented in insecure, poorly paid sectors and jobs that feature little training or prospects of progress (Bivand, 2012; EY, 2016).

Another common contemporary labour market experience for young people, and particularly those of low SES, is 'churning', which refers to the increasingly common experience of moving between unemployment and underemployment (MacDonald, 2009; Roberts, 2012). Underemployment and churning between it and unemployment was evident in many of the participants' experiences in this study. Heather, 17, who worked on a zero hours contract in a local café, described the unsettlingly erratic nature of her employment:

> I never know whether I'm working or not. Like, last week I got 4 hours, the week before that it was 20, like, I don't get it. I can't plan anything. I just literally have to wait for them to phone me, sometimes on the day they want me to show up[...] I was going to quit but I've realised this is basically all there is now, because my last job was like this too.

One of the older participants, Leigh, 26, described her lengthy and fragmented (under)employment since leaving school ten years ago at the age of 16. She described having 12 periods of unemployment and nine jobs during this time frame, with her employment typically very poorly paid and fixed-term. Since 2015, she had been relying on employment agencies to find her work as she was having no luck in the open market. While the agencies had managed to place her in several jobs, they were all temporary, poorly paid and unpredictable in terms of the number of hours required and where the jobs were located geographically. In her current temporary role in a bingo hall, Leigh had to commute to Stirling by train, which often left her cash- and time-poor.

The importance of public transport as a deliverer of, or barrier to, the inclusion and well-being of rural young people of low SES has been acknowledged in the literature (Mackett & Thoreau, 2015; Meek, 2008; Shucksmith, 2004), where it has increasingly been framed as a key factor in the social exclusion of working-class and/or rural youth. The issue of public transport was raised by several of the participants as a challenge of living in a rural area like Clackmannanshire without a car. The public transport was described as expensive, inefficient and confusing by several of the young people, while all of the practitioners raised it as a serious concern given the lack of local jobs available. Jane, who worked with youth in the Ochills area of Clackmannanshire expressed serious concerns about public transport in the area:

> It is rudimentary at best. We may have the train line up and running, which is great, but bear in mind that a lot of our young people don't live in Alloa, they live further out than that, and need to get little regional buses into Alloa before they do anything else, and this is the worry. These buses, they're expensive, unreliable, they're infrequent, they stop early[...] If we are going to expect our young people to go out of Clacks for work, we need to help them make that possible.

Indeed, a number of the participants described being actively encouraged and expected to seek work and education outside of Clackmannanshire, in what is an echo of Michael Corbett's (2007) research, *Learning to Leave*, which found that, instead of encouraging and establishing local opportunities and engagement, rural educators often teach their students to leave their rural homes for urban centres, implying their communities have nothing to offer them. Several of the participants had this experience in school, where teachers would encourage them to start planning a life outside of Clackmannanshire because of the lack of local opportunities available for young people. Moreover, this approach appeared to extend beyond the classroom, with participants mentioning its prevalence in their interactions with some job centre staff, career advisors and their relatives. Keith, 16, and his friend, Kian, also 16, had recently left school, and were keen to find an apprenticeship in a construction trade. When they mentioned this to their career advisor upon leaving school, they were advised to leave Clackmannanshire if they wanted to find work.

Keith and Kian were confused by, and actively resisted, the notion that they should leave Clackmannanshire in order to have a successful life. This was reflected in other participants' testimonies. Finlay, 27, had been unemployed for 4 years, and had been repeatedly admonished, and occasionally sanctioned, for declining to consider jobs outside of Clackmannanshire. Finlay, like several other participants, was keen to emulate the working lives of his parents, who had been employed in local, traditional industries. The participants seemed to mourn for a time and a labour market now largely past, measuring the nature and limited amount of opportunities open to them against the very different set of opportunities open to the previous generation. Joe, 24, who had been intermittently unemployed and underemployed for two years felt passionately that young people today were expected to work in low status, low wage jobs without complaint:

> Why shouldn't we want more? You know, I got in shit for saying I didn't want to be a cleaner the other week at the job centre, but was my dad ever asked to be a cleaner? No, he was doing proper, like, manual labour, so was my granddad with the ships [...] Nowadays you struggle to even get a crap job in McDonald's or something. Nah, it's not fair, it's not right.

Many of the participants felt strongly that they were the victims of intense distributive injustice or maldistribution. They attributed their poor outcomes to factors outside of their control, including the core lack of job or education opportunities in the area; the poor quality of existing opportunities; and to the prohibitively expensive and inefficient public transport system connecting them to opportunities elsewhere. As suggested in emerging literature with youth on generations, much of this perceived injustice was framed through a generational lens, with participants feeling strongly that their parents and previous generations had more and better opportunities when they were young than they do now, despite their social class backgrounds, and that they were not expected to have to leave their communities to find work, education or training as they are today. Indeed, the issues facing many young people today were clearly amplified for these participants by an intersection between their social class and their rurality.

INJUSTICES OF MISRECOGNITION: OVERLOOKED, MISUNDERSTOOD AND DEVALUED

Disadvantaged young people are the subjects of powerful discourses of 'problem youth' (Egan, Neary, Keenan, & Bond, 2013), which are perpetuated and sustained by their depiction in political rhetoric and the media as troublemaking no-hopers in need of strict regimes of social control (Neary, Egan, Keenan, Lawson, & Bond, 2013). These narratives give rise to powerful fears that young people of low SES today, who are more likely to struggle to access education and employment, will become anti-social, economically inactive adults tomorrow. As noted, young people of low SES are thus often the focal point for much scrutiny and concern, whether from the state via interventions in their EET, or via their characterization as 'folk devils' by the media (Pickard, 2014). As a result, young people, and especially those of low SES, typically possess very low social status.

Many of the participants described being keenly aware of the poor social status associated with being young and of low SES, with some arguing that they felt it played a direct role in their outcomes. Kylie, 21, a cleaner employed on a casual basis, described feeling stereotyped and pigeonholed by both her school and staff at the job centre:

> I swear, they hear your accent or know where you're from and they change. Like, I mind at high school when I said I wasn't sure what I wanted to do yet, they'd push me towards like the supermarkets and that, not even giving me a chance [...] Now with the job centre and that, they just do the same as in school. They never bother, they just chuck you into anything to get you off the books, and they wouldn't do that if I was from a different area or older or that.

Joanna, 29, felt that she had been stigmatized and brushed aside because of her youth and social class, claiming that she was actively discouraged from trying to access further or higher education by her teachers, and told instead to go straight into employment in retail and services. After 13 years of leaving school,

Joanna is finally pursuing higher education through an access to university course run at the local college for mature students, but she is still angry about how she was underestimated and overlooked as a younger person.

Many of the younger participants described feeling stigmatized and stereotyped by teachers, local residents and employers because of their age and social class. For Jason, 22, the low cultural status attributed to youth of low SES was most clearly obvious in the solutions prescribed to address the structural disadvantage described in the previous section. Jason, who had been NEET for a year since finishing an entry level course in carpentry and joinery at college, described being sent to the same employability skills course at college twice by the job centre, where they were lectured about hygiene, spelling and punctuality, and no mention was made of the lack of jobs available in the local area.

For Jason, this was a highly patronizing and ultimately unproductive experience, but one that he felt he was marshalled into because, in his words, young people 'have no choice' and are 'blamed for everything', chiming with Crisp and Powell's (2016) assertion that young people are increasingly compelled to believe that they are the problem and not the labour market. In the present context, unemployment is increasingly articulated as an individual problem caused by a lack of 'employability' rather than a structural condition characterized by a lack of employment (Crisp & Powell, 2016). Indeed, when Jason raised the fact that he had been at this course already to a member of staff at the job centre, they replied that as he was still unemployed, that suggested that he needed to get more advice.

Leo, a youth worker at a local organization, described what he perceived to be the cultural devaluation of young people, particularly of low SES, as a significant and common problem, and one with lasting implications. He discussed a 'growing anger' among the young people he came into contact with, who felt they were not listened to, consulted or taken seriously:

> They feel vilified, okay? They feel blamed for the shit situations they are in and they are at the age where they are resisting that. They're thinking, hang on, I'm looking for jobs all the time, or hang on, they keep sending me off to do these pointless training courses or placements and it never turns into anything, but I'm the bad person? It's our fault there's no jobs or decent courses in the area?

Leo went on to note that because of the relatively small size of Clackmannanshire, and the often quite close-knit towns and neighbourhoods within it, experiences tend to be shared, and emotion tends to build quickly and collectively. In the case of Clacks, Leo felt there was a mixture of 'depression and anger' among his young service users, who felt depressed by the lack of opportunities open to them, and angry that they were getting blamed for this rather than helped. This culture of blaming people for their own disadvantage has intensified in the neoliberal context, where social problems are heavily individualized and notions of personal responsibility are at the forefront of policy and political rhetoric (Crisp & Powell, 2016; Roberts, 2012).

Leigh, 26, whose fragmented (under)employment history was described earlier in the chapter, discussed being explicitly held to account for her disadvantage by numerous people, spanning from her parents, recruitment staff at the agency and job centre staff. In one instance, Leigh had gotten very upset at an appointment at the agency when she learned that her contract in a previous position was not going to be renewed, and a member of staff responding unkindly, suggesting it was Leigh's fault:

> I was literally crying, dreading telling my mum, dreading the stress and uncertainty of trying to find the next one, and she turned and said to me, come on, pull yourself together, you've got yourself into this mess, only you can get yourself out of it. Now, bear in mind I had a perfect employment record there, never been late, never missed a day, nothing, so how the hell is it my fault?

Upon probing, the member of staff clarified that she meant that Leigh had likely ended up in agency work through bad decision-making in school, leaving at the age of 16, and/or perhaps not being focused on studies and getting a job. These assumptions, based on common and highly problematic stereotypes around working-class youth and zero evidence, heavily shaped how a professional interacted with and delivered a service to a vulnerable young person. In several interviews, youth services and youth workers were heralded as the only non-related adults and institution that made the young people feel valued and respected. Harry, 18, who had recently started an entry level construction course at college, described the support he received from youth workers as 'vital' to him returning to education, for example. When asked why he found the support he received from youth workers so efficient, he said:

> They see you as a person [...] not a problem. They take each person as they come, like individuals, and for me they knew I'd been let down by the school and that I was drifting down the wrong path, so they built my confidence back up and helped me figure out what I wanted to do in life, but it all started with, I guess, making me feel, like, valuable and good about myself.

Here, unlike in the instances many of the participants described occurring between them and teachers, careers advisers, members of the public and job centre or agency staff, Harry felt taken seriously, understood and prioritized. In short, to use Fraser's (1998) terminology, he felt *recognised*, where in so many other situations he had been *misrecognised*. As with the structural disadvantage described in the previous section of this chapter, many of the participants framed their experiences of cultural injustice through a generational lens. They observed a disconnect between their experiences and perspectives and those of previous generations, who they felt misunderstood – and occasionally mistreated – them due to a lack of shared understanding about the different challenges facing them as young people of low SES in contemporary society.

INJUSTICES OF MISREPRESENTATION: VOICELESS AND DISCONNECTED

Finally, this chapter turns to Nancy Fraser's third dimension of social justice; that of political representation and participation. In the case of this study, rather than a literal focus on political participation, this was predominantly explored through how supported and represented the young people felt by older adults or institutions, and how connected or disconnected they felt to wider society. Almost all of the participants described feeling without support, representation or voice. Indeed, aside from their own personal connections with friends and family, and some relationships they had fostered with youth workers or teachers, the participants were at best ambivalent and worst scathing about the support available to them as young people living in working-class neighbourhoods in a rural location. Steven, 25, who had a young son and had been largely unemployed for seven years, was particularly angry about this:

> It just drives me mental. Like, I've really had to revise my expectations down from school and that, where they basically make out like that you're the future and all this, world's your oyster, all that [...] Then when you are actually out there living and stuff hits the fan, there is nobody to turn to. What can I do in my situation, like who can help me? [...] Nah, nobody cares.

Finlay, 27, who was long-term unemployed and living with a complex set of physical and mental health conditions, also expressed anger at the lack of support available to him and to fellow young people in the area, who he felt had no voice:

> When you think about it, we're living out here, and it's just a dot on the map to people, nobody cares [...] I don't think politicians know how bad it can be sometimes out here [...] Like, to try and get a job here, even if you're healthy, is so hard, and then add in some complications and the fact there is just nothing around, it's awful, and the worst thing is, we have nobody to vouch for us.

For Finlay, in an echo of a theme that is observable across much of the data, a lot of this problem was perceived to be generational, with older adults from previous generations unaware of the particular difficulties facing the current cohort of youth, who are transitioning into and through adulthood against the backdrop of a changed and narrowed labour market and a higher cost of living relative to wages.

Equally important was the issue of place and social class, which were identified as key issues in the battle for voice and fair treatment by several of the participants in both interviews and one of the focus groups. In this exchange, which occurred during an online focus group, three of the young people describe what they perceived to be at the root of some of their disadvantage and the reason behind their lack of progress towards better outcomes:

> Natalie (20): What I actually think is part of the problem is that people in charge of making decisions that could make a difference for us like putting more jobs and resources in the area and stuff usually don't live in the sort of areas we do
>
> Leigh (26): Ye and not just that they live in posher neighbourhoods but I also think because most people who are in charge live in places like Edinburgh and that
>
> Natalie (20): Yep, they don't necessarily understand what it means to live in Alva or Tullibody or any of these wee places, the challenges of it

Kylie (21): Totally agree

Leigh (26): Aye and they are all old as well!!

Natalie (20): Yes! So true

Researcher: Okay, so you think that the people who make decisions that impact your lives and other young people in Clacks basically can't relate to you?

Leigh (26): Ye, because they are old, posh and not from here, they don't know what it's like. How can they??

Many of the participants felt this way; that they, as young people from disadvantaged neighbourhoods in Clackmannanshire, were without representation. As noted previously, those people and institutions who they *did* feel understood and tried to advocate for them were often youth workers and youth organizations. Unfortunately, however, the availability of youth services in Clackmannanshire, and much of the UK, has significantly declined due to unprecedented levels of budget cuts by local authorities, with youth provision among the biggest casualties. This had hit many of the participants hard, and made them feel even less supported and represented than they had previously. Troy, 22, had benefited from youth services as a teenager, and was worried about the impact of its virtual disappearance from most of Clackmannanshire on young people:

> It's not good like, not good at all [...] I've got younger brothers, eh, and they're not on a good track right now, like me when I was their age, but difference is I had [the youth club], I had that relationship with them [...] A lot's happened in my life and they always looked out for me and tried to help me with jobs and with the job centre and everything, so I'm really gutted for the next young kids coming through, because there's barely anything for them. They're just basically being left to themselves.

Lindsay, an employee of Clackmannanshire Council who specializes in youth provision, expressed serious concerns about the cutbacks to youth services across the area, believing that the scale and immediacy of these cuts would have a negative impact on the poorest young people in most need of support and representation:

> These cuts are extremely worrying. The council's hands, and certainly my hands, are tied, you know, we've been told – you need to cut X amount of pounds by this date sort of thing – but I am very regretful that it's fallen so much on young people, who are already having a tough time of it as it is. These are relationships and services that have often been nurtured over years, you know, and very beneficial to a lot of young people in very tough situations, so it's not something you can replace or easily take away.

In terms of the other measure of the political dimension of social justice – a sense of connectedness to, and participation within, wider society – the participants were similarly negative, with many expressing that they felt completely uninvolved in life outside of their immediate social worlds. Interestingly, however, this was framed more diversely than previous issues were by the participants, with some actively perceiving their disconnection from wider society as an injustice, but others describing it as a conscious choice. In an echo of some of the participants' thoughts behind their perceived lack of representation, many of the young people in the study identified their age, social class and rural location as key factors in their exclusion from wider society or political participation. Some felt cut off and forgotten about, invisible to politicians and other key decision-makers, most crucially because of living in Clackmannanshire. Joanna, 29, spoke about this at length in her interview:

> You have to understand that [Clackmannanshire] is somewhere most people drive past, ken, drive through to get somewhere else. We aren't really somewhere a lot of people know about or think about and we have definitely suffered from that over the years [...] There is a definite sense of rejection, ken, like, of us being cut off from stuff going on in the rest of Scotland, or the UK, because you just feel invisible.

Lindsay, the employee of Clackmannanshire council, seemed to agree with this perspective in her interview, commenting that most funding is diverted away from Clackmannanshire to the bigger and more visible local authorities that surround it. Indeed, all of the practitioners commented upon the lack of resources dedicated to Clackmannanshire relative to nearby councils, and noted that this often felt like Clackmannanshire and the problems and needs of the people within it were neglected by the government.

A smaller group of the participants framed their perceived exclusion from wider society in more agentic terms, stating that they had little interest in life beyond Clackmannanshire. This often seemed to be the result of the participants reacting to the disinterest they perceived 'outsiders' to have in their life and reflecting this back, intensifying their emplacement within their local community. Research has illuminated the powerful ties that neighbourhoods, streets and towns can hold over young people, and particularly those from working-class backgrounds, which tend to be more close-knit (Pickering, Kintrea, & Bannister, 2012; White & Green, 2015). In these and similar studies, young people were found to attach strongly territorial caveats to their aspirations and life planning, often resulting in stronger connections to place and local networks, but also in significantly diminished opportunities and poorer structural outcomes.

A number of the participants expressed a strong and highly territorial attachment to Clackmannanshire, where many wanted to live and work for the rest of their lives. This not only manifested in disinterest in developments outside the local area, but also in a refusal to consider life or opportunities beyond it. For all of the practitioners, this was problematic, and was felt to be a key reason behind some young local people's struggles. Maya, who runs a volunteering initiative for youth in Alloa, described this situation as 'very problematic':

> I have a real concern about the lack of willingness I see in most of the young people I meet to move beyond the limits of Clacks, or their town or, in some cases, their street [...] If you ask them, they'll tell you, I don't want to leave, I'm not going, my family's here, what have you, but I think this is the product of a lack of confidence, a lack of knowledge, a lack of experience, and a lack of economic, social and cultural resources amongst the young people to access a world beyond this place, and they're doing themselves out of opportunities.

Some of the participants acknowledged they were likely limiting the opportunities open to them by not considering jobs or courses outside of Clackmannanshire, but most felt that they should not have to leave their homes and communities in order to achieve basic income or education. Only 3 out of the 16 young people in this study said they would currently consider moving elsewhere for EET or to make a new life, but the vast majority felt unwilling to do as seemingly everyone encouraged them to, which was to leave Clackmannanshire for an urban hub with more opportunities.

Their determination to stay not only departed from the advice given to them by many practitioners or relatives, but also from much of the literature on rural youth, which has consistently found evidence of high levels of out-migration of young people from rural areas into urban cities (Corbett, 2007; Nugin, 2014; Pedersen & Gram, 2016). However, for the participants in this study, cities outside of Clackmannanshire seemed alien, remote, unwelcoming and uninviting, and at a complete disconnect from their previous experiences and lifestyles. This sense of disconnection and exclusion from society beyond the area's limits explained diversely but felt broadly across the participants, contributed to a sense of insularity around Clackmannanshire, where notions of community were as powerful as feelings of being overlooked structurally, culturally and politically, and which were poorly acknowledged or responded to by policy approaches.

CONCLUSION

This chapter has used Nancy Fraser's tripartite theory of social justice, and its emphasis on social structure, cultural value and participation, to interpret the experiences and perspectives of working-class young people transitioning into and through adulthood in a rural area of Scotland. It has found examples of Nany Fraser's markers of injustice – maldistribution, misrecognition and misrepresentation – in each dimension of social justice it explored with the young people, whose structural outcomes and prospects were poor, whose social status and cultural value were low, and who described feeling disconnected from, and poorly represented by, wider society.

While the use of a critical theorist such as Fraser can be critiqued for simply delineating a problem rather than proposing how to address it, I would argue that, in the case of working-class youth, highlighting the range and extent of injustice experienced by young people is an important and often disregarded first step, because of the lack of attention given to the extent of their disadvantage, which continues to be largely normalized, either as a somehow 'natural' by-product of being young, or as the personal responsibility of the young people themselves. Moreover, with Catherine Robinson (2018), who has argued that the vulnerability of children and young people must be acknowledged rather than ignored, and in line with the work of France, Roberts, and Nood (2018), who argue that social class must feature more prominently in research with young people, this paper argues that young people, and particularly those from working-class backgrounds, must be recognized and prioritized as an oppressed *minority*, who experience significant and diverse forms of injustice.

The young people in this study had very low social status, as a result of the intersection between three widely devalued facets of their identities: low SES, youth and rurality. They felt at best invisible and at worst stigmatized and marginalized because of this, and were most hurt and angry by feeling blamed for their own disadvantage. The participants were also living highly precarious lives, where they lacked sufficient security, resources or opportunities to achieve distributive justice. Some had been largely unemployed for several years by their mid-twenties, and most had erratic (under)employment histories, characterized by churn and instability. Finally, the participants felt largely voiceless and without representation or visibility, both as individuals and as a group.

In sum, the young people in this study clearly fit the criteria for an application of Nany Fraser's theory of social justice. They are oppressed economically, culturally and politically, and thus are prevented from experiencing 'participatory parity' in social and civic life. They are *misrecognised* as aimless and apathetic, or as risks to be managed, rather than as a minority group in need of recognition; they are *misrepresented* by both a lack of literal representatives in positions of power and a failure to include their voices in decision-making; and they suffer acutely from *maldistribution* in that they are more likely to experience unemployment and underemployment than both older adults and their more affluent or urban-dwelling peers. Indeed, for the participants in this study, living in a rural area, and being of low SES clearly amplified the challenges facing many young people in the contemporary context, through a significant lack of quality EET opportunities, a rudimentary and inaccessible public transport network, and through major budget cuts greatly reducing youth services in a council area recently forecast to run out of cash reserves within three years (Audit Scotland, 2017).

Fraser's theory is also valuable in demonstrating how these dimensions of injustice interlink with and perpetuate one another. Indeed, it is because young people are misrecognized as incapable and risky that their maldistribution is legitimated as inevitable, for example. It is because young people lack effective representation and voice that they can be the victims of injustices that become normalized, invisible and unanswered. It is because they lack economic capital that they also lack cultural and social capital. The cultural, economic and political dimensions of public life, and of social justice, combine and are deeply imbricated with one another, in a symbiotic process of justification and perpetuation. For the working-class young people in this study, this meant that their oppression was structurally, culturally and politically reinforced. Each directs, makes possible and sustains the other, and changes in each of these dimensions are required for young people to begin to access meaningful social justice.

Before concluding, it is important to note that far from being purely the researcher's interpretation alone, the participants themselves felt strongly that they were the victims of injustice. Many expressed feeling profoundly misunderstood and misrepresented, with politicians and policymakers unaware of the challenges facing young people in specifically rural and low-income areas. Moreover, according to the participants, and in line with emerging youth literature that foregrounds issues of generation, much of this injustice was perceived to be generational in nature and cause, made possible by the gulf between the societal conditions they were living through versus those of previous generations, members of which work directly with the current cohort of young people in positions of power. While the size of this sample undoubtedly places limits on the generalizability of its findings, the extent and symbiotic nature of the injustices experienced and perceived by the young people in this study are considerable and valid in their own right. These findings suggest the need for more qualitative research in youth sociology that foregrounds social justice, social class and place in its exploration of youth transitions.

REFERENCES

Aaltonen, S. (2013). Trying to push things through: Forms and bounds of agency in transitions of school-age young people. *Journal of Youth Studies*, *16*(3), 375–390.

Abbott-Chapman, J. (2011). Making the most of the mosaic: Facilitating post-school transitions to higher education of disadvantaged students. *Australian Educational Researcher*, *38*, 57–71.

Alloway, N., & Dalley-Trim, L. (2009). 'High and dry' in rural Australia: Obstacles to student aspirations and expectations. *Rural Society*, *19*(1), 49–59.

Alloway, N. P., Gilbert, P., Gilbert, R., & Muspratt, S. (2004). *Factors impacting on student aspirations and expectations in regional Australia*. Canberra: Commonwealth of Australia.

Alston, M., & Kent, J. (2009). Generation X-pendable: The social exclusion of rural and remote young people. *Journal of Sociology*, *45*(1), 89–107.

Ansell, N., & Van Blerk, L. (2007). Doing and belonging: Toward a more-than-representational account of young migrant identities in Lesotho and Malawi. In R. Panelli, S. Punch, & E. Robson (Eds.), *Global perspectives on childhood and youth* (pp. 17–28). New York, NY: Routledge.

Ashby, J. S., & Schoon, I. (2010). Career success: The role of teenage career aspirations, ambition value and gender in predicting adult social status and earnings. *Journal of Vocational Behaviour*, *77*(3), 350–360.

Audit Scotland. (2017). *Local government in Scotland: Financial overview 2016/17*. Edinburgh: Audit Scotland.

Auer, P., & Cazes, S. (2003). *Employment stability in an age of uncertainty*. Geneva: Institute for the Study of Labour.

Bathmaker, A. M., Ingram, N., & Waller, R. (2013). Higher education, social class and the mobilisation of capitals: Recognising and playing the game. *British Journal of Sociology of Education*, *34*(5–6), 723–743.

Benjet, C., Hernandez-Motoya, D., Borges, G., Mendez, E., Medina-Mora, M. E., & Aguilar-Gaxiola, S. (2012). Youth who neither study nor work: Mental health, education and employment. *Salida Publica de Mexico*, *54*(4), 410–417.

Biletta, I., & Eisner, M. (2007). *Youth and work*. Dublin: European Foundation for the Improvement of Living and Working Conditions.

Birdwell, J., Gist, M., & Margo, J. (2011). *The forgotten half*. London: Demos.

Bivand, P. (2012). *Generation lost: Youth unemployment and the youth labour market*. London: Trade Union Congress.

Bragues, G. (2006). Seek the good life, not money: The Aristotelian approach to business ethics. *Journal of Business Ethics*, *67*(4), 341–357.

Bynner, J. M., & Parson, S. (2002). Social exclusion and the transition from school to work: The case of young people not in education, employment or training (NEET). *Journal of Vocational Behaviour*, *60*(2), 289–309.

Cartmel, F., & Furlong, A. (2000). *Youth unemployment in rural areas*. York: Joseph Rowntree Foundation.

Cavanagh, S. E., & Fomby, P. (2012). Family instability, school context, and the academic careers of adolescents. *Sociology of Education*, *85*(1), 81–97.

Charmaz, K. (2011). Grounded theory methods in social justice research. In N. K. Danzin & Y. S. Lincoln (Eds.), *The SAGE handbook of qualitative research* (pp. 359–381). Thousand Oaks, CA: Sage.

Cloke, P. (2005). Rurality and racialized others: Out of place in the countryside? In P. Cloke, T. Marsden, & P. Mooney (Eds.), *Handbook of rural studies* (pp. 379–387). London: Sage.

Corbett, M. (2007). *Learning to leave: The irony of school in a coastal community*. Halifax: Fenwood.

Corbett, M., & Forsey, M. (2017). Rural youth out-migration and education: Challenges to aspirations discourse in mobile modernity. *Discourse: Studies in the Cultural Politics of Education, 38*(3), 429–444.

Cote, J. E., & Bynner, J. M. (2008). Changes in transitions to adulthood in the UK and Canada: The role of structure and agency in emerging adulthood. *Journal of Youth Studies, 11*(3), 251–268.

Crisp, R., & Powell, R. (2016). Young people and UK labour market policy: A critique of 'employability' as a tool for understanding youth unemployment. *Urban Studies, 54*(8), 1784–1807.

Cuervo, H. (2011). Young people in rural communities: Challenges and opportunities in constructing a future. In S. Beadle, R. Holdsworth, & J. Wyn (Eds.), *For we are young and...? Young people in a time of uncertainty*. Melbourne: Melbourne University Press.

Cuervo, H. (2014). Critical reflections on youth and equality in the rural context. *Journal of Youth Studies, 12*(5), 544–557.

Cuervo, H., & Wyn, J. (2012). *Young people making it work: Continuity and change in rural places*. Melbourne: Melbourne University Press.

Duckworth, K., & Schoon, I. (2012). Beating the odds: Exploring the impact of social risk on young people's school-to-work transitions during recession in the UK. *National Institute Economic Review, 222*, 38–51.

Egan, M., Neary, J., Keenan, P. J., & Bond, L. (2013). Perceptions of antisocial behaviour and negative attitudes towards young people: Focus group evidence from adult residents of disadvantaged urban neighbourhoods (Glasgow, UK). *Journal of Youth Studies, 16*(5), 612–627.

Evans, K. (2007). Concepts of bounded agency in education, work, and the personal lives of young adults. *International Journal of Psychology, 42*(2), 85–93.

EY. (2016). *The employment landscape for young people in the UK: Challenges and opportunities*. London: EY Foundation.

Farrington, J., & Farrington, C. (2005). Rural accessibility, social inclusion and social justice: Towards conceptualisation. *Journal of Transport Geography, 13*(1), 1–12.

Farrugia, D. (2014). Towards a spatialized youth sociology: The rural and the urban in times of change. *Journal of Youth Studies, 17*(3), 293–307.

Farrugia, D., Smyth, J., & Harrison, T. (2014a). Rural young people in late modernity: Place, globalisation and the spatial contours of identity. *Current Sociology, 62*(7), 1036–1054.

Fenton, S., & Dermott, E. (2006). Fragmented careers? Winners and losers in youth labour markets. *Work, Employment and Society, 20*(2), 205–221.

Forsey, M. (2015). Learning to stay? Mobile modernity and the sociology of choice. *Mobilities, 10*(5), 764–783.

Forth Valley College. (2018). *Alloa campus*. Retrieved from https://www.forthvalley.ac.uk/about-us/getting-here/alloa-campus/. Accessed on December 5, 2018.

France, A., Roberts, S., & Nood, B. (2018). Youth, social class and privilege in the Antipodes: Towards a new research agenda for youth sociology. *Journal of Sociology, 54*(3), 362–380.

Fraser, N. (1998). Social justice in the age of identity politics: Redistribution, recognition, participation. *WBZ Discussion Paper, No. FS198-108*.

Fraser, N. (2000). *Rethinking recognition*. Retrieved from https://newleftreview.org/II/3/nancy-fraser-rethinking-recognition. Accessed on November 29, 2018.

Fraser, N. (2007). Feminist politics in the age of recognition: A two-dimensional approach to gender justice. *Studies in Social Justice, 1*(1), 23–35.

Fraser, N. (2008). Reframing social justice in a globalising world. In K. Olson (Ed.), *Adding insult to injury: Nancy Fraser debates her critics* (pp. 273–295). London: Verso.

Furlong, A., Woodman, D., & Wyn, J. (2011). Changing times, changing perspectives: Reconciling 'transition' and 'cultural' perspectives on youth and young adulthood. *Journal of Sociology, 47*(4), 355–370.

Goodman, R., & Burton, D. (2012). What is the nature of the achievement gap, why does it persist and are government goals sufficient to create social justice in the education system? *International Journal of Primary, Elementary and Early Years Education*, *40*(5), 500–514.

Goos, M., & Manning, A. (2003). *Lousy and lazy jobs: The rising polarisation of work in Britain*. London: Centre for Economic Performance, London School of Economics.

Gray, P. (2007). Youth justice, social exclusion and the demise of social justice. *The Howard Journal of Crime and Justice*, *46*(4), 401–416.

Gregg, P., & Tominey, E. (2004). *The wage scar from youth unemployment*. Bristol: CMPO.

Harris, A. (2015). Transitions, cultures, and citizenship: Interrogating and integrating youth studies in new times. In D. Woodman & A. Bennett (Eds.), *Youth cultures, transitions and generations: Bridging the gap in youth research* (pp.84–99). Basingstoke: Palgrave Macmillan.

Haukanes, H. (2013). Belonging, mobility and the future: Representations of space in the life narratives of young rural Czechs. *Young*, *21*(2), 193–210.

Holscher, D. (2014). Considering Nancy Fraser's notion of social justice for social work: Reflections on misframing and the lives of refugees in South Africa. *Ethics and Social Welfare*, *8*(1), 20–38.

Hoolachan, J., McKee, K., Moore, T., & Soaita, A. M. (2017). Generation rent and the ability to 'settle down': Economic and geographical variation in young people's housing transitions. *Journal of Youth Studies*, *20*(1), 63–78.

Hurst, Y. G., & Frank, J. (2000). How kids view cops: The nature of juvenile attitudes toward the police. *Journal of Criminal Justice*, *28*, 189–202.

Irvin, M. J., Byun, S., Meece, J. L., & Farmer, T. W. (2012). Educational barriers of rural youth: Relation of individual and contextual difference variables. *Journal of Career Assessment*, *20*(1), 71–87.

Jentsch, B., & Shucksmith, M. (Eds.). (2017). *Young people in rural areas of Europe*. Abingdon: Routledge.

Johns, D. F., Williams, K., & Haines, K. (2017). Ecological youth justice: Understanding the social ecology of young people's prolific offending. *Youth Justice*, *17*(1), 3–21.

Keddie, A. (2012). Schooling and social justice through the lenses of Nancy Fraser. *Cultural Studies in Education*, *53*(3), 263–279.

Knight, A. (2015). Democratising disability: Achieving inclusion (without assimilation) through 'participatory parity'. *Hypatia: A Journal of Feminist Philosophy*, *30*(1), 97–114.

Krestos, L. (2010). The persistent pandemic of precariousness: Young people at work. In J. Tremmel (Ed.) *A young generation under pressure?* (pp. 3–23). Berlin: Springer.

Leyshon, M. (2008). The betweeness of being a rural youth: Inclusive and exclusive lifestyles. *Social and Cultural Geography*, *9*(1), 1–26.

MacDonald, R. (2009). Precarious work: Risk, choice and poverty traps. In A. Furlong (Ed.), *Handbook of youth and young adulthood: New perspectives and agendas* (pp. 167–176). Abingdon: Routledge.

MacDonald, R. (2011). Youth transitions, unemployment and underemployment: Plus ca change, plus c'est la meme chose? *Journal of Sociology*, *47*(4), 427–444.

Mackett, R. L., & Thoreau, R. (2015). Transport, social exclusion and health. *Journal of Transport & Health*, *2*(4), 610–617.

Maguire, S. (2013). Will raising the participation age in England solve the NEET problem? *Research in Post-Compulsory Education*, *18*(1–2), 61–76.

Malik, S., & Barr, C. (2016). *UK faces permanent generational divide, social mobility tsar warns*. Retrieved from https://www.theguardian.com/world/2016/mar/11/uk-faces-permanent-generational-divide-social-mobility-tsar-warns. Accessed on December 4, 2018.

McKee, K. (2012). Young people, home ownership and future welfare. *Housing Studies*, *27*(6), 853–862.

Meek, R. (2008). Young people, social exclusion and intergenerational tension in a rural Somerset town. *Children & Society*, *22*(2), 124–135.

Mendes, P., Baidawi, S., & Snow, P. C. (2014). Young people transitioning from out-of-home care in Victoria: Strengthening support services for dual clients of child protection and youth justice. *Australian Social Work*, *67*(1), 6–28.

Muncie, J. (2006). Governing young people: Coherence and contradiction in contemporary youth justice. *Critical Social Policy*, *26*(4), 770–793.

Murphy, K. (2015). Does procedural justice matter to youth? Comparing adults' and youths' willingness to collaborate with police. *Policing and Society*, *25*, 53–76.

Nayak, A. (2006). Displaced masculinities: Chavs, youth and class in the post-industrial city. *Sociology*, *40*(5), 813–831.

Neary, J., Egan, M., Keenan, P. J., Lawson, L., & Bond, L. (2013). Damned if they do, damned if they don't: Negotiating the tricky context of antisocial behaviour and keeping safe in disadvantaged urban neighbourhoods. *Journal of Youth Studies*, *16*(1), 118–134.

Ng, E. S., Lyons, S. T., & Schweitzer, L. (2017). Millennials in Canada: Young workers in a challenging labour market. In E. Parry & J. McCarthy (Eds.), *The Palgrave handbook of age diversity and work* (pp.325–344). London: Palgrave Macmillan.

NOMIS. (2018a). *Labour market profile – Clackmannanshire*. Retrieved from http://www.nomisweb.co.uk/reports/lmp/la/1946157409/printable.aspx. Accessed on November 30, 2018.

NOMIS. (2018b). *Labour market profile – Edinburgh*. Retrieved from http://www.nomisweb.co.uk/reports/lmp/la/1946157416/printable.aspx. Accessed on November 30, 2018.

Nugin, R. (2014). 'I think that they should go. Let them see something.' The context of rural youth's out-migration in post-socialist Estonia. *Journal of Rural Studies*, *34*, 51–64.

Panelli, R., Punch, S., & Robsen, E. (Eds.). (2007). *Global perspectives on rural childhood and youth: Young rural lives*. New York, NY: Routledge.

Pedersen, H. D., & Gram, M. (2016). 'The brainy ones are leaving': The subtlety of (un)cool places through the eyes of rural youth. *Journal of Youth Studies*, *21*(5), 620–635.

Peiro, J. M., Hernandez, A., & Ramos, J. (2015). The challenge of building human capital and benefiting from it: A person-centric view of youth unemployment and underemployment. In L. M. Finkelstein, D. M. Truxillo, F. Fraccaroli, & R. Kanfer (Eds.), *Facing the challenge of a multi-age workforce: A use-inspired approach* (pp.83–108). New York, NY: Routledge.

Pickard, S. (2014). The trouble with youth these days: 'Deviant' youth, the popular press and politics in contemporary Britain. *French Journal of British Studies*, *19*(1), 89–121.

Pickering, J., Kintrea, K., & Bannister, J. (2012). Invisible walls and visible youth: Territoriality among young people in British cities. *Urban Studies*, *49*(5), 945–960.

Punch, S. (2015). Possibilities for learning between childhoods and youth in the minority and majority worlds: Youth transitions as an example of cross-world dialogue. In J. Wyn & H. Cahills (Eds.), *Handbook of children and young adulthood* (pp. 689–701). Singapore: Springer.

Quintini, G., Martin, P., & Martin, S. (2007). *The changing nature of the school to work transition process in OECD countries*. Bonn: Institute for the Study of Labour.

Raffe, D., & Croxford, L. (2015). How stable is the stratification of higher education in England and Scotland? *British Journal of Sociology of Education*, *36*, 313–335.

Roberts, K. (2012). The end of the long baby-boomer generation. *Journal of Youth Studies*, *15*(4), 479–497.

Robinson, C. (2018). *In defence of vulnerability*. TASA 2018 Conference, Deakin University, November 21, 2018.

Roscigno, V. J., & Crowley, M. L. (2001). Rurality, intersectional disadvantage, and achievement/attainment. *Rural Sociology*, *66*, 268–293.

Sandel, M. (2009). *Justice: What's the right thing to do?* London: Penguin.

Serracant, P. (2012). Changing youth? Continuities and ruptures in transitions into adulthood among Catalan young people. *Journal of Youth Studies*, *15*(2), 161–176.

Shucksmith, M. (2004). Young people and social exclusion in rural areas. *Sociologia Ruralis*, *44*(1), 43–59.

Stern, E., & Turbin, J. (1986). *Youth unemployment and unemployment in rural England*. London: The Development Commission.

Stewart, A., & Abbott-Chapman, J. (2011). Remote island students' post-compulsory retention: Emplacement and displacement as factors influencing educational persistence or discontinuation. *Journal of Research in Rural Education*, *26*(6), 1–16.

Strand, S. (2014). Ethnicity, gender, social class and achievement gaps at age 16: Intersectionality and 'getting it' for the white working class. *Research Papers in Education*, *29*(2), 131–171.

Thissen, F., Fortuijn, J. D., Strijker, D., & Haartsen, T. (2010). Migration intentions of rural youth in the Westhoek, Flanders, Belgium and the Veenkolonien. *Journal of Rural Studies*, *26*(4), 428–436.

Thomas, A., Lowe, B., Fulkerson, G., & Smith, P. (2011). *Critical rural theory: Structure, space, culture*. Lanham, MD: Lexington Books.

Thompson, R. (2011). Individualisation and social exclusion: The case of young people not in education, employment or training. *Oxford Review of Education*, *37*(6), 785–802.

Walther, A. (2006). Regimes of youth transitions: Choice, flexibility and security in young people's experiences across different European contexts. *Young*, *14*(2), 119–139.

White, A., & Green, A. E. (2015). The importance of socio-spatial influences in shaping young people's employment aspirations: Case study evidence from three British cities. *Work, Employment and Society*, *29*(2), 295–313.

Wierenga, A. (2009). *Young people making a life*. New York, NY: Palgrave Macmillan.

Woodman, D. (2009). The mysterious case of the pervasive choice biography: Ulrich Beck, structure/agency, and the middling state of theory in the sociology of youth. *Journal of Youth Studies*, *12*(3), 243–256.

Woodman, D., & Wyn, J. (2011). Youth research in a changing world. In S. Beadle, K. Holdsworth, & J. Wyn (Eds.) *For we are young and...? Young people in a time of uncertainty*. Melbourne: Melbourne University Press.

Woodman, D., & Wyn, J. (2015a). Class, gender and generation matter: Using the concept of social generation to study inequality and social change. *Journal of Youth Studies*, *18*(10), 1402–1410.

Woodman, D., & Wyn, J. (2015b). *Youth and generation: Rethinking change and inequality in the lives of young people*. London: Sage.

Yates, S., Harris, A., Sabates, R., & Staff, J. (2011). Early occupational aspirations and fractured transitions: A study of entry into 'NEET' status in the UK. *Journal of Social Policy*, *46*(3), 513–534.

Yates, S., & Roulstone, A. (2013). Social policy and transitions to training and work for disabled young people in the United Kingdom: Neo-liberalism for better and for worse? *Disability & Society*, *28*(4), 456–470.

RELUCTANCE TO REGISTER UNDER THE JJ ACT AMONG CHILD CARE INSTITUTIONS IN MALAPPURAM DISTRICT OF KERALA

Raneesh C. and Mohan A. K.

ABSTRACT

Purpose – *According to Juvenile Justice (Care and Protection) Act, 2015 Act, the registration of Child Care Institutions (CCIs) is compulsory, but the registration process all over the country is being prolonged on the part of the NGOs and other private welfare agencies. Against this background, the researcher intends to study the reasons for reluctance to registration by the CCIs.*

Methodology/Approach – *The researcher adopted exploratory approach to find the reasons behind the reluctance towards JJ registration. There are 112 children's homes in Malappuram district, among which 40 institutions did not apply or get JJ Registration. Among these 40, the researcher selected 20 (50%) by simple random sampling. The respondents were one among the institution's Secretary/President or staff. The method used for extracting data was interview schedule and the collected data were coded and analyzed with the help of the SPSS software.*

Findings – *The CCIs apprehend that their organizational freedom would be limited after registration. Another observation of this study is most of the children's homes are managed by religious organizations and most of them are worried that registering their institution under this act might adversely*

Human Rights for Children and Youth: Sociocultural Differentiation, Resistance and Unity
Sociological Studies of Children and Youth, Volume 24, 221–233

ISSN: 1537-4661/doi:10.1108/S1537-466120190000024012

affect their religious sentiments. About 60% of the CCIs concern about the financial burden and 85% of them have difficulty to implement the new rules and regulation.

Research Limitations – *This study covered the 20 children's Home and all those institutions are run by Muslim religious management, so the situations of child care institutions run by other management (Hindu, Christian, Secular) is not covered by this study.*

Keywords: Reluctance; child care institutions; orphanages; juvenile justice; children; registration

INTRODUCTION

India realized the importance of children by enacting two national child policies and several legislative and welfare schemes. The first national child policy proclaimed, 'The nation's children are a supremely important asset. Their nurture and solicitude are our responsibility' (National Child Policy, 1974). The country recognized the importance of children through national policies in the year 1974 and 2013. Besides that, after the ratification of the UNCRC in 1992, India was obliged to the international community to protect and develop a healthy situation for the child population in the country. Precedent to the ratification of the UNCRC, several juvenile acts had been in existence in the arena of juvenile justice system of the country. The Juvenile Justice (Care and Protection) Act 2015 was the latest in its kind. It had been in existence in the form of a comprehensive legislative measure and re-enactment as Juvenile Justice (Care and Protection) Act, 2000.

Juvenile justice in India is firmly supported by proper legislative measures, policies, and programs. After the UNCRC in 1989, a remarkable change happened in juvenile justice all over the world. In 1992, India ratified the CRC and took measures to achieve its objectives. The Juvenile Justice (Care and Protection) Act 2000, brought about structural changes in the approach towards children and is considered as more child friendly as it ensures the civil, political, cultural, economic, and social rights of children, irrespective of their entitlements. It is a fact that only a country or society can achieve justice and not its legislative measures. But at the same time, the legislature provides a legitimate path to accomplish the objectives. After the enactment of the Juvenile Justice Act, 2000, the Supreme Court formed a one-man committee headed by the Honourable Justice Madan B. Lokur in 2013 to ensure the effective implementation of the JJ Act. The committee's prime focus was to find the structural and administrative deficiencies that inwardly affected the implementation of the JJ Act, 'To identify challenges/gaps/ deficiencies/ bottlenecks in the implementation of the Act' (UNICEF, 2016). The committee's recommendation was to bring all types of Child Care Institutions under the umbrella of the JJ Act, which was considered as most promising and advanced in concern with juvenile justice. During that time, the JJ Act, 2000, was repealed, and in 2015, a new JJ Act came into existence.

REQUISITE OF JJ REGISTRATION IN INDIA

What is the need of registration of orphanages in India? This question leads to several tangible and intangible factors, among its most prerogative reasons are:

- the vacuum of data on orphans and orphanages; and
- the human rights violations and abuse in child care institutions.

The number of orphan children in India is still vague even decades after independence; the orphans in India have not come under the radar of the official system. Not a single census or sample survey has been conducted specifically for orphans and abandoned children. The huge data vacuum on orphan and abandoned children affects the country's policies and programs for ensuring the welfare of these children. The existing data on orphan and abandoned children is largely dependent on private organizations and other international agencies. These organizations also depend on secondary sources, while estimating the orphan population of India. For instance, SOS (a charity organization) estimates that '4 percentage of India's child population are orphans and abandoned children (2011)'. This study was based on the samples of India's National Family Health Survey – 3 (2005–2006) and had correlated the data with the national census. Up to this moment, there has been no extensive information on orphans and orphanages. In a book on orphans in India, Shukala and Pavini say 'a state wise comprehensive list of orphanages, which would include orphanages registered as well as those which are not registered or are avoiding registration, has never been prepared by the Government of India' (Shukla & Pavini, 2015). So this initiative on behalf of the Supreme Court will fill the gap on the information regarding orphans, abandoned children, and Child Care Institutions.

Another important reason which led to the compulsory registration of Child Care Institutions was the vast number of human rights violations and abuse happening in these institutions since only minimum number of cases comes to the notice of the general public. Recently, an incident awoke the conscience of the Indian society and the world at large. In a shelter home for girls in Muzaffarpur, Bihar, among 44 girls, 29 were raped and had experienced other forms of sexual abuse and violence. In response to this incident, Mrs Maneka Gandhi, Minister of Women and Child, ordered a social audit of Child Care Institutions all over the country (Nair, 2018).

CHILDREN IN NEED OF CARE AND PROTECTION

It is understood that children who are in difficult circumstances need supplemental care that should cover the drawback they face due to different reasons. There are a lot of measures taken by the government to ensure the welfare of children in difficult circumstances. The Juvenile Justice Act (2015), differentiates these children into two categories as Children in Need of Care and Protection (CNCP) and Children in Conflict with Law (CCL). In India, the welfare of children has a history of legislative mechanism that works for the betterment of children from the Reformatory Schools Act, 1897 to the Juvenile Justice (Care and Protection) Act, 2015. Between these two acts, it was not a sudden leap to child welfare, instead it consisted of sequential activities and programs incorporated and initiated by different parties, which included international organizations such as the UN, UNICEF, etc., different acts and policies and programs by the Government of India, civil society, NGOs, welfare organizations, activists, etc. Everyone has their own role in this development. It is not a finishing point in child welfare, instead as said by Robert Frost in his famous poem 'Miles to go before I sleep and Miles to go before I sleep' (Frost, 1923). At the same time, the JJ Act, 2015, is considered as a landmark in legislations that deal with child welfare. That is why this Act was overwhelmingly received by the organizations and people, who were working for the betterment of children in the country, but some sections of the people, were also opposing the implementation of this Act. It is not a wonder in India that a new legislation got a rage from the society but most of opposition is arising from the same people who are committed to child welfare. Mostly the dissent was on the part of welfare organizations operating children's homes (Orphanages, Destitute Home for Children, and Bala-Balika Sadans).

CHILD CARE INSTITUTIONS IN KERALA

According to the JJ Act, 2015, Child Care Institutions means Children's Home, Observation Home, Shelter Home, Place of Safety and fit facility recognized under this Act for providing care and protection of needy children. The life of a child in institutions more often comprises of unabated sorrow. There are several studies and reports on the difficulties faced by children in these institutions. While discussing on the re-conceptualization of juvenile justice in the country, the existing condition of child care institutions always came into the first priority. There will be always a wide gap between rhetoric policies and ground realities. After the firm intervention of the Supreme Court of India in response to a PIL submitted by a social activist demanding attention towards the issues of Child Care Institutions in Tamil Nadu, directing all state parties to implement the JJ Act, 2015, and in the same judgement Supreme Court set a deadline for registration of orphanages on before 31 December 2017. 'The orphanages all over the country were asked to register under the JJ Act by the Supreme Court through an order on 5th May 2017. The deadline set by the court for registration is 31st December 2017' (Raveendran, 2017). It is prevalent in the field of child welfare in Kerala because the JJ Act, 2000, was also not implemented in Kerala. 'Nineteen states in India have already brought children's homes under the Juvenile Justice (Care and protection of children) amendment Act 2006 (JJ Act), Kerala, even after taking initial steps in this regard in 2007, is yet to take a final decision on bringing children's homes under JJ Act' (Sree, 2013). There was large outcry by welfare organizations, especially by NGOs and other charity-based organizations in Kerala against the bringing of orphanage under the JJ Act. According to the latest statistics, in Kerala, there are 1100 children homes, and among which 315 are not registered either because they are illegal or have been closed down.

While discussing justice for juveniles, it is significant to give priority to children in need of care and protection. In this Act, there are safeguards to assure to minimize the plight of these children, who stayed away from their family such as children's home, short stay home, etc. due to different circumstances they faced in their life. It is undeniable that care and protection must be the first priority of these children. It is a proven fact that children who live in institutions are exposed to different kinds of exploitation and institutional abuse. A research conducted by the Ministry of Women and Child Welfare revealed that 56.37% of children in institutions were subjected to physical abuse by the staff members of these institutions. The same study exposed that Kerala was one among the states which showed the highest rate (63.50%) of physical abuse towards institutionalized children (Study on Child Abuse: India, 2007). It also reported that institutional care children faced the highest incidence of sexual assault. It is a known fact that Child Care Institutions are not a promising place for a child to grow up, but unfortunately this situation continues in India as other alternative care such as foster care, adoption, kinship care, etc. are not much welcomed in the country.

So, proper procedures, legislations and monitoring mechanism are needed to ensure a standard care in Child Care Institutions. The JJ Act, 2015, has guaranteed facilities and standard of care in Child Care Institutions based on the statistics of the inmates of the said institutions. All these mechanisms are to assure the rights of a child in need of care and protection, but the first one must be to bring all Child Care Institutions under the legal and official system of the country. It is a fact that most of the institutions are not registered under the JJ Act, and recently a judgement of the Supreme Court observed:

> in this context, it is necessary to draw attention to section 41 of the JJ Act which mandates, notwithstanding anything contained in any other law for the time being in force, that all institutions, whether run by government or by voluntary organizations or NGOs which are meant, either wholly or partially, for housing children in need of care and protection shall be registered under the JJ Act in such manner as may be prescribed within six months of the commencement of the said act. The JJ Act came in to force on 15th January, 2016 but we were informed that the process of registration is underway and not yet complete. (State of Tamil Nadu v. Union of India, 2017)

The evolution of child right approach in the Indian society has been resolutely strengthened by legislatures and policies. It could evidently be seen from the Guardians and Wards Act, 1890 to the Juvenile Justice (care and protection of Children) Act, 2015. There are different layers of multiple stakeholders related with juvenile justice. Among these stakeholders, Child Care Institutions are prominent. While debating the issue of justice of children in need of care and protection, bring the institutions under the government purview registration is essential. But in India the registration process is lagging behind hence the honourable court raises it's voice against the lackadaisical approach of concerned state governments for delaying the registration process. Simultaneously the association of orphanages and charitable homes in Kerala raised their dissent on implementation of JJ Act 2015. In this situation the researcher asked: what are the reasons for reluctance towards JJ registration in the part of child care institutions? It is a fact that these institutions are historically evolved to take care of the marginalized children. Why this hesitancy? What are the problems they faced to shift into the new enactment? These are the fundamental questions this research tries to find answers for.

METHODOLOGY

In the present study, the researcher adopted the exploratory approach to find the reasons behind the reluctance towards JJ registration by the Child Care Institutions in Malappuram district. This district is located in the southern part of the Indian state of Kerala at 75° to 77° East longitude and 10° to 12° North latitude. The district came into existence in the year 1969 and is the most populous district in the state. The total population is 4,112,920 and ranks third-wise. The district ranks sixth for its child sex ratio in the state and the literacy rate is 93.57%, positioning it in the ninth place in the state (Government of India, 2011). There are 112 children's homes in Malappuram district, among which 40 institutions did not apply for or get JJ Registration. Among these 40, the researcher selected 20 (50%) for study. The sampling was by done by simple random sampling. The respondents were one among the institution's Secretary/ President or staff. The method used for extracting data was interview schedule and collected data were coded and analyzed with the help of the SPSS software.

ANALYSIS AND INTERPRETATION

The table represents the demographic details of the respondents and reveals that 30% belong to the age group of 31–40 years, 20% are in the age group of 51–60 years, 15% belong to the age group of 21–30 years, and the same percent of respondents belong to the age group of 71–80 years. About 40% respondents had studied up to high school, 20% were graduates and post graduates, and 10% had primary education. The occupation of the respondents varied from business to working as a coolie in which 10% had their own business, 40% were working in the private sector, 5% were coolies, and the remaining 40% were retired government employees (Table 1).

This table represents the association or relationship of the respondents with the Child Care Institutions. For this study, the researcher included the respondents on the basis of two categories, one as an office bearer in the Child Care Institution such as for the president or secretary and the second as the working staff in the Child Care Institution. Thus, it was found that 65% of the respondents had worked with the Child Care Institution in the range of 1–10 years, 20% for 11–20 years, and 15% for 21–30 years. The table also shows that 80% of the respondents held the post of manager/staff in the institution, 15% held the post of secretary of the institution, and only 5% of that of a president (Table 2).

Table 1. Demographic Profile of the Respondents.

Variables	Classification	Frequency	Percent
Age (in years) (N = 20)	21–30	3	15.0
	31–40	6	30.0
	41–50	3	15.0
	51–60	4	20.0
	61–70	3	15.0
	71–80	1	5.0
Gender (N = 20)	Male	20	100
Education (N = 20)	Primary	2	10.0
	High School	8	40.0
	Higher Secondary	2	10.0
	Under Graduation	4	20.0
	Post-graduation	4	20.0
Occupation (N = 20)	Business	2	10.0
	Private Job	8	40.0
	Coolie	1	5.0
	Professional	1	5.0
	Retired Government Employee	8	40.0

Table 2. Association with CCIs.

Variables	Classification	Frequency & Percent (N = 20)	
Association with CCI (in years)	1–10	13	65.0
	11–20	4	20.0
	21–30	3	15.0
Position in CCI	Secretary	3	15.0
	Manager/Staff	16	80.0
	President	1	5.0

Table 3. Religious Affiliation of CCIs.

Variable	Classification	Frequency (N = 20)	Percent
Religion	Muslim	20	100

This table represent the religious affiliation of Child Care Institutions, and it was found that all the institutions (100%) belong to the Muslim religion (Table 3).

The table shows the intake capacity of the institutions, that is, the number of children that the institutions can accommodate. It reveals that 25% of the

Table 4. Intake Capacity of CCIs.

Variable	Classification	Frequency (N = 20)	Percent
Intake Capacity of CCIs	1–50	5	25.0
	51–100	7	35.0
	101–150	5	25.0
	151–200	3	15.0

Table 5. Source of Income of CCIs.

Variable	Classification	Frequency (N = 20)	Percent
Source of Income	Contribution from society	3	15.0
	Grant in aid and contribution from society	7	35.0
	Contribution from society and self- income generation	1	5.0
	Grant in aid, own income, and contribution from society	9	45.0

Table 6. District Authority for JJ Implementation.

Variable	Classification	Frequency & Percent (N = 20)	
Authority of JJ Implementation	DCPU	16	80.0
	Social Justice Department	3	15.0
	Don't know	1	5.0

institutions have intake capacity of 1–50 children, 35% of 51–100 children, 25% of 101–150 children, and 15% of 151–200 children. No institution has an intake capacity of above 200 children (Table 4).

The table reveals that 15% of the institutions' source of income was through contribution from society; for 35%, it was grant in aid and contribution from society; for 45%, it was through grant in aid, own income and contribution from society, and 5% depended on contribution from society and own income (Table 5).

This table represents the awareness of respondents regarding district authority for JJ implementation. About 80% of the institutions responded that the DCPU was the authority, 15% regarded the Social Justice Department as the authority, and 5% were unaware of it (Table 6).

This table represents the awareness of the respondents towards registration under the JJ Act. For the variable 'Registration ensures child rights', 25% replied 'Yes', 10% replied 'No', and 65% did not know anything about it. To the

Table 7. Awareness of JJ Act.

Variables	Classification	Frequency & Percent (N = 20)	
Registration will ensure the rights of the child	Yes	5	25.0
	No	2	10.0
	Don't know	13	65.0
Registration is unnecessary	Yes	7	35.0
	No	3	15.0
	Don't know	10	50.0
Government motives for compulsory registration	Welfare of children	1	5.0
	Child rights violations in institutions	7	35.0
	Supreme Court intervention	2	10.0
	Don't know	10	50.0
Registration will positively change the life of a child	Yes	2	10.0
	No	6	30.0
	Don't know	12	60.0

variable 'Registration is unnecessary', 35% replied 'Yes', 10% replied 'No', and 50% replied 'Don't Know'. Regarding 'Registration will positively change the life of the children', 10% replied 'Yes', 30% replied 'No', and 60% replied 'Don't know' (Table 7).

This table represents the awareness of the registration process on the part of the respondents. It shows that 80% of them know where to submit the application for registration, 10% provided the wrong answer, and 10% were unaware of where to submit the application. Regarding the status of their institution's application, 95% had not applied for registration and 5% had started the application process. Regarding the challenges faced while preparing application for registration, 10% faced difficulty to summon the documents, 25% failed to meet the requirements demanded by the JJ Act, 5% claimed procedural ignorance, 45% found it to be not applicable to them as either they had not still decided to apply for it or were least bothered about it, and 15% were still undecided. All the respondents were satisfied by the friendly approach of the DCPU officials.

On expectation of the type of help from DCPU, 40% and 25% respondents demanded technical support and relaxation from the requirements, respectively, and 35% unaware about it. In response to the difficulty on compulsory registration, 5% replied as building, 50% as staff, 40% replied both, and 5% replied as other (Table 8).

The table reveals information about government support for CCI registration. While answering as to how many times the government officials visited the respective CCIs, 55% replied once, 5% as two times, 10% as three, and 30% that government officials had not visited their institution. Among the respondents,

Table 8. Awareness of Registration Process.

Variables	Classification	Frequency & Percent (N = 20)	
Place of application submission	District Child Protection Unit	16	80.0
	Social Justice Department	2	10.0
	Don't know	2	10.0
Status of application submission	Yes/Has been initiated	1	5.0
	No/Not initiated	19	95.0
Challenges faced while submitting/preparing application	Summon documents	2	10.0
	Failed to meet requirements	5	25.0
	Procedural ignorance	1	5.0
	Not applicable	9	45.0
	Other	3	15.0
Response of DCPU officials	Friendly	20	100.0
Type of assistance expected from DCPU	Technical support	8	40.0
	Relaxation of requirements	5	25.0
	Not yet thought of/Unaware	7	35.0
Difficult part in JJ registration	Building	1	5.0
	Staffing/Staff	10	50.0
	All of the above	8	40.0
	Other	1	5.0

20% attended one meeting and another 20% attended three meetings regarding registration, 15% had attended more than three meetings, 10% had no knowledge about these meetings, and 35% had not attended any meeting. About 85% of the respondents had participated in the awareness programme on the JJ Act and registration and 15% had not attended it. About 10% of the respondents had attended a training programme related to registration and 90% had not attended any type of training programme. Replying to the query as to whether the government had provided any financial assistance to the CCIs for conducting awareness programme in their own institutions, 100% had not received any assistance (Table 9).

FINDINGS

The researcher broadly classified the area of differences of the respondents into four categories (Table 10).

Religious Obligation

About 80% of the respondents believed that the JJ Act would affect their religious sentiments and principles, particularly the protection of orphan children. Child care institution's major differences are relate with adoption of child,

Table 9. Support of Government to the CCI for Registration.

Variables	Classification	Frequency & Percent (N = 20)	
No. of visits by officials	One	11	55.0
	Two	1	5.0
	Three	2	10.0
	Nil	6	30.0
No. of meetings conducted by officials	One	4	20.0
	Three	4	20.0
	More than three	3	15.0
	Don't know	2	10.0
	Nil	7	35.0
Participation in awareness programme	Yes	17	85.0
	No	3	15
Participation in training	Yes	2	10
	No	18	90

Table 10. Major Differences of Respondents.

Variables	No. of Respondents
Religious obligation	16 (80%)
Financial problems	12 (60%)
New regulations and procedure	17 (85%)
Affects the autonomy of the institution	12 (60%)

according to JJ Act when a child is legally proclaimed as a child in need care and protection is automatically came into a be ready for adoption. But acording to Islamic law, adoption is against their religious belief; besides that some families or parents sent their children to the institution so that they receive a better education. These children regularly visit his/her family (weekly/monthly/vacation time, etc.). So the main argument of institutions is that it is not practical to declare these children as orphans, and they fear that the government may allow these children to be adopted.

Another concern was the expenditure of the contributory money. The main source of income for these institutions is the contribution from the people, who do so on the condition that it be spent for the protection of Yatheems (Orphans), and the use of this money for another purpose is against their belief. In Islamic tradition, people contribute to Yatheemkhanas (orphanage) for the protection of orphans as they believe that this will help them attain heavenly life. Hence, the institution can only use this money according to the will of the deceased person, but the institutional representatives doubt that while implementing the JJ Act, the institutions are compelled to admit other categories of children such as beggars, vagrants, children from other than their religious background and children in conflict with law. So they have to use the money that people gave to them for protecting Yatheems (orphans) for other children too. This will be considered as sacrilege of religious vow.

Financial Problems

Prabhakar (2014) observed that one of the major reasons for the failure of Indian NGOs or the voluntary sector was the lack of funds. In another article, 'Non- governmental organizations problems and remedies in India', Latha and Prabhakar (2011) stated that lack of funds was the dominant problem faced by the voluntary sector. Likewise in this study, 60% of the respondents said that the reason for reluctance to register was the financial burden due to the implementation of the JJ Act, especially since the auxiliary sources of these CCI are donations from community people. In this study, 15% of the institution's source of income was from contribution from society; for 35% of institutions, it was grant in aid; for 45% of institutions, it was grant in aid, own income and contribution from society, and for 5% of institutions, it was contribution from society and own income.

CONCLUSION AND RECOMMENDATIONS

Child Care Institutions in Malappuram have a long history of service to the destitute and orphan children. Now it is time to revamp the structure and functions of these institutions. Registration under the JJ Act is the law of the land and not a single institution can circumvent the process. It is the responsibility of each and every institution to obey it as soon as possible. But it is also important that the reluctance by the CCIs should be taken care of by the government department in a more inclusive manner. It is presumed that these institutions will continue their welfare work for several more years with a strong religious and moral conviction. It is the duty of the government to strengthen these types of non-governmental and welfare organizations. All these years they have continued their work in their own way and now the new enactment affects their basic tenets that have helped them to survive. So they face difficulties in dealing with it and an effective government mechanism could help them cope with the change with proper technical assistance.

The unawareness of the JJ Act among the institutional persons revealed by this study was shocking. The government and all other child care organizations should focus on improving their awareness regarding the JJ Act among all stakeholders of child welfare and the society at large. Bearing in mind all these factors it is undoubtedly the duty and responsibility of society to ensure that standardized facilities and resources are available in each Child Care Institution. A child does not enter an institution willingly, but comes in to it due to factors such as death and desertion of parents, abuse, poverty, negligence of parents, etc. of which the child may or may not be aware of it, so it is the duty of government and welfare agencies to provide a healthy atmosphere to these children to lead a positive life.

Under these circumstances, this study put forward some recommendations. They are: to conduct effective awareness and training programs exclusively for the institutional heads and staff; increase financial assistance to the CCIs; give assistance to the CCIs to modernize their activities and approaches; give technical assistance to the CCIs to encourage the registration process; and conduct community programs to awaken community conscience on the JJ Act.

REFERENCES

Frost, R. (1923). *Stopping by woods on a snowy evening.* Retrieved from https://www.poetryfoundation.org/poems/42891/stopping-by-woods-on-a-snowy-evening

Government of India. (2011). *Census of India.* Directorate of Census Operations, Kerala. Retrieved from http://censusindia.gov.in/2011census/dchb/3205_PART_B_MALAPPURAM.pdf

Latha, L. K., & Prabhakar, K. (2011). Non-government organizaations: Problems and remedies in India. *Serbian Journal of Management, 6*(1), 109–121. doi:10.5937/sjm1101109L

Nair, S. (2018). *In the running of children's homes, the rules that apply or do not. The Indian Express.* Retrieved from https://indianexpress.com/article/explained/child-shelter-home-muzaffarpur-deoria-home-sexual-abuse-maneka-gandhi-juvenile-justice-act-5298332/

National Child Policy. (1974). Department of Social Welfare. New Delhi. Retrieved from https://www.childlineindia.org.in/CP-CR-Downloads/national_policy_for_children.pdf

Prabhakar, K. (2014). *Voluntary organisation and its challenges in India, 2*(3), 567–581.

Raveendran, A. (2017, November 30). *Orphanages on the verge of shutdown.* The Hindu. Retrieved from http://www.thehindu.co/todays-paper/tp-national/tp-kerala/orphanages-on-the-verge-of-shutdown/article21159375.ece

Shukla, A., & Pavini, P. (2015). *Weakest on earth: Orphans of India.* New Delhi: Bloomsbury Publishing India Pvt. Ltd.

Sree, M. K. (2013, September 9). *In Kerala, delay in implementing the Juvenile Justice Act on orphanages a boon for offenders. The Times of India.* Retrieved from https://timesofindia.indiatimes.com/city/kozhikode/In-Kerala-delay-in-implementing-the-Juvenile-Justice-Act-on-orphanages-a-boon-for-offenders/articleshow/22434855.cms

State of Tamil Nadu v. Union of India. WP(C)102 of 2007, 2017.

The Juvenile Justice (Care and Protection of Children) Act 2015. (2015, December 31). Retrieved from http://wcd.nic.in/sites/default/files/JJ%20Act%2C%202015%20_0.pdf

UNICEF. (2016). *Consolidated report of second round of regional level round table conferences.* Retrieved from http://unicef.in/Uploads/Publications/Resources/pub_doc116.pdf

WEBSITES

http://censusindia.gov.in/2011census/dchb/3205_PART_B_MALAPPURAM.pdf

https://census2011.co.in/census/district/275-malappuram.html

https://www.soschildrensvillages.ca/india-now-home-20-million-orphans-study-finds

INDEX

Printed and bound by CPI Group (UK) Ltd, Croydon, CR0 4YY

13/09/2026

14961059-0006